Demographic and Structural Change

Recent Titles in
Contributions in Sociology

Demographic and Structural Change

THE EFFECTS OF THE 1980s ON AMERICAN SOCIETY

EDITED BY
DENNIS L. PECK
AND J. SELWYN HOLLINGSWORTH

Contributions in Sociology, Number 114

GREENWOOD PRESS
Westport, Connecticut • London

Library of Congress Cataloging-in-Publication Data

Demographic and structural change : the effects of the 1980s on
   American society / edited by Dennis L. Peck and J. Selwyn
   Hollingsworth.
         p.   cm.—(Contributions in sociology, ISSN 0084–9278 ; no.
   114)
      Includes bibliographical references and index.
      ISBN 0–313–28744–9 (alk. paper)
      1. United States—Social conditions—1980–   2. United States—
   Population.   3. United States—Economic conditions—1981–
   I. Peck, Dennis L.   II. Hollingsworth, J. Selwyn.
   III. Series.
   HN59.2.D46   1996
   301—dc20   95–37332

British Library Cataloguing in Publication Data is available.

Library of Congress Catalog Card Number: 95–37332
ISBN: 0–313–28744–9
ISSN: 0084–9278

First published in 1996

Greenwood Press, 88 Post Road West, Westport, CT 06881
An imprint of Greenwood Publishing Group, Inc.

Printed in the United States of America

The paper used in this book complies with the
Permanent Paper Standard issued by the National
Information Standards Organization (Z39.48–1984).

10 9 8 7 6 5 4 3 2 1

This book is dedicated to my daughters, Heather Kathleen, whose determination, hard work, and talent should ensure future success, and Shannon Marie, the "cheerleader," whose disposition and humanness serve as an inspiration to others. It is my wish that the future will provide them with the opportunity of which each is so deserving.

Dennis L. Peck

This book is dedicated in honor of my father, Clyde Hollingsworth, and in memory of my mother, Alma Clark Hollingsworth. Their wise teachings instilled in me a lasting sense of values that have served me well, even through the most difficult of times. Their love, prayers, support, and encouragement have been a constant source of comfort throughout my life. Without their sage counsel, my accomplishments in this life would have been much more meager.

J. Selwyn Hollingsworth

Contents

Contents

Figures and Tables

FIGURES

TABLES

Preface

Changes in the population dynamics of a nation, region, state, or locality occur not within a vacuum, but within a dynamic entity. Therefore, changes in the demographic characteristics result in concomitant changes in the larger unit. The reverse is also true—changes in the larger context result in changes in related demographic factors. The pragmatic consequences of these changes affect not only the present generation, but have implications for the future of the community as well. The structural and social significance of some of these changes are captured in this collection of essays, which focus primarily on demographic change in the United States during the 1980s.

The 1980s serve as an important example of how demographic and structural changes affect societies. The task of sociologists is to establish an appropriate understanding of these dynamics of human behavior through an objective identification of organized patterns of social change. They must likewise establish a partial contextual meaning that can be attributed to the processes that lead to such change. The purpose of this edited volume is served by the various assessments of political, economic, technological, and population change that occurred during the 1980s. The authors also consider the patterns that are predicted to emerge during the course of this final decade of the twentieth century. The content provided herein is intended to provide an assessment upon which community analysts and other planners may develop a more comprehensive understanding of future growth and development of the American society.

Three questions serve to unify the chapters that follow:

1. What are the major changes that occurred during the 1980s?
2. What changes in structure created these social changes?
3. What consequences result from these changes?

This collection of essays covers issues important to theorists of social change, public policy-makers, and to all students of society. Included are chapters relating to theoretical explanations of social change, social and ecological effects of high population density, and change in population diversity of composition, as well as analysis of U.S. fertility, mortality, and migration patterns. In addition to these traditional demographic discussions, this book provides insights on issues relating to community development, poverty, and changing patterns in the family.

As is the case with all efforts of this nature, the success of this initiative is due to the contributors, whose vast knowledge of population dynamics is aptly demonstrated through an extensive record of research and publication in learned journals, government reports, and scholarly books. Their contribution to this collection is acknowledged with appreciation. Their positive response to the invitation to participate in the project, as well as their continuing support throughout the rather long period involved, underscores a strong commitment to scholarship.

A special thank you to Sandra Arnold, Shelby Chandler, Pamela Chesnutt, and Dina Eady, each of whom assisted in the preparation of communiqué and various components of this project. Of course, ultimately this book would not have been finalized without the assistance of the Greenwood Publishing Group, most notably acquisitions editor Lynn Flint, whose considerable talent and effort enhanced the quality of presentation.

Introduction

DENNIS L. PECK AND J. SELWYN HOLLINGSWORTH

From the time of Aristotle, analysts of society have been interested in the sources, properties, and directions of social change (Nisbet 1969, p. 16). The noted analyst William F. Ogburn (1937, p. 330) wrote that the concept of social change represents a scientific perspective based on objective description devoid of implied values. Inventions and their accumulation, according to Ogburn, represent the driving force behind social change. As the number of inventions increase, social change occurs more rapidly. Of course, other factors also account for social change. More recently, Boudon (1986) posed that the study of social change represents a basic, fundamental area of analysis within the social sciences and history. Moreover, the study of social change represents a strength as well as what Friedrichs (1970) identified as the most important problem facing the field of sociology. Like the political, ideological, and economic changes that have recently restructured the institutions of Eastern Europe, the conservative ideology holding sway in the United States for the past fifteen years has led to a process that has important consequences for social institutions that, in turn, prompt renewed efforts to clarify the position of sociological theory. Such efforts, according to Ritzer (1990), are integrative in nature, representing a theoretical synthesis of micro and macro sociological theory.

Although this collection of essays can be evaluated within a global context, the focus of this book is specifically directed to demographic and structural change in the United States during the 1980s. Demography is not only important, it is basic to understanding population dynamics and patterns that serve as a requisite condition to forecasting. Future social policies are dependent upon accurate predictions based on past and current fertility, mortality, and migration patterns.

The 1980s represent a decade of rapid social change—change that perhaps was the most dramatic experienced in human history. To some analysts, the rapidity of this change may not yet be comprehensible, while others, such as Baker (1993) and Francis (1993), suggest that the so-called chaos experienced during this period can be organized into an appropriate theoretical context. Theoretical efforts to explain social change are, according to contributor Lakshmi Bharadwaj, best understood when demography and human ecology are combined, leading in turn to enhanced understanding of the social change process as well as the adaptation/accommodation to change.

Similar to the structural disruptions and reorganization caused by political and social anomalies, the cumulative nature of scientific understanding is, as noted by Kuhn (1962) and Friedrichs (1970), the result of change in the scientific world view. Students of the functionalist perspective, for example, attempted to establish theories of change, but when functionalism and functionalists such as Ogburn became relegated to minor status within sociology, the effect of this exploration for social change also was diminished. According to Nisbet (1969, p. 283), however,

The best of functionalism lies exactly in what critics have mistakenly condemned it for—its emphasis upon those processes which are involved in equilibrium and stability. For these are real processes and powerful processes in human behavior.

The world changed rapidly during the 1980s and early 1990s. Witness the struggle of the various governments of the former USSR to convert their political ideologies and form of economic exchange. The sociological effort to address such change is dramatic, but it is not dissimilar to the progress of science and the development of the scientific models as noted by Kuhn and Friedrichs. It is also noteworthy that much of what has been identified as sociological theory is in fact written by analysts who are more interested in promoting social change than they are in understanding the process and effects of such change. Maintaining a scholarly separation between these activities is as important today as it was throughout the developmental stages of sociology, an activity that has frequently come under attack by humanists and others interested in changing the nature of the human condition (see, for example, Coser and Rosenberg 1989; Martindale 1988).

Change involves crisis, as Nisbet (1969, pp. 282–283) noted, but persistence and fixity is vital to understanding social change. The goal of sociology, and indeed the goal of scientific inquiry, is the identification of repetitive patterns of human behavior. Moore (1974, p. 13) noted that ''although we cannot meet the challenge of history, if by that we mean accounting for unique events, we must attempt to identify recurrent combinations of antecedents and consequences.'' Making assumptions of repetition and continuity allows social scientists to account for social change.

Social change also is cause for crisis; that is, anomalies arise in the expected patterns that challenge the current explanations. Such anomalies occur because of outcomes that differ from those anticipated. It is not unusual in the field of population studies, for example, for demographers to operate from several sets of assumptions upon which to build their predictive models. When social change occurs, these assumptions can be, and often are, placed in question, thereby challenging the ability to predict, estimate, or forecast population trends.

Once anomalies appear, the pattern expected is broken, making prediction impossible. However, sociologists can and do utilize data in the effort to account for change. New categories are necessary since the old ones, based on previous taken-for-granted patterns, are no longer useful. Social change also inhibits or at least constitutes a major challenge to the establishment of general laws pertaining to human behavior. Thus, Nisbet (1969) argues that the task is to develop a dynamic vision that builds change into its very fabric.

Despite problems such as these, governments are interested in the insights offered by social scientists regarding population dynamics and social change. As Weinstein (1976, p. 12) observed,

Governments, in seeking to keep abreast of critical developments in nature and society, support and receive information from organized science, especially those branches of organized science that may be especially useful in formulating policies about population, sustenance, and technology.

Similar to the 1960s, when ''a renewed interest in social-trend analysis . . . coincided with a rise in public concern regarding domestic social problems'' (Rossi and Gilmartin 1980, p. 11), events of the 1980s suggest that concern over domestic social problems and related issues is increasing. The challenge to sociologists is, therefore, to create the understanding of the dynamics of human behavior by identifying the organized patterns of change and the contextual meanings in the process leading to change. If population analysts assume anything, perhaps they should build on Nisbet's idea that everything is processual, everything is law governed in that the pattern is repeated, thereby making the future predictable. Important to this task is an understanding of persistence and fixity because, as Nisbet (1969, pp. 282–283) noted, persistence and fixity are vital to understanding change evolving from crisis.

The decade of the 1980s should serve as an important exemplar to how demographic and structural changes affect society in terms of both persistence and crisis. The ideological, political, economic, technological, and population changes that occurred during the 1980s may not yet be fully appreciated. However, the content of this volume is intended to provide some assessment upon which future analysts can build a more comprehensive understanding of growth and development in U.S. society and its changing institutions. Such understanding will undoubtedly underscore the effect of other important changes in the way society and culture are viewed; it will also serve to stimulate further theoretical development within the social sciences.

The conservative ideological shift within society during the 1980s may also be responsible for the revival of the consensus approach in sociology and a renewed interest in functionalism to explain social change and the social change process. Such social change could be attributed to what Coleman identified as a diminishing primordial social organization, be partially spontaneous in nature, or represent a constructed social organization (Bourdieu and Coleman 1991, pp. 1–14). Whatever the reason, organizational change did occur; the change was rapid, and it has had a profound effect on American society.

The hue and cry heard from social and cultural critics throughout the 1980s pertain to a decline in the moral codes of conduct, an increasing incidence of crime, and the need to respond more harshly to this perceived rationality of conduct (crime). The declining influence of so-called traditional family values and an increasing incidence of divorce, deadbeat dads, and so on are identified as exemplifying the breakdown of the social fabric. On the other hand, Ogburn (1937, p. 333) would point out that such problems are more appropriately characterized as resulting from a period of great social change and the changing values that are implied in progress. Thus, the 1980s demonstrate that significant social change, especially in advanced societies, is, at least for the present condition, considered to be a normal rather than an exceptional process (see, for example, Calhoun 1991).

The contributors to this volume draw upon several theoretical orientations to explain the demographic and structural changes that evolved during the 1980s. This decade is pivotal within the discipline of sociology as well. With a renewed interest in macro-level theoretical explanations and, as noted by Ritzer (1990), the concerted effort to synthesize sociological theory and social theory, the contents of this volume are intended to provide explanations for the demographic and structural issues addressed. The book's purpose is to offer insights into the social change process, demonstrating, in turn, that the 1980s was indeed a pivotal period. Perhaps the contents of this edited volume also will assist in some small way by responding to Coleman's (1990) challenge to develop theory that is useful to policy analysts and to present findings that will aid policy-makers to respond to a new social organization.

While the sources of social change are defined as being exogenous in nature, some of the changes discussed in this volume can also be considered of endogenous origin. Social systems are affected by external sources, while organizations can generate change(s) in their own structure(s). According to Swanson (1971, p. 3), "change refers to a difference in a structure, the difference occurring over time and being initiated by factors outside that structure." On the other hand, if one thinks in terms of function, development and, as will be discussed in this set of readings, process, then Swanson argues that what is being referred to are "differences within a structure . . . that appear over time and that are initiated by factors already present within that structure.'' Thus, change is different from other processes in that whatever sources bring about change lie outside that structure that changes (Swanson 1971, p. 5).

Social change, according to Kornblum (as cited in Jaffee 1990, p. 4), ''refers to 'variations over time in the ecological ordering of populations and communities, in patterns of roles and social interactions, in the structure and functioning of institutions, and in the cultures of societies.' '' Social change, then, represents a complex, multidimensional process affecting change at both the cultural (individual beliefs and values) and organizational levels (roles and patterns of interaction). Based on these statements, three questions serve as a unifying theme:

1. What are the major changes that occurred during the 1980s?
2. What changes in the American structure (or elsewhere) created these responses?
3. What are the consequences of these changes?

In Chapter 1, Lakshmi K. Bharadwaj identifies social change as one of the dominant issues of the contemporary experience. In establishing the framework for the demographic and structural change thesis of this book, he emphasizes the important effects of social, cultural, and demographic change on the human experience. However, structural change influences these experiences because of the relationships of humans and their organizations with the environment, ranging from the primary areas of demographic concern to family and community development issues. Although the current contributors cover only some of the many issues and problems identified in Chapter 1, the author's examples are illustrative of the significant role demographers play in their unending quest to provide both data and explanation to governments and organizations dependent on such information.

Although Bharadwaj's well-reasoned historical acknowledgment is directed primarily toward Emile Durkheim's contributions to the understanding of social change, it is noteworthy that Max Weber also is recognized by students of social change as a major contributor to this worthy area of analysis (Weber 1968). Durkheim's erudite contributions are significant; it can also be argued that the writings of Weber and Karl Marx offer much to our historic sociological understanding of social and demographic changes.

Bharadwaj's argument juxtaposes demographic and structural change issues, namely human ecology and environmental sociology. Although theoretical in exposition, the author addresses numerous social problems that have garnered significant attention in the sociological literature. Examples include the population resource crisis, the human ecological approach, and internal migration. Nicely summarizing the concerns and suggested future implications on the overall well-being of the American population, the author sensitizes the reader to better appreciate the importance of social issues currently being debated by policy-makers. If, as Bharadwaj notes, human ecology and demography do constitute the core of sociological inquiry and evaluation, then the focus of this collection of topics may serve to demonstrate this point.

William H. Frey and Elaine L. Fielding address several of the demographic trends referred to in the opening chapter as they relate to urban-suburban demographic change. As noted throughout Chapter 2, the population profiles of older industrial cities are changing, leading in turn to large social and economic disparities between newly arrived inner-city residents and other portions of metropolitan area populations. The new changes highlighted in this chapter pertain to immigration-related minority gains, recent urban and regional restructuring, and a suburban domination in Standard Metropolitan Areas (SMAs). These distribution-related developments of the past decade have contributed to the economic growth and political independence of suburban cities.

The effects of immigration experienced during the 1980s, which was the largest number since the first decade of this century, are substantial. As Frey and Fielding report, the data for the 1980s indicate that a disparity between minority and majority growth rates is quite evident. Although the resultant demographic patterns appear to be dramatic, they are also shown to be distinctive by geographic region, especially for states such as California and New York where large numbers of Asian and Latin American immigrants reside. In other sections of the United States, the distinctive patterns of high internal migration and high out-migration patterns are discussed, as are the race and status effects associated with migration dynamics relating to growth and decline. For example, the authors explain some of this change within the context of growth and decline provoked during the 1980s by manufacturing decline, disinvestment, agricultural surpluses, and a loss of labor-intensive industry in the Northeast, Midwest, and South, as well as the attendant effects caused by growth in the recreation and retirement industry in the Southeast, New England, and Northwest.

The policy concerns that emerge from the demographic changes discussed in Chapter 2 are the substance of which sociology is made. Residential segregation, multilingual education, concentrated poverty, and diversity are associated with the kinds of population dynamics highlighted in this well-orchestrated chapter. On the other hand, the change in economic functions that led to state and regional transformations should not be overshadowed. The restructuring of the U.S. economy during the 1980s, especially in the service sector, represents an important element in the redistribution of the population as well as the rebound from population decline experienced previously in some large cities.

The suburbanization of America, according to the authors, also is distinctive. The data brought to bear on this process again demonstrate the disparity between majority and minority groups. But this disparity also is shown to hold within the minority populations, especially among black and Hispanic Americans, when levels of education are controlled. That is, social class and area of metropolitan residence are of historical consequence, and this pattern continues to the present.

In the final section, Frey and Fielding report on and assess the demographics of poverty conditions and trends. As a major policy issue of the 1990s, the authors clearly demonstrate why the poverty trends of the 1980s have led to the intense dialogue surrounding this problem (see, also, Chapter 8).

In Chapter 3, Donald W. Bogie provides several sets of data pertaining to age and racial structure over a 200-year period beginning in 1850 and projecting to the year 2050. As a complement to the work of Frey and Fielding, this chapter also includes information on the country of origin for the large influx of immigrants to the United States during the 1980s and the racial distribution, diversity, and growth of the U.S. population by geographic region. Placing the analysis of these data within the various features of current demographic patterns and projected future changes, Bogie's discussion emphasizes the important role of demography in the planning engaged in by representatives of governments, community organizations, and business.

Bogie's chapter also includes information useful to students interested in aging trends and age projection for a 100-year period. The population pyramids and sex ratios based on the 1990 census data offer important insights into what the age distribution of the United States will look like for the first half of the twenty-first century.

Other important features of Chapter 3 include a brief discussion of cultural change, such as the increased likelihood that members of various minority groups will identify themselves as minorities. This apparent change, suggests the author, holds important implications for public policy. Differences in present levels of educational attainment, employment, income, and family size and stability also are important to understanding the significance of Bogie's concluding discussion of the next American minority (see also Chapter 9).

In Chapter 4, Dudley L. Poston, Jr. and Hong Dan discuss changing patterns of fertility. U.S. fertility rates have decreased from more than eight children per woman in 1790 to 1.8 children by the 1980s. This trend is evaluated within the context of the demographic transition, complementing the discussion of this theory in Chapter 1. An important feature of the assessment offered by Poston and Dan is their consideration of the effects of urbanization, technology, and the changing role of women upon the fertility rates.

However, the primary focus of Chapter 4 is on fertility trends and societal change. Comparing fertility and mortality rates throughout U.S. history with the demographic transition, the authors show what population growth could have occurred without the intervening effects of cultural, social, economic, and technological changes. Important historical events, such as war, economic vicissitudes, a Supreme Court ruling, and the introduction of more efficient contraception are skillfully introduced as a means to explain the fertility rates for various time periods.

Consistent with the previous two chapters, Poston and Dan note the influence of global change. In this instance, technological change born of the Industrial Revolution had an effect on the demographics of developed and developing nations alike. More efficient technology in particular has, in the words of the authors, "had a major influence on the social fabrics of other European countries, as well as on that of the U.S.'' One major effect was on family size. Mortality declined as sanitation, health, and general living conditions improved. Other more recent factors include the introduction of child labor laws, compulsory mass education, urbanization, increased participation of women in the labor force, and increased consumption. In addition to these economic factors, the authors suggest that noneconomic forces may also have been operating to influence the declining birth rates.

Finally, fertility differentials are evaluated. However, as an extension to Bogie's discussion, these differences are also addressed by introducing religion, urban verses rural residence, and more precise income levels.

Chapter 5, coauthored by David W. Coombs and Stuart A. Capper, has important public policy implications relating to mortality. The authors contend that during the 1980s, the U.S. public health system was in ''disarray.'' The contention that the disease prevention efforts of public health officials may have been less than effective is supported by a number of factors affecting public service delivery; and these, in turn, serve as the focal point of this chapter. Change affected the structure of public health systems, their environments, and the quality of life of the American people during the 1980s. The authors effectively demonstrate their knowledge of this area with a thoughtful and constructive assessment of this important system.

The initial portion of Chapter 5 is a description of federal, state, and local public health systems and a delineation of the costs involved in basic and comprehensive health care service delivery and prevention. A lack of consistency in the structure and function of state health agencies prevents the authors from undertaking an important comparison of these agencies, but a discussion of increased costs per year from 1980 to the late 1980s is revealing. Such information is also quite suggestive as to reasons why the nation's health care systems and service delivery have been topics of debate during the 1990s.

In the second portion of this chapter, Coombs and Capper assess the success or failure of targeted reductions in mortality, morbidity, risk factors, and disease, and a general social awareness of major health problems. The authors used the 226 specific objectives identified in 1980 by a panel of health experts as a guide for assessing progress in achieving what was identified as the life stage goals. These objectives were then subject to a set of assumptions that took into consideration the projected effects of new regulations, technology, and the social and political climates. The authors' candid assessment of progress made during the 1980s takes into consideration that many health-related goals are highly correlated with specific behaviors and overall life styles, as well as newly identified problems.

Two serious public health issues are discussed in detail, namely infant mortality and the AIDS epidemic. The former problem was well known in 1980, whereas the latter was unanticipated. In both instances, the extent of human knowledge of the complex, interrelated factors involved is framed within the diverse attitudes and beliefs held by individuals of differential educational, social, and economic backgrounds. As noted, structural and behavioral problems are characteristic of both the health care delivery system as well as the clients for whom this system is intended to serve. The problems are also affected by change in policy, programs, and expectations.

The complexity and number of social factors involved in enhancing the health of Americans is not ignored by the authors. They skillfully weave the issues together, taking into consideration the demographic and structural change issues that serve as the theme for this book. In this regard, Coombs and Capper relate their own interest in health behavior to macro social change theory and structural change. They then move on to extensively discuss the micro-level models used to evaluate the costs and effectiveness of current public policy and strategy initiatives to promote changes in attitudes that correspond to unhealthy, anti-social behavior. Returning to a macro-level approach, the authors conclude their discussion with an assessment of the barriers and the potential to be realized as health care officials and practitioners diligently strive to create structural and environmental change that will enhance the health and well-being of special interest groups and the entire American population.

The changing role of women in the American labor force, briefly discussed in Chapters 2 and 4, is more fully elaborated upon by Teresa A. Sullivan in Chapter 6. This insightful work highlights the large influence of technology on change. In the opening pages, Sullivan raises a number of important questions pertaining to whether improved technology enhances or diminishes job opportunities or whether both of these approaches occur. These social change related questions certainly were germane during the 1980s, affecting, in turn, employment opportunities for the American labor force of the 1990s.

Employing the ''cashier complex'' concept, the author explores answers to whether dual or segmental labor markets resulted from changes in technology. That is, the cashier complex concept, in the words of Sullivan, ''enhances our understanding of those labor force changes that are influenced by a continuing shift into a service market, substitution of capital for labor, the lessening of skill requirements for workers, and the shifting proportion of demographic groups among entry level workers.''

Chapter 6 is a fine example of how the sociological imagination can be employed using aggregate data from a portion of the labor market to generalize about other components of that market. Use of a diagram of occupational types and specific occupational areas enhances this generalization, the more focused discussion of structural and environmental change in the work place, and future occupational growth trends during the 1990s and beyond.

The cashier complex illustrates the dramatic change in the knowledge and skill levels required of workers. Technology, in this instance, has led to reductions in these areas, a decrease in staffing needs, and a decline in client-oriented business practices. On the other hand, demographic characteristics are more positive. Cashiers have not only increased in number, but the occupation is now less gender segregated and more racially diverse than in the past, and the income levels for males and females are more equitable.

Gentrification represents an important demographic process. The concept was introduced into the literature to assist in explaining the urban redevelopment of the 1970s and beyond. It is employed in Chapter 7 by Frank Harold Wilson, who addresses urban redevelopment and the post-industrial city. As part of the effort of governments to focus on revitalization of downtown areas, conservation, rehabilitation, slum clearance, and general upgrading of private housing and public and commercial buildings, gentrification represents one critical process involved in the economic restructuring and environmental change of large, old U.S. central cities. Known as the new urbanization, this process, according to Wilson, contributes to "increased middle class home ownership, taxes, and an improved quality of life [while also leading to] rising housing costs, tightening of renter markets, speculation, and displacement."

The author examines urban redevelopment and the specific role of gentrification in this process and the effect the process has had on the population and housing within the context of economic restructuring, regional development, and post-industrial urbanization. The implications of the changes described in terms of theory, research, and public policy also are discussed.

Wilson begins his discussion by describing the divergent trends that characterized post–World War II American cities. Population gains and losses of suburban and central cities characterize the patterns observed on a national and regional basis. Using U.S. census data, a thorough assessment of the trends serves the author well as he documents primary and secondary population trends through the 1980s, tying these tendencies to the distinctive economic structures existing in various portions of the country. Again, gentrification serves as a focal point for Wilson's analysis as he points out that, contrary to popular belief, gentrification is most salient in cities where national and regional administrative centers are located and where post-industrial transformation to new economies, such as service and government, is taking place.

Various relationships between gentrification and structural change are covered at length, including changes in housing, population, social class, and racial-ethnic patterns and characteristics. In this area, Wilson's chapter is complementary, though more extensively developed, to a portion of material presented in previous chapters.

Wilson observes that the economic restructuring and growth that has occurred in the United States since 1970 has had important consequences for population growth in regions and metropolitan areas. He also argues that this growth is not only correlated to national and regional economies but to a global economy as well. Again, the influence of globalization looms large and ties in well with the gentrification thesis developed by Wilson in this well-written and comprehensive chapter. The author concludes with an overview of the vast number of social problems that have long characterized many central cities, but these problems are highly correlated to changes in technology, economic restructuring, and the gentrification process that have had important consequences for demographic and structural change in the post-industrial city.

Poverty is identified as a major problem in areas of large U.S. cities that are characterized by redlining, disinvestment, the absence of a middle class, few jobs, older and deteriorated housing, and abandonment. In Chapter 8, Kirsten W. West more directly addresses the poverty trends observed among a significant proportion of the U.S. population. Several areas of interest to students of demographic and structural change are examined, including income distribution, the size and characteristics of the working underclass, and relative income.

Comparing income data from the 1970s and 1980s, West characterizes poverty in the United States as a phenomenon increasing both in absolute numbers and in rates. Utilizing core demographic variables, the author identifies numerous trends in the pattern of poverty by urban-rural areas, geographic regions, levels of education, age, family status, occupational attainment, unemployment, and differences by race and ethnic background. Noteworthy findings are reported throughout, but, on several occasions, the author also addresses some myths about poverty. Examples include the observations that the feminization of poverty is not new and that poverty is found in all educational groups.

The author also identifies the restrictions and limitations imposed upon analysts who use the official definition of poverty in their work for comparative purposes. In this portion of her discussion, West notes the many issues involved in evaluating poverty when changes occur in the elements identified as relevant to its measurement. These changing elements, it can be inferred from the discussion, result from the influence of a changing political ideology and economy. These ideological perspectives are also identified as being grounded in diverse views pertaining to the influence of social structure upon individuals who are denied access to the labor market or earn low wages, as opposed to the characteristics of individuals who live in poverty, including their values and attitudes.

Structural change, including public aid programs that were severely cut in level of funding during the 1980s, have contributed to the increase in poverty. In other instances, the assistance level for those who qualify is not sufficiently high to move recipients out of the poverty category. This includes the elderly and disabled as well as families receiving Aid to Families with Dependent Children (AFDC). Unemployment trends in certain core areas such as construction and the decline in unemployment insurance coverage also contribute to increases in poverty. Structural change, according to West, can be identified as a factor in the changing characteristics of poverty, but the growth of service sector employment, identified by many analysts as an example of the working poor, is not considered to be a contributor to the observed poverty increase.

The inequality measure and the relative income distribution reported serve as yet further indicators of the widening gap between those with the highest level of income and the proportion of the U.S. population having the lowest level of income. With the exception of the elderly, the proportion of inequality among the poor of working age increased during the 1980s, as did the proportion of the population with the highest level of income. West concludes that the prevailing economic structure has decreased job opportunities for many, and that it offers low wages and increased unemployment. But the efforts to reduce poverty within the same structure have not been conducive to achieving this goal. As observed by West, "There are many causes and many sources of structural change reflected in the incidence of poverty."

In Chapter 9, coauthored by Louie Albert Woolbright and J. Selwyn Hollingsworth, a relatively new demographic issue is presented within the context of the demographic and structural change focus that serves as the theme for this book. Cultural change and changing social values have, according to the authors, led to a significant problem, a problem that is induced by agency denial of self-identity. That is, official applications and questionnaires used by governments do not allow individuals born of mixed racial unions to respond to categories that reflect their true racial heritage. In response, the authors present data for the purpose of assessing the increase in cross-racial births in the United States at the more general level. This assessment addresses macro-level social change in race relations since the 1960s and a concomitant change in a micro-level social identity.

Tracing the history of cross-racial persons in the United States and elsewhere and the official government reaction to relations among members of different racial groups, Woolbright and Hollingsworth draw from important events such as World War II, the civil rights movement, and the assimilation model to explore the degree of increased interrelationships between racial and ethnic groups that led to growth in the incidence of cross-racial marriage and parentage. The authors also explore the intellectual literature of the past to establish, in part, the societal reactions to this phenomenon and that of the specific individuals involved.

Attempts to distribute individuals born of mixed racial unions into specific racial categories for official purposes may succeed in generating data useful for demographic analysis. The authors contend, however, that such attempts to establish parsimonious organizational classification schema hold deleterious effects for those involved. Self-image represents a contending position, and this hypothesis is supported by several case studies of biracial individuals' testimony as well as aggregate data gathered by the National Center for Health Statistics. These data focus on the extent of occurring mixed-race births.

Whether the governments involved will respond to an increasing reality is not a matter of contention. That the need exists for such change is perhaps beyond argument. In any event, Woolbright and Hollingsworth do submit that a predicted increased growth in mixed-marriage births will be substantial and that this increase will occur because of another prediction, which is a huge decrease in the percentage of the non-Hispanic white majority in the United States.

REFERENCES

Baker, Patrick L. 1993. "Chaos, Order, and Sociological Theory." *Sociological Inquiry* 63:123–149.

Boudon, Raymond. 1986. *Theories of Social Change* (trans. by F.C. Whitehouse). Berkeley, Calif.: University of California Press.

Bourdieu, Pierre and James S. Coleman (eds.). 1991. *Social Theory for a Changing Society.* Boulder, Colo.: Westview Press.

Calhoun, Craig. 1991. "Social Change." Pp. 1807–1812 in Edgar F. Borgatta (ed.), *Encyclopedia of Sociology,* vol. 4. New York: Macmillan.

Coleman, James S. 1990. *Foundations of Social Theory.* Cambridge, Mass.: Harvard University Press.

Coser, Lewis A. and Bernard Rosenberg. 1989. *Sociological Theory: A Book of Readings.* Prospect Heights, Ill.: Waveland Press.

Francis, Roy G. 1993. "Chaos, Order, and Sociological Theory: A Comment." *Sociological Inquiry* 63:239–242.

Friedrichs, Robert W. 1970. *A Sociology of Sociology.* New York: The Free Press.

Jaffee, David. 1990. *Levels of Socio-economic Development Theory.* New York: Praeger.

Kuhn, Thomas S. 1962. *The Structure of Scientific Revolutions.* Chicago: University of Chicago Press.

Martindale, Don. 1988. *The Nature and Types of Sociological Theory.* Prospect Heights, Ill.: Waveland Press.

Moore, Wilbert E. 1974. *Social Change* (2nd ed.). Englewood Cliffs, N.J.: Prentice-Hall.

Nisbet, Robert A. 1969. *Social Change and History: Aspects of the Western Theory of Development.* New York: Oxford University Press.

Ogburn, William F. 1937. "Social Change." Pp. 330–334 in Edwin R.A. Seligman (ed.), *Encyclopedia of the Social Sciences.* New York: Macmillan.

Ritzer, George. 1990. *Frontiers of Social Theory: The New Synthesis.* New York: Columbia University Press.

Rossi, Robert J. and Kevin J. Gilmartin. 1980. *The Handbook of Social Indicators: Sources, Characteristics, and Analysis.* New York: Garland STPM Press.

Swanson, Guy E. 1971. *Social Change.* Glenview, Ill.: Scott, Foresman and Co.

Weber, Max. 1968. *Economy and Society: An Outline of Interpretive Sociology.* New York: Bedminster Press.

Weinstein, Jay. 1976. *Demographic Transition and Social Change.* Morristown, N.J.: General Learning Press.

Demographic and
Structural Change

Theories of Demographic Change

LAKSHMI K. BHARADWAJ

Change has become a predominant issue of our times: "Everywhere change has become central to people's awareness, and there is a commitment to change that is irreversible, irresistible and irrevocable" (Vago 1980, p. 4). Generally speaking, change refers to a discontinuity between the structure of a society at two different points in time. One way to conceptualize change, therefore, is to view it as the "significant alteration of social structures" (Moore 1960, p. 3). While the judgment of what is significant may well lie with the observer, some characteristics of the social structure must persist through time for it to be identified as the same entity. On the other hand, a major structural transformation, or the destruction of structure brought about by revolutionary or cataclysmic change, may be such that it may no longer be possible to say that the entity being studied is the same.

Harper (1989, p. 5) has identified five types of alterations of structure of interest to sociologists: changes in personnel due to the continual turnover of membership; changes in the way parts of structures relate, including changes in role relationships; changes in the functions of structures; changes in the relationships between different structures; and, lastly, changes that lead to the emergence of new structures. The difference between the first four types of changes and the last one is clearly that between changes *in* and a change *of* structure.

In this connection, it is also instructive to keep in mind the important distinction that can be drawn between the idea of development, whose roots can be traced to the doctrines of classical antiquity and early Christian thought, and the idea of change. Nisbet (1970) has drawn this distinction most succinctly as follows:

We become aware of change through our perception of differences in time within a persisting entity. All three of these elements are necessary: differences, time, and persisting entity. A mere array of differences does not betoken change, only differences. (Nisbet 1970, p. 177)

While the essence of change involves a succession of differences in the original structure of a persisting identity from one time to another, development results from differences generated from within the structure itself. The crucial distinction here is that "[whereas] change alone may be the consequence of external, intrusive factors, of random events or catastrophes, development is a process that proceeds from the thing itself" (Nisbet 1970, p. 177).

Notwithstanding deep differences in the way they have attempted to grapple with the dynamics of social change, most social scientists have subscribed to certain common constitutive assumptions that derive largely from their particular understanding of evolutionism, the nature of nature and of human nature, and the nature of the scientific enterprise itself. In the scientific view, nature as well as all social reality is viewed in processual terms. Behind the seemingly accidental, haphazard, and chaotic appearance of reality, the underlying processes themselves are seen as repetitive, recurrent, and regular, hence patterned and law-governed. The discovery of these laws has been the prime task for both natural and social scientists in their unending quest for the understanding, prediction, and control of the incessant processes of changes in the natural and social worlds.

THE DEMOGRAPHICS OF CHANGE

Changes in the composition and characteristics of population affect, and are in turn affected by, the dynamic process of ever-changing relationships of humans and organizations to their environments. Among the contributions made by demographers to the understanding of demographic change, one could cite the explication of changes in *family composition* (the rise in the frequency of divorce, cohabitation, late marriage, number of people living alone, the number of single-headed households, and the decline in household size); in *fertility, mortality, migration, and mobility* (the aging of the baby boom generation and the graying of America, the feminization of work and poverty, the growing racial and ethnic diversity of the American population due to immigration); and in *population distribution* (white-flight and suburbanization, urban renewal and gentrification, metropolitanization and variations in the density of settlement in different parts of the country). Demographers are also interested in spelling out the socio-economic impact and policy implications of these interdependent changes in terms of the mounting costs of housing, schooling, medical care, unemployment, and welfare, as well as of social security, health care, and insurance programs for the elderly. For the students of population dynamics, Winsborough (1991, p. 13) projects the documenting of "how these changes occur,

understanding their workings, and testing hypotheses—perhaps cross-nation-
ally—about why they come about,'' as one of the likely major research programs in the next century.

Sociological attempts to account for the demographics of change have, by
and large, relied on the contributions made by Durkheim in his classic study on
the division of labor in society (1932). To account for the change from mechanical to organic solidarity in functionalist terms, Durkheim paid special attention to the underlying factors that govern the master process of differentiation.
In addition to the increase in demographic density (the concentration of population in a given area) as the necessary condition, Durkheim identified moral or
dynamic density (the intensity of contact or interaction among the differentiated
parts) as the sufficient condition for the shift from mechanical to organic solidarity. He argued that *mechanical solidarity* is characteristic of preindustrial
societies with their segmental division of labor and a solidarity based on simi-
larity and likeness. *Organic solidarity,* on the other hand, is a characteristic of
modern societies in which intense competition gives rise to a highly differentiated and complex division of labor and a solidarity grounded in the interdependence of the specialized parts.

Schnore (1965, p. 9) points out that within what is essentially a demographic
theory of change, Durkheim viewed modern divisions of labor as arising out of
the operation of the Darwinian struggle for existence in the human realm, but
saw in the division of labor a mechanism for resolving competition and an
alternative as much to Darwinian natural selection as to Malthusian checks. The
moderating effect of the modern division of labor prevents the differentiated
parts from destroying each other. On the contrary, since the parts are engaged
in the pursuit of different ends in common, they actually contribute to the maintenance and survival of much larger populations.

In the same context, Schnore (1965, pp. 12–13) also draws our attention to
the fact that *differentiation* is only one of several modes of resolving competition
over scarce resources. He therefore offers a number of alternative survival strategies that may involve one or a combination of the following: *demographic
changes* resulting in the elimination of excess numbers (increase in the death
rate, decrease in the birth rate, and outward migration); *technological changes*
that allow for the expansion of the resource base (the exploitation of unused or
existing resources, availability of new areas and new resources, and resource
substitutions); and *organizational changes* that allow for the support of larger
numbers (occupational and territorial differentiation, revolutionary changes that
redistribute the surplus among the many, and reduction in the general level of
living to support increased numbers).

Moore (1960, p. 814) has identified three change-producing societal strains
that result from demographic imbalances, universal scarcity situations, and the
dialectic conflict between normative alternatives. As examples of demographic
strains, Vago (1980) points to the mismatch between trends in birth rates and
plans for building schools or the entry of migrants and the ability of the receiv-

ing area to absorb them in the current labor forces. Similarly, changes in the composition of the population can have an effect on the size of the economically active population. Furthermore, the concentration of population in urban areas contributes to a plethora of problems, including traffic congestion. Imbalances in the supply and distribution of foodstuffs are also created by population growth. The growth of population likewise affects the degree of utilization of other resources.

The Population-Resource Crisis

What lends urgency to the current population-resource crisis is the fact that while human numbers are declining, or standing still at best, in industrial societies, they are increasing in the rest of the world, a world divided today not only economically and socio-politically, but also demographically. The technological mastery of the world has resulted in a higher material standard of living in the West, but it has also spelled economic polarization, ecological ruin, and environmental disasters worldwide. At the same time, hunger, famine, poverty, and overpopulation raise critical issues of equity, justice, security, and human survival. While the close link among poverty, population growth, and environmental degradation is invariably highlighted in the literature, the impact of unsustainable patterns of consumption and production on environment and resources does not receive equal emphasis. No less disconcerting is the fact that the use of the population argument tends to divert attention away from the role of exploitative and oppressive social institutions and arrangements. On the basis of the available evidence, Humphrey and Buttel conclude that

[one] of the most important findings to come from the study of the relationship between population size and the environment is the misplaced importance given to world population size as cause of natural resource scarcities and pollution. . . . [We do not] imply that world population growth should be . . . neglected as a cause of environmental problems, [but] a fixation on it as the major reason for pollution and energy crises would be sociologically misguided. (1982, p. 60)

Depending on their particular theoretical orientation, the three dominant approaches to the population-resource dynamic place differential emphases on the alternative modes of resolving competition over scarce resources. In the context of actual and perceived resource scarcities in a highly fluid and uncertain international situation, neo-Malthusianism has gained ascendance since the 1970s over the older theories of demographic transition and human ecology (expansionism), which were dominant through the 1960s. The ascendance of one or the other approach is closely tied to the shifting fortunes of the American economy within the context of changing demographic and international equations. Thus:

In the expansionary sixties, society was perceived to be a "variable sum game" in which all could benefit. During the seventies decade of scarcity, limits, and economic stagnation, society came more to be perceived as a "zero-sum game" in which one person's gain was another person's loss. (Thurow 1980; quoted in Harper 1989, p. 44)

The Neo-Malthusian Approach

Based on the Malthusian notion that population invariably outruns food supply because of a lag between the simple arithmetic increases in resources and the exponential rates of population growth, the neo-Malthusians bring in the notion of *carrying capacity* to identify overpopulation as the main threat to human planetary survival. The notion implies competition among species over scarce or limited resources, so that the more of one entails the less of the other. However, in spite of.the fact that there is no exact or objective formula for determining the optimum population, the neo-Malthusians tie in the notion of carrying capacity—the optimum population that a given environmental resource base can support at a given time—with the idea of an acceptable quality of life that one insists on living. The theory of demographic transition has also been invoked to explain why western societies were able to avoid the Malthusian apocalypse by joining declining death and birth rates with increasing standards of living. Contrary to the tenets of the theories of modernization and development, however, it is now asserted that nonwestern societies will be unable to do so, given the least likelihood of their ever achieving western levels of industrial and economic development. Even otherwise, the possibility of their duplicating the western experience is foreclosed, given the impossibility of supporting everyone in the world to live at U.S. standards within the constraints imposed by the finite nature of the earth's resources (Daley 1979).

To restore the population-resource balance, with global economic development, equitable distribution of resources, and the perfectibility of man and society now largely ruled out, the neo-Malthusians rely on sophisticated computer models to prescribe the end to development and limits to economic and demographic growth; others favor sustained environmental development. Still others despair of the effort to avert disaster through population control or the *preventive checks* of moral restraint proposed by Malthus. Instead, they invoke the operation of the Malthusian *positive checks* (wars, famine, pestilence, and natural disasters) and raise the specter of massive famines and die-offs to justify triage, war, secessionist movements, adding sterilants to drinking water, forced sterilization, nuclear holocaust, and even genocide. A few, on the other hand, question the modern equation of improvements in quality of life with ever-expanding levels of consumption, and blame the latter for the destruction of the environment as well as the exhaustion of the world's resources. Thus, Miller (1972, p. 122) identifies the megaconsumers and the megapolluters "who occupy more space, consume more of each natural resource, disturb the ecology more and pollute directly and indirectly the land, air, and water with ever-increasing thermal, chemical, and radioactive wastes,'' as the ones threatening our life-support system.

The Theory of Demographic Transition

A central question for demographers pertains to the reasons why demographic changes assume the forms they do and the differential consequences that accompany these changes. If Malthus is right, improvements in income and productivity should cause populations to grow. Since the demographic changes that occurred in Europe during the nineteenth century failed to follow this Malthusian path, the theory of demographic transition was proposed to cover the anomalous results. The theory was also offered as a ''stage'' model for the kind of changes that were likely to occur in the rest of the world. It specifies declining fertility as a consequence of modernization and economic development. In terms of this theory, population is kept stable in the initial stage as high birth rates are matched by high death rates due to the operation of the positive checks of famine, pestilence, war, etc. In the second stage, population increases sharply as death rates decline while birth rates remain high due to increases in food supply and improvements in health care. In the third stage, birth rates decrease faster than death rates due to the widespread use of family planning and birth control measures. In the final stage, low birth rates and low death rates again stabilize the population, but at a lower level of change.

However, the assumptions of demographic transition theory have not always followed to course as predicted. For example, population changes in the United States and some other industrialized nations have gone through a three-phase trend since the turn of the century: the decline in fertility levels between 1900 and 1940, which was interrupted unexpectedly by the high fertility decade of the baby boom years, was resumed again only after the 1960s. Significantly, this upsurge in births recorded in the 1950s and 1960s not only caught the demographic profession by complete surprise, it eludes a satisfactory explanation to our own day. Public discussion in the 1960s and 1970s was once again dominated by the threat of overpopulation: ''So massive was the boom in births and so high were fertility rates, both in more and in less developed countries, that the demon of overpopulation seemed to have once more broken out of his chains'' (Grebenik 1989, p. 11). In the intervening years, fertility rates in industrialized countries have again neared or been below replacement levels. Despite significant reductions, however, fertility rates in nonwestern countries continue to be high, especially in areas where there is less, not more, food to eat. While the United States is currently said to be in the final stage of the transition, with an ''aging'' population raising concerns about social and political costs of the ''graying of America,'' the nonwestern world is still experiencing relatively high rates of reproduction, with a larger proportion of its population in the early childbearing stage.

Since the fertility decline in the West began long before modern contraceptives became available, Weinstein (1976) believes that the general reason for the decline in fertility relates to the normative dimension of childbearing practices. Evidence of resistance to change in fertility practices also indicates that high fertility in nonwestern nations "is neither the result of ignorance nor lack of technique but a part of historical context resistant to piecemeal change" (Weinstein 1976, p. 84). In the West itself, smaller families became the norm as a result of reduced levels of living that affected newly affluent families during the Depression. Overall, the western experience still appears to confirm the association of declining fertility rates with rising levels of material well-being. Weinstein identifies some of the factors that are implicated in a downward fertility transition worldwide: the declining role of tradition and religion with increasing industrialization and urbanization; rising levels of income, women's education, and outside employment; and the awareness and availability of fertility control measures.

However, many of these generalizations have proved to be culturally and historically specific. The 1950s and 1960s reversed the educational differences in fertility in industrial societies, with better educated women producing families well above the average size. Grebenik (1989, p. 15) points out that, as a result, none of these generalizations have proved helpful in constructing a general theory of fertility behavior. Although urban and industrial growth and fertility decline occurred concurrently in western nations, it is virtually impossible to say whether it was declining mortality or economic growth that caused the decline in fertility (Weinstein 1976, p. 91). In any case, based on the absence of any evidence that a particular threshold level of development was necessary for this change to occur and the finding that fertility decline could occur under conditions of little economic development (as in parts of rural France and Hungary), little of the original transition model remains intact. This diversity is characteristic today of the nonwestern countries as well (Simmons 1988). Simmons, however, sees a lack of broad consensus on what conceptual framework might replace transition theory as an explanation of population change.

The Human Ecological (Expansionist) Approach

Another group of thinkers espouses a human ecological *expansionist* (or pro-growth) view on the population-resource problem. To explain the growth patterns of modern society, this approach draws upon its Durkheimian heritage and also combines elements of biological theory, Marxian historical materialism, and modern systems theory (Lenski 1979). This chapter shall discuss the views of Amos Hawley (1979, 1984, and 1986) in some detail, for he not only provides a concise exposition of the expansionist view, but his version of human ecology, with its focus on population growth and differentiation as significant processes of continuous change, is also "perhaps the most viable of the functional perspectives" (Turner 1991, p. 151).

Hawley (1986, p. 52) strongly objects to the application of the Malthusian argument regarding carrying capacity to human populations, even though it may be appropriate for plant and animal populations. Asserting that resource supplies are finite but unbounded, Hawley (1986, pp. 110–111) questions the neo-Malthusian assumption that overpopulation and overuse will soon exhaust a declining supply of fixed resources. While acknowledging the threats of over-population and pollution to the quality of the environment, he points to tech-nological advances that have resulted in a long history of resource expansion through more efficient extraction and the use of new and existing resources, new resource development, and resource substitutions. With regard to global food producing resources, he presents evidence to show that the amount of arable land, and its productivity and agricultural output, can be increased ahead of the rate of population growth. Hawley blames poverty and the structural conditions that generate it for the chronic food shortages in parts of the world. He points to the indispensability of further increments of growth and the creation of a central organization capable of tackling these and other environmental problems.

To avoid the circularity involved in the attempt to define an equilibrium state as adaptive, Hawley (1986) views adaptation as a process rather than as an end state. He follows the same strategy to counter criticisms of the convergence hypothesis based on the principle of isomorphism: convergence upon a common form of system structures that interact frequently should be regarded as a process rather than a consummation.

Focusing on the way human populations organize for survival or viability in given environments, Hawley (1986) views polities and human populations as inherently expansive, not only in numbers but also in their propensity to seize opportunities to enlarge their resource base. The demographic processes of birth, death, and migration are seen by him as the basic mechanisms employed by a population to maintain its size and its ability to provide sustenance. However, contrary to the Malthusians, he holds that the expansive power of population, alone, does not cause war, resource depletion, or environmental degradation. This occurs only under specific *organizational* circumstances. Hawley views these outcomes as the result of maladaptation or malfunctioning of organization, with disequilibrium opening the possibility for evolutionary change through a movement to a higher level of complexity. He discards the older views of linear evolution, the arbitrary sequences and definitions of evolutionary stages, and the conceptualization of ecological succession as a series of stages leading to a final stage. However, unwilling to give up the notion of directionality, even though change occurs in fits and starts (Nisbet 1969), he emphasizes the multilinear as well as the cumulative character of evolutionary change.

Hawley (1984) has identified the following propositions pertaining to *adaptation, growth,* and *evolution,* which affirm the interdependence of demographic and structural factors, as constituting the core of the human ecological paradigm:

1. Adaptation to environment proceeds through the formation of a system of interde-pendences among the members of a population;

2. system development continues, ceteris paribus, to the maximum size and complexity afforded by the existing facilities for transportation and communication;

3. system development is resumed with the introduction of new information which increases the capacity for movement of materials, people, and messages and continues until that capacity is fully utilized. (p. 905)

The four ecological principles of *interdependence, key function, differentiation,* and *dominance* define the processes of system functioning and change. A system is viewed as made up of functioning parts that are related to one another. Functions designate recurring behaviors, while patterned interactions constitute relationships. The ecosystem is conceptualized as an adaptive mechanism that emerges out of the interaction of environment, population, and organization. Adaptation to the environment involves the development of interdependence among members, which increases their collective capacity for action. Differentiation allows human populations to restore the balance between population and environment, which is upset by competition or improvements in technologies of communication and transportation. System change occurs as the number and kinds of functions shift or are reorganized in other combinations. The problem of integration caused by increasing specialization and expanding division of labor is solved by the hierarchical ordering of units in terms of the functions they perform for the system as a whole. As adaptation proceeds through a differentiation of environmental relationships, one or a few functions come to mediate environmental inputs to all other functions. Functional units that have a direct relationship with the environment perform the key function of regulating and determining the functions of units having indirect relationship with the environment. Since power follows function in Hawley's view, dominance attaches to those units that control the flow of sustenance into the ecosystem. The productivity of the key function, which controls the flow of sustenance, determines the extent of functional differentiation. As a result, the dominant units in the system are more likely to be economic than political.

Since the environment is always in a state of flux, every social system is continuously subject to change. Hawley defines change in terms of *any nonrecurrent alteration of a social system considered as a whole.* He therefore excludes from his definition rhythmic events, such as the cycles of daily activities or the succession of generations, that sustain rather than alter a given pattern of relationship. For all participants, change alters the life conditions to which they must adapt in order to remain in the system. One of the most significant nonrecurrent alterations is *cumulative change,* involving both endogenous and exogenous changes as complementary phases of a single process. Treating the relationship of individual purpose to collective outcomes as a moot issue, Hawley skirts the micro-macro issue and the question of intended and unintended effects by focusing on events or circumstances that lead inexorably toward cumulative change.

Cumulative change implies the ideas of *irreversibility, evolution,* and *expan-*

sion. Though irreversibility does not preclude the possibility of decline or even disappearance, it does mean that the succession of events by which a system was brought to a given stage cannot be followed backward to a starting point (Hawley 1979). While evolution implies a movement from simple to complex, proceeding through variation and natural selection, cumulative change refers to an increase in scale and complexity as a result of increases in population and territory. Territorial expansion is viewed by Hawley as a function of the limits afforded by improvements in facilities for movement and increase in population resulting from natural increase (which followed the sequence described by the theory of demographic transition in the West), migration, and the absorption of the population of outlying areas. Whether the process leads to growth or evolution depends on the concurrent nature of the advances in scale and complexity.

Generalizing the process of cumulative change as a principle of expansion, Hawley (1979 and 1986) applies this framework to account for growth phases that intervene between stages of development. Expansion, driven by increases in population and in knowledge, involves the growth of a center of activity from which dominance is exercised. When scale and complexity advance together, the normal conditions for growth or expansion arise from the colonization process itself. The evolution of the system takes place when its scale and complexity do not go hand in hand. Change is resumed as the system acquires new items of information, especially those that reduce the costs of movement from its environment. Thus, an imbalance between population and the carrying capacity of the environment may create external pressures for branching off into colonies and establishing niches in a new environment. Since efficiencies in transportation and communication determine the size of population, the scope of territorial access, and the opportunity for participation in information flows, Hawley (1979) identifies the technology of movement as the most critical variable. In addition to governing accessibility and, therefore, the spread of settlements and the creation of interaction networks among them, it determines the changes in hierarchy and division of labor. In general, the above process can work on any scale and is limited only by the level of development of the technologies of communication and transportation. Hawley takes the position that systems possessing similar efficiencies in transportation and communication are subject to similar principles of organization.

Hawley (1986, pp. 104–106) points out how, with the growth of a new regional and international division of labor, these states now draw sustenance from a single biophysical environment and are converted to subsystems in a more inclusive world system by the expansion process. In this way, free trade and resocialization of cultures create a far more efficient and cost-effective global reach. The result is a global system thoroughly interlinked by transportation and communication networks. The key positions in this international network are occupied by the technologically advanced nations with a monopoly of information and rich resource bases. However, as larger portions of system territories are brought under their jurisdiction, the management of scale becomes highly problematic. In the absence of a supranational polity, a multipolar international pecking order is then subject to increasing instability, challenge, and change. With mounting costs of administration, the system again tends to return to scale, resulting in some degree of decentralization and local autonomy, but new information and improvements in the technologies of movement put the system in fresh gear and start the growth process all over again.[1]

In the modern period of "ecological transition" (Bennett 1976), a large portion of the biophysical environment has progressively come under the control of the social. At the same time, Hawley points out that modern expansionism shies away from direct political domination and aims instead at structural convergence along economic and cultural axes. The process of modernization and the activities of the multinational corporations are given as prime examples of this mode of system expansion, which undermines traditional modes of life and results in the loss of autonomy and sovereignty of individual states.

Convergence of divergent patterns of urbanization is brought about by increased economic interdependence among nations and the development of compatible organizational forms and institutional arrangements. This approach, as Wilson (1984) points out, is based on the assumption that convergence is mainly a result of market forces that allow countries to compete in the world on an equal basis. He cites evidence that shows how the subordinate status of nonwestern nations has, on the other hand, hindered their socio-economic development, sharpened inequalities, increased rural-to-urban migration, and led to the expansion of squatter settlements.

As the process moves toward a world system, all the limiting conditions of cumulative change are reasserted at a higher level. On the one hand, a single world order with only a small tolerance for errors harbors the seeds of totalitarianism (Giddens 1990). On the other, there is the grave danger that a fatal error may destroy the whole system (Bharadwaj 1992). Human ecologists, however, rely on further expansion as the sure remedy for the problems created by expansion. To restore ecological balance, they put their faith in the creation of value consensus, rational planning, trickle-downs, market mechanisms, technological fixes and breakthroughs, native "know-how," and sheer luck.

Post-1980 Internal Migration in the United States and Concluding Comments on the Population-Resource Problematic. An understanding of the applicability as well as the limitations of the human ecological perspective can be gleaned from a study of the international dimensions of post-1980 internal migration in the United States. Murdock et al. (1991) found that some of the post-1980 migration and metropolitan growth patterns were similar to those of the 1960s (the more rapid growth of the metropolitan areas and of metropolitan areas in proximity to the metropolitan core) and could be explained by theories of metropolitanization and ecological expansion. However, subsequent events of the 1980s (the decline in parts of metropolitan areas showing general patterns of rapid growth or population decline as a result of the decline in functional economic and sustenance base) contradicted the trends established by these theories during the 1970s. The authors utilize the central human ecological concepts of sustenance activities, key functions, and dominance, but within an expanded international perspective, to account for these changes. They found support for their main argument that areas vary in their ability to obtain, retain, and control resources necessary to support population and, therefore, in their level of net migration, depending on (1) the sphere of operation (national or international ecosystem) of the key sustenance activity and (2) the activity's dominance in the ecosystem:

The loss of United States' dominance in such sustenance activities as manufacturing in the 1980s thus affected all areas in which that activity was dominant. . . . On the other hand, in areas . . . in which the United States retained international dominance during the 1980s, such as electronics, the sustenance level supporting the population remained unchanged or increased. (Murdock et al. 1991, p. 493)

By expanding the ecological perspective on migration into the international realm, their study led them to conclude that the key element in economic and demographic growth and revitalization may lie not in the diversification of the economy alone, but in the ability to pursue activities for sustenance specialization within a more diversified economic base. Thus, as a matter of policy, the authors recommend that for optimal results, the preferred strategy in international economic matters is to pursue only those activities in which the United States has dominance.[2]

Frey (1993) has recently pointed to the opportunities and challenges of the emerging urban system, at once more interconnected and responsive to global influences but ever more sharply differentiated internally. As a consequence, he continually raises concerns about equity in access to jobs, housing, schools, and social services. In addition to drawing attention to the increasing pressures of immigration and multiculturism and the sharpening of racial and ethnic clevages and conflicts, Grebenik (1989) points to the considerable stress, generated by a rapidly aging population, on health, housing, education, and welfare costs, and the prospects of generational conflicts over scarce resources.

To Greer (1979, p. 315), the rapid growth of American society, made possible by the increase in societal scale, has led to the following Durkheimian dilemma: "Increasing interdependence requires more cultural integration than we can manage; growth itself has undermined the cultural support system. While bureaucratization may increase order within a segment of the society, what is to guarantee order among segments?" In the absence of the spirit of consensus generated by war, economic disaster, or a universalized humanity, Greer feels that symbiosis rather than cultural integration may best remedy the fragmentation accompanying the discontinuities of societal growth. Such an approach, he believes, would not only emphasize trading partners, controlled markets, and formal and informal cooptation, but [given] the increasing number of role players who do not "know their place," from white working-class men to black college-educated women, such a system will take an awful lot of work by leaders, middlemen, and fixers, as well as some luck. (Greer 1979, p. 316)

While warning about the threat that population decline due to decreasing fertility ("birth dearth") can pose to democracy, Grebenik's (1989) keen awareness of the power of numbers prompts him to conclude that the opposite, over-population, is a much greater danger that should be the thrust of our concerns. Favoring collective action to modify unfavorable trends, Grebenik is also painfully aware of the inadequacies in our understanding of the determinants of demographic behavior and of the tentative nature of demographic projections that are statistical extrapolations of present trends rather than predictions of what will actually happen in the future.

The nature and shape of these projections vary with the assumptions that underlie each model with respect to factors that are held constant, even as the present trends are assumed to hold their own for changes in other factors. Since the trends are projected on the basis of the assumption that the future will be like the past, Grebenik is convinced that

policies can be framed only by trial and error, and we must be prepared to accept that some of the attempts which will be made to modify present trends may prove to be ineffective or mistaken, or entail unforeseen consequences. (1989, p. 21)

CONCLUSION

This last consideration brings out the fact that a lack of access to a "theoretically driven model" has often forced demographers to extrapolate from historical trends and forecast their "best-guess projections along with ranges of plausible outcomes [in order to] provide a certain amount of cover when things go wrong" (Winsborough 1991, pp. 1–2). It has also been argued that, in contrast to its current and past reliance on the neo-Malthusian model, demography has much to gain by making common cause with human ecology, its theoretically sophisticated sister discipline.[3]

While demographers are primarily interested in population structure and dynamics and their determinants and consequences, human ecologists are mainly concerned with how populations organize and use technology to win sustenance from the environment. Population size, composition, and distribution, as well as the changes in population structure that result from changes in such factors as fertility, mortality, migration, and mobility, constitute the subject matter of demography; the study of population, organization, environment, and technology, viewed as an interdependent whole (the "ecological complex"), provides the central focus for human ecology. Since demographic factors become salient in the way they interact with socio-economic forces, a comprehensive approach would require demographers to pay particular attention to the socio-economic and organizational linkages of population structure and change, and human ecologists to take into account the demographic dynamics involved in organizational interactions. In view of their overlapping interests and concerns, a marriage between their respective disciplines is, therefore, said to hold the greatest promise for the study of societies and social systems (Namboodiri 1988).

Since the study of organizational dynamics as well as the structure and dynamics of population are at the core of sociology, Namboodiri (1988) claims that rather than being peripheral to sociology, human ecology and demography constitute its core. As a result, he contends that the hybrid "ecological demography" promises the most systematic and comprehensive handling of a common core of sociological problems (analysis of power relations, conflict processes, social stratification, societal evolution, and the like) than any other competing sociological paradigm:

It provides a framework for fruitful application of the demographic perspective to the study of human, as well as organizational, populations. . . . It provides a powerful perspective for a careful examination of intersocietal dependence, the focus of world-system theorists. No other single approach in contemporary sociology does all these so well. (Namboodiri 1988, p. 631)

However, though human ecologists recognize the possibility of other pairwise interactions in addition to competition and even highlight the points of convergence between the human ecological and the Marxist points of view (Hawley 1984), human ecology as such does not directly focus on conflict in a central way. In this connection, Namboodiri (1988) points out how the very expansionist imperative of humans and social systems, identified as a central postulate by human ecologists, generates the possibility of conflict between the haves and the have-nots, far more so in a milieu of frustrated expectations, felt injustice, and a growing awareness of entitlements, which include claims to a higher standard of living by the deprived populations. How these factors affect the development and distribution of resources and the relationships among populations by sex, race, ethnicity, and other stratifiers should obviously be of concern to human ecology. While the tendency of human ecologists "not to confront policy matters directly" (Hawley 1986, p. 127) may be a defensive response to avoid espousing unpopular positions, it diverts their attention away from the fate of those at the receiving end of expansionism. Borgatta (1989), on the other hand, feels a strong need for a "proactive sociology" that would bridge the gap between theory and practice and help ensure the relevance of sociology for social policy and action.

The general neglect of the role of norms and agency in human and organizational interaction has also been a cause for concern to many sociologists. While some latitude is provided for incorporating social norms in specific analyses (for example, in the relationship between group membership and fertility behavior), their macro-orientation and focus on whole populations compels the demographers and human ecologists to ignore the role of the subjective values and purposes of individual actors in ecological and demographic processes (Namboodiri 1988, pp. 625–627). The use of micro-economic models of fertility by the "New Home Economics," on the other hand, is viewed by Winsborough (1991) as an effort to patch up the Malthusian model: "In the initial model, economic hardship affected fertility only because of delayed marriage. The 'New Home Economics' further endogenizes fertility, allowing women to adjust their fertility to maintain their level of living"[4] (1991, pp. 3–4).

Despite major gains in our understanding of human ecology and population dynamics, the fast pace of social and demographic changes, coupled with the uncertain and unsettling impact of these changes on the structure and organization of family and social life, makes it difficult to disagree with Winsborough's prognosis of "a long period of change, experimentation, and normative confusion before a new set of patterns appears" (1991, p. 13).

NOTES

1. The nature and direction of this process is hardly as cumulative or clear-cut as it is made out to be. Luckmann (1979) states that the quest for modernization is not a straightforward matter of economic policy. It is rather one of the most complex processes in history. In it, transnational ideologies and nationalistic aspirations, and deep moral concerns, as well as individual stupidity and bureaucratic incompetence, inexorable structural developments, and accidental meanderings of local history can only be distinguished with some difficulty. Perhaps this passionate engagement in a global lottery will some day find a Gibbons. For us, it is too soon to know the true nature of the prizes for which we are striving (Luckmann 1979, p. 3). At the same time, Gellner (1964) makes it quite clear that it is not a "fair" (tacit) global referendum that has decided on the striving for industrialization and affluence but an (unwittingly) "rigged" one: those who opt out, or pursue change ineffectively, are eliminated, rendered powerless if not physically destroyed. This is a referendum in which all those who vote no see their votes, or indeed themselves, destroyed (1964, p. 70, footnote 1).

2. Murdock et al. (1991, pp. 492–493) define sustenance activities as "the complex of organizational means used by a population to extract a living from the environment" or, alternatively, as "the entire set of social, economic, and cultural factors which determine, interrelate with, and result from the activities used to extract a living (sustenance) from a set of environmental resources." The key function is then defined as the key sustenance activity "most likely to determine the level of resources available to area residents, thus affecting the area's pattern of net migration." Finally, dominance determines "how sustenance activities affect the flow of resources to an area's population."

3. As noted earlier, the human ecological and neo-Malthusian orientations are contrasting positions—the former in consonance with the capitalist expansionary imperative, the latter responding to the actual and perceived limits to planetary carrying capacity and the impossibility of duplicating western patterns of growth and living standards in the rest of the world within the context of the earth's finite resources.

4. Winsborough (1991) points out that with the decline of work in fertility, interest

has now turned to household and family demography and to the analysis of population composition and the other components of change in size: "Interest in mortality analysis appears to have increased somewhat in recent years, in part due to the AIDS epidemic in Africa and elsewhere but also in part due to methodological advances. . . . The difficult issue of undocumented aliens, well-founded complaints about the data system, and just plain good work have contributed to a renewed interest in international migration in this country (1991, p. 7).

REFERENCES

Bennett, John. 1976. *The Ecological Transition: Cultural Anthropology and Human Adaptation.* Oxford, England: Pergamon.

Bharadwaj, Lakshmi K. 1992. "Human Ecology and the Environment." Pp. 848–867 in Edgar F. Borgatta and Marie L. Borgatta (eds.), *Encyclopedia of Sociology,* vol. 2. New York: Macmillan.

Borgatta, Edgar F. 1989. "Toward a Proactive Sociology." Paper presented at the 29th International Congress of the International Institute of Sociology, Rome, Italy.

Daley, Herman E. 1979. "Ethical Implications of Limits to Global Development." Pp. 37–57 in William F. Finnin, Jr. and Gerald Alonzo Smith (eds.), *The Morality of Scarcity: Limited Resources and Social Policy.* Baton Rouge: Louisiana State University Press.

Durkheim, Emile. [1893] 1932. *The Division of Labor in Society* (trans. by George Simpson). Glencoe, Ill.: The Free Press.

Frey, William H. 1993. "The New Urban Revival in the United States." *Urban Studies* 30:741–774.

Gellner, Ernest. 1964. *Thought and Change.* London: Weidenfeld and Nicholson.

Giddens, Anthony. 1990. *The Consequences of Modernity.* Stanford, Calif.: Stanford University Press.

Grebenik, E. 1989. "Demography, Democracy, and Demonology." *Population and Development Review* 15:1–22.

Greer, Scott. 1979. "Discontinuities and Fragmentation in Societal Growth." Pp. 308–316 in Amos H. Hawley (ed.), *Societal Growth: Processes and Implications.* New York: The Free Press.

Harper, Charles L. 1989. *Exploring Social Change.* Englewood Cliffs, N.J.: Prentice-Hall.

Hawley, Amos H. (ed.). 1979. *Societal Growth: Processes and Implications.* New York: The Free Press.

———. 1984. "Human Ecological and Marxian Theories." *American Journal of Sociology* 89:904–917.

———. 1986. *Human Ecology: A Theoretical Essay.* Chicago: University of Chicago Press.

Humphrey, Craig R. and Frederick R. Buttel. 1982. *Environment, Energy, and Society.* Belmont, Calif.: Wadsworth.

Lenski, Gerhard. 1979. "Directions and Continuities in Social Growth." Pp. 5–18 in Amos H. Hawley (ed.), *Societal Growth: Processes and Implications.* New York: The Free Press.

Luckmann, Thomas. 1979. "Comments." P. 3 in Charles F. Gallagher (ed.), *Modernization, Economic Development, and Cultural Values: A Bellagio Conference.* New York: The Rockefeller Foundation.

Miller, G. Tyler. 1972. *Replenish the Earth: A Primer in Human Ecology.* Belmont, Calif.: Wadsworth.

Moore, Wilbert E. 1960. "A Reconsideration of Theories of Social Change." *American Sociological Review* 25:810–818.

———. 1967. *Order and Change: Essays in Comparative Sociology.* New York: Wiley.

Murdock, Steve H., Kenneth Backman, Sean-Shong Hwang, and Rita R. Hamm. 1991. "International Dimensions of Post-1980 Internal Migration in the United States: The Role of Sustenance Specialization and Dominance." *Sociological Inquiry* 61: 491–504.

Namboodiri, Krishnan. 1988. "Ecological Demography: Its Place in Sociology." *American Sociological Review* 53:619–633.

Nisbet, Robert A. 1969. *Social Change and History: Aspects of the Western Theory of Development.* New York: Oxford University Press.

———. 1970. "Developmentalism: A Critical Analysis." Pp. 167–204 in John C. McKinney and Edward A. Tiryakian (eds.), *Theoretical Sociology: Perspectives and Developments.* New York: Appleton-Century Crofts.

Schnore, Leo F. 1965. *The Urban Scene: Human Ecology and Demography.* New York: The Free Press.

Simmons, Ozzie G. 1988. *Perspectives on Development and Population Growth in the Third World.* New York: Plenum Press.

Thurow, Lester. 1980. *The Zero-Sum Society.* New York: Penguin.

Turner, Jonathan H. 1991. *The Structure of Sociological Theory.* Belmont, Calif.: Wadsworth Publishing Company.

Vago, Steven. 1980. *Social Change.* New York: Holt, Rinehart and Winston.

Weinstein, Jay A. 1976. *Demographic Transition and Social Change.* Morristown, N.J.: General Learning Press.

Wilson, Franklin D. 1984. "Urban Ecology: Urbanization and System of Cities." *Annual Review of Sociology* 10:283–307.

Winsborough, Halliman. 1991. "Demography in the Next Century." *Center for Demography and Ecology (CDE) Working Paper 91-22.* Paper presented at the 54th Annual Meetings of the Southern Sociological Society. Madison: University of Wisconsin–Madison.

2

New Dynamics of Urban-Suburban Change: Immigration, Restructuring, and Racial Separation

WILLIAM H. FREY AND ELAINE L. FIELDING

NEW CONTEXTS FOR URBAN DEMOGRAPHIC CHANGE

The contexts for urban demographic change in the 1980s and 1990s have led to sharper divisions in growth prospects, diversity profiles, and economic inequalities across space. Some of the worst consequences of these new demographic growth trends are borne by inner-city residents in selected parts of the Rustbelt and also in coastal areas that serve as "ports-of-entry" for the surging immigrant flows that have accelerated over the course of the 1980s. Yet, sharp differences in population gains and race-ethnic compositions are also emerging *across* broad regions and metropolitan areas. The regions surrounding the high immigration areas—in California, Texas, South Florida, and New York—are becoming distinct from other parts of the country as a result of the growth of "new" minority populations. The "whiter," interior parts of the country are also becoming more strongly differentiated by patterns of economic growth and decline.

This chapter provides a backdrop for understanding the changing population profiles of urban America by focusing on the forces that shape key demographic trends across broad regions and within metropolitan areas. It then goes on to show how these trends have led to disparities in area growth and decline and in socio-demographic change. The new changes in the nation's urban landscape are strongly influenced by three elements (Frey 1993a):

1. *Immigration-related minority gains.* The expanded role of minority populations has important influence on internal redistribution within the United States. The heightened

Figure 2.1
U.S. Metropolitan Growth Trends, 1960–1990

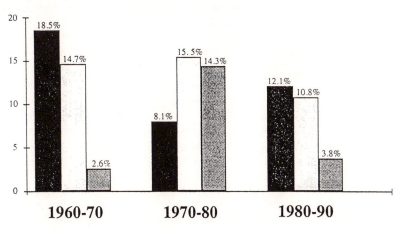

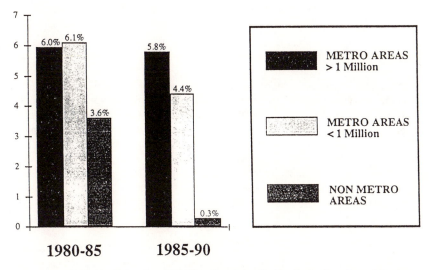

Source: Compiled at the University of Michigan Population Studies Center from decennial censuses.

immigration from Latin America and Asia has contributed to a marked growth disparity between the minority and majority (non-Hispanic) white populations for the United States as a whole (see Figure 2.1). However, these nationwide "majority-minority" trends are not replicated for each region and local area. Although minorities (Hispanics, blacks, Asians, Native Americans, and others) have dispersed to a greater degree than in earlier decades, minority growth is predominantly focused on particular regions and metropolitan areas. For example, fully one-fifth of the total minority growth over the 1980s accrued to just one metropolitan area—Los Angeles. Over half of the decade-wide minority growth accrued to just nine metropolitan areas. In contrast, the vast majority of the nation's metropolitan areas have relatively low minority percentages. These disparities across broad regions and metropolitan areas in race and ethnic profiles can be linked to similar disparities in their age structure and their skill-level and poverty compositions.

2. *Urban and regional restructuring.* The 1980s brought a revival of urbanization against the backdrop of the "rural renaissance" 1970s. The latter is now seen to be a result of exogenous or cyclical economic and demographic forces that temporarily increased the growth of small and nonmetropolitan areas. It also resulted from an industrial restructuring that reduced the employment-generating capacities of several northern industrial metro areas. The new urban growth patterns are clearly not a return to the past. Rather, they follow new industrial structure shifts that favor "knowledge-based" advanced service industries in metropolitan areas that serve as corporate headquarters or with otherwise highly diversified economies. Growth has also occurred in recreation and retirement centers catering to the large waves of retired elderly. Still, many smaller and rural areas, particularly in the interior parts of the nation, did not fare well as a consequence of 1980s economic downturns, and these areas now rely on less-than-competitive industries. In sum, urban and regional restructuring has led to more marked patterns of growth and decline for regions and metro areas.

3. *A suburban-dominated society.* A third important distribution-related development of the 1980s is the continued outward spread of population and jobs away from the historically dominant central cities of metropolitan areas. While the "urbanization of the suburbs" is not a new theme, and the suburban office boom was already noticeable in the 1970s, most urban residents now live and work within the suburbs. The growth of the suburban portion of the metropolitan areas resulted both from the relocation of activities outside of central cities in older northern and eastern metropolitan areas, as well as the recent growth within suburban areas of southern and western metropolitan areas where central cities never dominated, as completely, their areas' economic and residential landscapes (Cervero 1989; Stanback 1991) (see Figure 2.2). This is not to devalue a focus of central city demographic dynamics. On the contrary, it underscores their plight as places which house a plurality of the nation's minorities and disproportionate shares of urban poverty and recent immigrant populations.

Each of these three broad trends—the increased growth of minorities, the new disparities in urban growth and decline, and the suburban dominance of metropolitan activities—are signature characteristics of contemporary urban America. These trends serve to shape evolving patterns of growth, decline, and minority concentration across broad regions, as well as within selected metropolitan areas. These evolving patterns are discussed in greater detail below. Because minority concentration is occurring both across regions and within metropolitan areas, the roles of immigration and national minority growth, and their selective impact on the internal redistribution of minorities is first discussed.

Figure 2.2
Distribution of U.S. Population by Central City, Suburb, and Nonmetropolitan Status, 1960–1990*

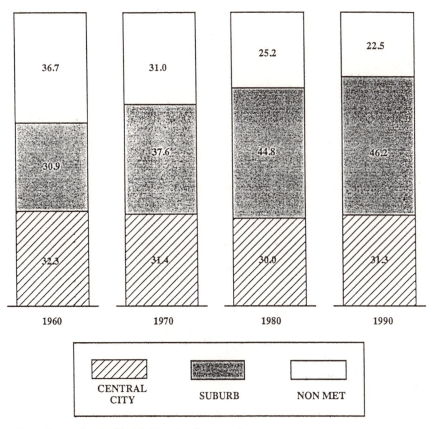

*Categories consistent with definitions in effect at each census.
Source: Compiled at the University of Michigan Population Studies Center from decennial censuses.

IMMIGRATION AND MINORITY GAINS—NATIONAL AND LOCAL IMPACTS

Immigration's Role in National Growth

The nation's population continues to grow at about one percent a year. The most pronounced shift is linked to the greater role of international migration, which accounted for more than one-third of national population growth between 1980 and 1990. During the 1980s, approximately 10 million immigrants entered the United States as either legal aliens, undocumented aliens, or refugees (Fix and Passel 1994). This represents the largest numeric increase via the immigration route since the 1900–1910 decade.

The greater immigration component of national population growth can, to a large degree, be attributed to high numbers of undocumented, illegal aliens from Mexico and Central and South America, as well as to refugees who immigrated here from Southeast Asia, Cuba, and other countries. It is not likely that this higher 1980s immigration will taper off, however. Although the Immigration Reform and Control Act of 1986 (IRCA) was intended to stem further undocumented immigration, it is estimated that between 100,000–300,000 illegals will continue to immigrate annually. Moreover, the Immigration Reform and Control Act of 1990 will also have the effect of increasing the number of legal immigrants. The immigration experience of the 1980s decade has led the Census Bureau to revise its projections for future population growth (Day 1993). Primarily because of new immigration assumptions, the projected year 2050 population was revised from 300 million to 392 million. This projection, compiled in 1993, assumes a net annual immigration of 880,000 (including 200,000 illegal aliens) for each year of the projection. The earlier 1989-based projection assumed an annual net immigration of 500,000.

These immigration gains have contributed substantially to recent growth in the nation's minority (other than non-Hispanic white) population. This is because the 1965 immigration legislation effectively decreased immigration allotments from Europe and Canada and increased allotments for developing countries, particularly in Asia. As a result, the share of legal immigrants originating in Asian countries increased from 13 percent during the 1960s to about 44 percent during the 1980s. Latin American countries, especially Mexico, continue to account for 40 percent of legal immigrants, and almost again as many illegal immigrants. As a consequence, the expanded immigration that is anticipated over the 1990s will be disproportionately from Latin American and Asian origins.

The disparity between minority and majority growth rates is evident from 1980s statistics that showed the non-Hispanic white "majority" population to grow by only 4.4 percent during the decade—in contrast to a +30.9 percent growth for the combined minority populations. About three-quarters of the Asian populations' 108 percent growth can be attributed to immigration over the decade. Once heavily dominated by Japan, China, and the Philippines as countries of origin, recent Asian growth encompasses a much wider array of national origin populations (including India, Korea, and Viet Nam, among others). About one-half of the Hispanic population's 53 percent growth can be attributed to immigration, with the remainder accounted for by natural increase (the surplus of fertility over mortality). Mexicans made up 13.4 million of the 22.3 million Hispanic population in 1990. The remainder consisted of Puerto Ricans (2.7 million), Cubans (1 million), and other Central and South American origins (about 5 million).

Although Asians and Hispanics represent the fastest growing minorities, the black population remains the most dominant—comprising about 30 million and 12.1 percent of the 1990 U.S. population. However, this continued sharp disparity between the growth rate for blacks and higher immigration-generated rates for Asians and Hispanics will lead to an increasingly smaller representation of blacks among both the minority and total populations. For the first time in 1990, blacks comprise less than half of the combined minority population. In fact, the Census Bureau's projections for the year 2050 portray a population that is 21 percent Hispanic, 15 percent black, 10 percent Asian, and 1 percent Native American. Under this scenario, "majority," non-Hispanic whites would constitute only 53 percent of the total population.

Impacts on States—Migration Dynamics

This nationwide picture camouflages distinctly different patterns for broad regions and individual states as a consequence of their divergent immigration and internal migration experiences. A significant distinction is whether the state's dominant migration flow is comprised of immigration from abroad or internal migration from other states. The geographic patterns of gains from these two sources, by and large, do not overlap. Led by California and New York, states that are the dominant destinations for abroad migrants tend to be those with large existing settlements of earlier immigrants from Latin America and Asia (Bean and Tienda 1987; Barringer, Gardner, and Levin 1993). A somewhat different grouping of states constitutes the greatest internal migrant "magnets"—which are located largely in the South Atlantic and the Pacific and Mountain regions. These maps also illustrate an overlap that *does* exist between states that *lose* large numbers of internal migrants and those that *gain* significantly from immigration.

To clarify these distinctions, a typology of states is presented based on their dominant migration sources of change (Frey 1993b; 1994b) (see Figure 2.3 and Table 2.1). States classed as "high immigration states" include the six states with largest 1985–1990 migration from abroad, where the immigration component overwhelms net internal migration—California, New York, Texas, New Jersey, Illinois, and Massachusetts. In fact, all of these states, except California, lost internal migrants to other states during the 1985–1990 period. (Note: although California ranked seventh among states in attracting internal migrants during this period, its growth dynamics are clearly dominated by migration from abroad.)

The six states classed as "high internal migration states"—Florida, Georgia, North Carolina, Virginia, Washington, and Arizona—displayed greatest net increases in their migration exchanges with other states over the 1985–1990 period. Moreover, in each case, these net internal migration gains significantly exceeded those of the immigration component. (This is also the case for Florida, despite its strong attraction for immigrants.) The attraction of these states for internal migrants is their growing economies and, in most cases, climatic and other amenities that serve as additional "pulls" for elderly retirees (Frey 1992; Taeuber 1992).

Figure 2.3
U.S. Immigration and Internal Migration, 1985–1990

Migration From Abroad 1985-90

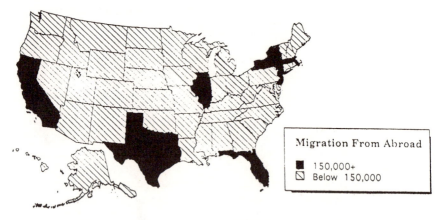

Net Interstate Migration 1985-90

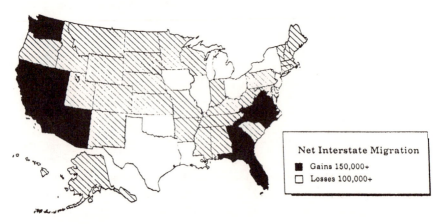

Source: Frey (1994c).

The third class of states shown in Table 2.1 are five "high out-migration states"—Louisiana, Michigan, Ohio, Oklahoma, and Iowa. These are states that displayed the greatest net out-migration in their exchanges with other states and were not recipients of large immigration from abroad. Although several of the high immigration states experienced greater levels of net internal out-migration (e.g., New York, Illinois, Texas, and New Jersey) than some of the latter, their demographic dynamics are much more influenced by the immigration component.

Table 2.1

Classification of States by Dominant Immigration and Interstate Migration Contributions to Population Change, 1985–1990

Rank	State	Migration from Abroad	Net Interstate Migration**
		Contribution to 1985-90 Change (1000s)	

I HIGH IMMIGRATION STATES[a]

Rank	State	Migration from Abroad	Net Interstate Migration**
1	California	1499	174
2	New York	614	-821
3	Texas	368	-331
4	New Jersey	211	-194
5	Illinois	203	-342
6	Massachusetts	156	-97

II HIGH INTERNAL MIGRATION STATES[b]

Rank	State	Migration from Abroad	Net Interstate Migration**
1	Florida	390	1071
2	Georgia	92	303
3	North Carolina	66	281
4	Virginia	149	228
5	Washington	102	216
6	Arizona	80	216

III HIGH OUT-MIGRATION STATES[c]

Rank	State	Migration from Abroad	Net Interstate Migration**
1	Louisiana	30	-251
2	Ohio	69	-141
3	Michigan	74	-133
4	Oklahoma	32	-128
5	Iowa	17	-94

Source: Compiled from 1990 Census files at the Population Studies Center, The University of Michigan

* 1990 State residents who resided abroad in 1985
**1985-90 In-migrants from other States minus 1985-90 Out-migrants to other States

[a]States with largest 1985-90 migration from abroad which exceeds net interstate migration
[b]States with largest 1985-90 net interstate migration and exceeds migration from abroad
[c]States with largest negative net interstate migration and not recipients of large migration from abroad

Source: Frey (1994b).

Although this migration classification of states is based on the dominant immigration/internal migration component of population change, it is intended to serve as a vehicle for characterizing the race and status selectivity associated with these distinct migration dynamics. Sharp differences in the race-migration dynamics are associated with each class of states. The characteristic dynamic

for most high immigration states is a large, primarily minority immigration
stream—coupled with a significant, largely white net internal out-migration.
Although California's internal migration is positive, it too sustained selective
net out-migration of important white population segments (discussed below).
Clearly, the substantial minority immigrant flows dominate demographic change
in all of these states.

The characteristic migration dynamics for the high internal migration states
contrast sharply with these. Here, the strong white internal migration gains dominate growth over the 1985–1990 period. Almost the reverse pattern characterizes the race-migration dynamic in high out-migration states. For these, it is a
large net out-migration of whites that dominates migration over the 1985–1990
period. In fact, with the exception of Louisiana, the minority component of total
net out-migration from these states is extremely small. They are losing large
numbers of whites that are not being compensated for by immigration from
abroad.

The above dynamics, if continued, suggest a situation where a few immigrant
destination states will continue to gain larger minority populations, while losing
(predominantly white) internal migrants to other prosperous areas. These different processes serve to maintain or even exacerbate a polarized pattern that
could lead to regional and state differences in racial compositions, age structures,
and other demographic characteristics that separate the largely minority immigrant populations from the white majority population that dominates internal
migration streams. These dynamics will be highlighted in the discussions that
follow.

REGIONAL AND METROPOLITAN TRENDS

Growth and Decline in the 1980s

Although immigration has an important impact on metropolitan population
growth, areas that gained primarily from internal migration have benefited from
economic gains owing to both national and worldwide economic restructuring.
The patterns of gains and losses associated with restructuring have led to a
resurgence in urban growth in some metropolitan areas, especially larger areas
on the coasts. However, many smaller metropolitan and rural areas in the nation's interior have not benefited from this regional restructuring.

Growing metropolitan areas tend to be those that successfully transformed
their economies from manufacturing to advanced services, FIRE (finance, insurance, and real estate), high-tech research and development, and growing new
industries (Noyelle and Stanback 1984; Frey 1987). Less stable growth prospects
occurred in smaller, nonmetropolitan areas engaged in peripheral, routine production activity that could be phased out by decision-makers located in corporate
or (in the case of defense activities) government centers. Nonetheless, much of
the deindustrialization-related "urban decline" of the 1970s turned around for

the 1980s. Of the eight large "million-plus" metropolitan areas that lost population in the 1970s, three (New York, Philadelphia, and St. Louis) began gaining in 1980–1985, and an additional three (Detroit, Milwaukee, and Buffalo) showed gains in 1985–1990. Only Pittsburgh and Cleveland continued to lose population through the 1980s.

The economic bases of the fastest gaining metropolitan areas are tied to expanding economic sectors and do not have histories of "heavy industry" manufacturing. They also tend to be located on the coasts. The following list of large metropolitan areas, whose population growth rates exceeded two and a-half times the national rate for the respective period, illustrates these points:

1970–80	1980–85	1985–90
Phoenix MSA	Phoenix MSA	Orlando MSA
Tampa–St. Petersburg MSA	Dallas–Ft. Worth CMSA	Sacramento MSA
Houston CMSA	Houston CMSA	San Diego MSA
Miami MSA	Tampa–St. Petersburg MSA	Phoenix MSA
San Diego MSA	Atlanta MSA	Atlanta MSA
Denver CMSA	San Antonio MSA	Los Angeles CMSA
Sacramento MSA	San Diego MSA	Seattle CMSA
	Sacramento MSA	Washington, D.C. MSA
		Miami CMSA
		Charlotte MSA
		Tampa–St. Petersburg MSA
		Dallas–Ft. Worth CMSA

Note: MSA = Metropolitan Statistical Area.
       CMSA = Consolidated Metropolitan Statistical Area.

Yet, the national trend toward 1980s reurbanization has been coupled with a *deceleration* of redistribution to the Sunbelt, when examined from a thirty-year perspective. While 1980s South and West regional growth continued to outpace Northern growth by a wide margin, the differential has become reduced—particularly for the South. This shift suggests that some of the strong period-related draws of small Sunbelt places have diminished over the 1980s and that several large Snowbelt metropolises benefited from restructuring or better economic times.

A Coastal-Interior Dichotomy

The Snowbelt-Sunbelt (or Northeast and Midwest versus South and West) dichotomy continues to be useful for distinguishing large absolute differences in population decline and growth between these two broad regions. Yet, an additional geographic distinction is useful for analyzing the recent *changes* in urbanization patterns for these regions. This distinction separates the "interior" portion of each region from its "coastal" portion. This way of dividing regions shows that the observed growth declines in both the South and the West are concentrated heavily in their interior sections. These growth slow-downs are most severe for 1985–1990 in small metropolitan areas in the interior South (see Figure 2.4).

Small and nonmetropolitan areas in the northern part of the country also displayed disparate patterns for interior (Midwest) and coastal (Northeast) regions. While these areas showed lower levels of 1970s growth than their counterparts in the Sunbelt, Midwest small areas fared even worse in the 1980s— particularly in the early part of the decade. Nonmetropolitan areas in this section registered negligible—then negative—growth as the decade wore on. In contrast, Northeast small and nonmetropolitan areas showed increased growth in the 1985–1990 period. These categories of North coastal areas grew faster than the large metropolises of the region.

The interior growth slow-downs of small and nonmetropolitan areas in both the Sunbelt and Snowbelt are strongly linked to economic period influences. The worldwide and cyclical forces that stimulated the sharp 1970s growth rises in smaller interior areas also provoked declines during the 1980s. The weak early-1970s dollar served to stimulate labor-intensive manufacturing in the South's eastern interior region and many small Rustbelt areas, but the dollar became stronger in the early 1980s with a change in the balance of trade. This, combined with the recessions, led to reduced demand and, hence, increased unemployment and disinvestment in these activities and areas. Likewise, the worldwide agricultural shortages that stemmed the decline of farming areas in the 1970s turned into an agricultural surplus in the 1980s—effecting widespread population declines in the rural and small-town Midwest and selected parts of the South.

Still, it was the changing fortunes of the mining and petroleum industries that had the most severe impact on communities of all sizes—in Appalachia, the Mountain West, and, in particular, the Southwest. Many of these areas grew at exceptionally high rates during portions of the 1970s and early 1980s. However, with the fall of worldwide petroleum prices toward mid-decade, growth was sharply curtailed in several interior metropolitan and nonmetropolitan areas.

The generally higher levels of growth for smaller and nonmetropolitan areas in the coastal sections of their respective regions draw from particular economic specialties, such as the recreation and retirement industry in Florida, New England, and the Pacific Northwest. They are also explained by the more diversified economies that these areas possess because of their stronger links to broader urban networks in the coastal portions of their regions. Some of these areas (such as the Allentown, Lancaster, and Reading MSAs in eastern Pennsylvania) lie at arm's length from major metropolises and were able to attract both employers and residents in search of somewhat lower labor and housing costs.

The growth prospects for large coastal metropolises in all three regions improved considerably over the 1980s decade. Areas that serve as national or re-

Figure 2.4
Geographic Pattern of Population Change in Metropolitan Areas of the United States over Four Intervals between 1960 and 1990

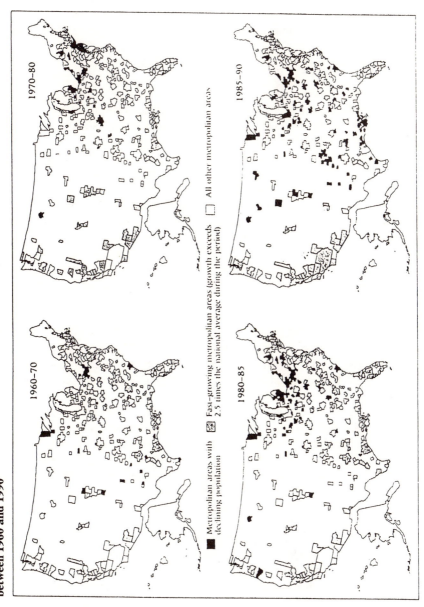

Source: Frey and Speare (1992), p. 136.

gional advanced service centers have shown the most steady population gains over the 1980s. Other metropolitan areas specializing in recreation and resorts that show spectacular but fluctuating growth levels (such as Miami and Tampa–St. Petersburg) are also located in coastal regions. Together, both types of areas help to account for the steadily rising 1980s growth levels in the nation's coastal regions.

Racial Disparities in Metropolitan Growth

Just as the immigration-driven growth of "new minorities" has led to disproportionate minority gains in high immigration states, these impacts are also observed for metropolitan areas. Immigrant minorities historically have tended to locate in traditional "port-of-entry" areas, or areas with already large concentrations of their ethnic group. In contrast, recent white majority migration streams tend to follow the "pushes" and "pulls" associated with regional restructuring-related economic gains. This can be seen by comparing metropolitan areas with the greatest non-Hispanic white population increases over the 1980s with those that show the greatest increases in the combined minority population (see Table 2.2.). The former areas—strong economic magnets—attracted whites in search of employment opportunities. The latter areas constitute the nation's largest "port-of-entry" metropolitan areas for immigrants, or areas with established minority concentrations.

Black distribution patterns differ from other minorities. Metropolitan areas that constituted traditional northern destinations for earlier southern-origin black migrants—New York, Chicago, Philadelphia, and Detroit—still rank among the black metropolitan concentrations (see Table 2.3). These traditional destinations still house almost a quarter of the nation's black population and the twelve metropolitan areas with more than a half million blacks are home to more than two-fifths of the black population.

Still, recent black redistribution shifts, even among these twelve areas, demonstrate a shift toward the Sunbelt. Chicago's metropolitan black population decreased during the 1980s, and slow black growth characterized Philadelphia and Detroit. In contrast, the "new South" metros—Atlanta, Miami, and Dallas—displayed substantial gains. Other fast-growing areas not on the list include these South Atlantic areas: Orlando, Raleigh-Durham, and Tampa–St. Petersburg. This is consistent with the recent attraction of South Atlantic states as Sunbelt destinations for blacks.

Hispanics and Asians are even more strongly concentrated in large metropolitan areas than blacks. The nine metropolitan areas with the largest numbers of Hispanics contain almost three-fifths of the nation's Hispanic population. The four areas with the largest Asian populations contain just over half of the *nation's* Asian population. Unlike the situation with blacks, metro areas with greatest 1990 Hispanic and Asian populations should also continue to experience the largest numerical gains. This is because they are key "port-of-entry" areas for recent immigrants.

Table 2.2

Metropolitan Areas with Greatest 1980–1990 Increases: Total Population, Non-Hispanic Whites, Minorities

Metro Area	Increase (1000s)
I. *AREAS WITH GREATEST TOTAL INCREASE*	
1. Los Angeles CMSA	+3,034
2. Dallas-Fort Worth CMSA	+ 955
3. San Francisco CMSA	+ 885
4. Atlanta MSA	+ 695
5. Washington DC MSA	+ 673
II. *AREAS WITH GREATEST WHITE INCREASE*	
1. Dallas-Fort Worth CMSA	+ 487
2. Atlanta MSA	+ 414
3. Phoenix MSA	+ 412
4. Tampa-St. Petersburg MSA	+ 345
5. Seattle CMSA	+ 324
III. *AREAS WITH GREATEST MINORITY INCREASE*	
1. Los Angeles CMSA	+2,795
2. New York CMSA	+1,398*
3. San Francisco CMSA	+ 787
4. Miami CMSA	+ 635*
5. Houston CMSA	+ 484

*Area experienced gain in minority population and loss in white population.
Source: Frey (1993a).

Still, the spread of these groups is evident in the fact that twenty-nine metropolitan areas had more than 100,000 Hispanics in 1990 (up from twenty-two in 1980), with high levels of growth displayed in areas like Washington, D.C., Boston, Phoenix, Orlando, and Tampa–St. Petersburg. Areas with Asian populations of greater than 100,000 have grown to twelve in 1990 (up from five in 1980). High Asian growth rates are seen in the majority of the nation's metropolitan areas (from small population bases). Hence, there is both concentration and some spread of these populations. The areas with high percentages of Hispanics tend to be located in the West and in Texas. Only two metropolitan areas have Asian populations that exceed 10 percent—Honolulu (62.9 percent) and San Francisco (14.8 percent).

The explosion of minority populations—both homegrown and immigrant—is leading to a much more diverse national population. However, the trends for regions and metropolitan areas point up the sharp disparities that have emerged. Some parts of the country—smaller sized communities in the North and Midwest—are becoming increasingly "whiter" and older than the national popu-

Table 2.3
Metropolitan Areas with 1990 Populations of Blacks, Hispanics, Asians, and Other Races, Exceeding 500,000

Metropolitan Area	1990 Pop. (1,000s)	Percent Change 1980-90	Minority Proportion of Total Pop.
Blacks			
1. New York CMSA	3289	+ 16.4	18.1
2. Chicago CMSA	1548	-- 0.6	19.2
3. Los Angeles CMSA	1230	+ 16.1	8.5
4. Philadelphia CMSA	1100	+ 6.5	18.6
5. Washington, DC MSA	1042	+ 19.7	26.5
6. Detroit CMSA	975	+ 5.9	20.9
7. Atlanta MSA	736	+ 40.0	25.9
8. Houston CMSA	665	+ 17.8	17.9
9. Baltimore MSA	616	+ 9.8	26.7
10. Miami CMSA	591	+ 50.1	18.5
11. Dallas CMSA	555	+ 32.4	14.2
12. San Francisco CMSA	538	+ 14.8	8.6
Hispanics			
1. Los Angeles CMSA	4779	+ 73.4	32.9
2. New York CMSA	2778	+ 35.4	15.4
3. Miami CMSA	1062	+ 70.9	33.3
4. San Francisco CMSA	970	+ 47.0	15.5
5. Chicago CMSA	893	+ 41.3	11.1
6. Houston CMSA	772	+ 70.2	20.8
7. San Antonio MSA	620	+ 28.8	47.6
8. Dallas CMSA	519	+109.4	13.4
9. San Diego MSA	511	+ 85.6	20.5
Asians and Other Races			
1. Los Angeles CMSA	1339	+138.3	9.2
2. San Francisco CMSA	927	+103.9	14.8
3. New York CMSA	873	+135.5	4.8
4. Honolulu MSA	526	+ 15.9	62.9

Source: Compiled at the University of Michigan Population Studies Center from decennial censuses.

lations. At the same time, growing multicultural "port-of-entry" metropolitan areas are taking on a much different demographic character. If current trends continue, the majority-minority polarization across regions, areas, and communities will intensify. Moreover, intra-metropolitan concerns associated with residential segregation, multilingual education, and concentrated poverty will be heightened in those parts of the country that have served as magnets for minorities.

INTRA-METROPOLITAN CITY-SUBURB TRENDS

The demographic dynamics *within* metropolitan areas have also taken significant turns. The majority of America's metropolitan population now lives in the suburbs. Although central cities once dominated, such that their population characteristics were more representative of the nation's demographic profile, this is no longer the case. Now many central cities, particularly in the older regions of the country, show demographic profiles that are quite distinct from those of their suburbs and from the nation as a whole. They are more racially diverse and have higher percentages of young adults and elderly and a greater incidence of poverty. During the manufacturing-to-services transformation of the nation's economy, some cities survived better than others. Still, even in these surviving cities, the kinds of white-collar professional jobs that have grown are often not consistent with the lower skill and educational levels of large segments of their resident populations (Frey and Speare 1988; Kasarda 1988). This section discusses the broad outlines of central city growth and decline as a prelude to subsequent discussions of race-ethnic suburbanization, as well as the concentration of poverty and its associated demographic characteristics in the nation's central cities.

City Gains and Declines

The 1980s rise in metropolitan growth served to moderate the declines and growth slow-downs many large cities sustained during the 1970s. This is evident from Table 2.4, which shows trends for the central cities and surrounding areas (suburbs) of the nation's twenty-five largest metropolitan areas. (The central city-suburb comparisons in this section pertain to central cities and metropolitan balances of 320 Primary Metropolitan Statistical Areas [PMSAs], MSAs, and New England County Metropolitan Areas [NECMAs] defined by the Office of Management and Budget as of June 30, 1990.) Of the eighteen central cities that lost population during the 1970s, six (New York, Boston, Minneapolis–St. Paul, Kansas City, San Francisco–Oakland, and Seattle) displayed gains in the 1980s, and all but one (Denver) of the remaining areas showed smaller losses than in the 1970s.

There are two primary reasons why the larger central cities have rebounded from their 1970s losses. One has to do with the economic functions some of these cities possess, which dovetailed with secular patterns of corporate growth and related advanced service industries during the 1980s. Cities that serve as headquarters of corporations and related FIRE industries tended to grow in employment and population. A case in point is New York, where the metropolitan area's population growth became strongly concentrated within the central city where many of these employment opportunities grew. On the other hand, those cities located within metropolitan areas where such industries with ''new'' agglomeration economies are less prominent did not grow as strongly.

Table 2.4
Percent Change in Central City(ies) and Suburbs of the 25 Largest Metropolitan Areas by Region, 1960–1990

Region & Metropolitan Area*	Central City Percent 10-Yr. Change			Suburbs Percent 10-Yr. Change		
	1960-1970	1970-1980	1980-1990	1960-1970	1970-1980	1980-1990
NORTHEAST						
New York	1.4	-10.4	3.5	22.0	2.3	1.7
Philadelphia	-3.1	-13.5	-5.8	25.1	6.4	8.4
Boston	1.5	-7.4	2.9	16.1	2.2	3.5
Pittsburgh	-14.1	-18.5	-13.0	4.2	-1.4	-5.8
MIDWEST						
Chicago	-4.7	-10.7	-6.7	39.8	13.1	7.4
Detroit	-8.5	-19.2	-13.0	30.9	9.5	2.5
Cleveland	-14.3	-23.6	-11.9	27.0	0.9	0.0
Minneapolis-St. Paul	-2.4	-12.5	0.5	51.2	22.4	22.8
St. Louis	-10.9	-22.4	-8.7	30.8	8.7	7.2
Cincinnati	-9.8	-15.0	-5.6	21.9	8.8	7.1
Milwaukee	-1.8	-9.3	-0.2	27.4	9.9	5.1
Kansas City	20.1	-6.9	1.0	8.2	17.3	16.8

SOUTH

Washington, DC	0.6	-14.2	-0.1	64.9	16.6	27.7
Dallas	30.6	8.0	15.6	56.2	56.2	48.0
Houston	34.3	27.3	2.6	53.0	82.6	48.3
Miami	24.3	12.2	8.6	44.8	39.5	25.1
Atlanta	1.8	-12.7	-3.9	58.1	44.8	42.4
Baltimore	-2.8	-12.5	-6.0	34.5	19.7	16.8
Tampa-St. Petersburg	11.5	8.8	3.6	69.4	82.4	42.5

WEST

Los Angeles	11.8	4.7	17.9	21.7	7.7	19.2
San Francisco	-3.3	-5.1	6.6	29.6	5.7	8.6
Seattle	-0.5	-5.2	7.8	64.4	26.2	31.1
San Diego	28.0	28.1	29.7	35.7	47.7	38.7
Phoenix	-66.9	44.1	35.7	-4.6	104.4	55.7
Denver	4.2	-4.3	-5.0	61.6	58.3	23.4

*Metropolitan areas, central cities and suburbs are based on MSA, PMSA and NECMA definitions as designated on June 30, 1990.

Source: Compiled at the University of Michigan Population Studies Center from decennial censuses.

A second continuing source of city growth in selected "port-of entry" cities draws from immigration. Immigrant minorities are more likely to locate in the central city than is the general population. As a result, large immigrant streams to areas like Los Angeles, New York, San Francisco, and Miami contributed significantly to these central cities' growth.

City Losses by Race

Although several large central cities have somewhat rebounded demographically over the past decade, many central cities of all sizes continue to experience declines in their populations. This is a result of continued suburban spread as well as industrial restructuring patterns that adversely affect many central city employment bases. While population losses of whites in selected cities are countered by gains in immigrant populations, this is not the dominant pattern. Central city population loss is addressed in Table 2.5, which shows rankings of absolute and percentage loss between 1980 and 1990 for the total, non-Hispanic white, black, and Hispanic populations.

Cities with greatest absolute losses are heavily concentrated in the Midwest and interior Northeast. Chicago leads the pack with a loss of 208,000 people. Other losers include three large East Coast cities (Philadelphia, Newark, and Baltimore) and three Southern cities (New Orleans, Memphis, and Louisville). Most of these cities also lost blacks, except for Detroit and Memphis, which gained blacks over the 1980s. The numbers for Hispanics are striking: Chicago's loss would have been much greater without the influx of 130,000 Hispanics between 1980 and 1990. Philadelphia, Newark, and Denver also partially offset their losses with gains of Hispanics.

Ranking cities by percentage loss produces a different top fifteen list—one that includes many cities in small metropolitan areas, in addition to the large cities common to both lists. Most of the declining small cities have heavy manufacturing or mining-based economies and are located in the region where Ohio, Pennsylvania, and West Virginia meet (Johnstown, Pennsylvania; Wheeling, Huntington, and Parkersburg, West Virginia; and Steubenville, Ohio). In none of these cities were losses offset by black or Hispanic gains.

About half of the top fifteen losers of non-Hispanic whites also appear on the total population list. The others are all cities that lost non-Hispanic whites but gained members of one or more minority groups. Many of these cities registered *gains* in total population between 1980 and 1990. New York City is a case in point; it lost just over a half a million non-Hispanic whites and gained over 300,000 each of blacks and Hispanics, as well as 270,000 Asians (data not shown), resulting in a total population gain of 253,000 (some of these blacks and Asians may have also been Hispanic). Several other immigration-magnet cities attracted Hispanics and Asians while losing a substantial number of non-Hispanic whites (Los Angeles, Houston, Miami, and Minneapolis).

In terms of non-Hispanic white percent population loss, new cities on the list

Table 2.5

Rankings of Absolute and Relative Population Loss, 1980–1990, for Total, Non-Hispanic White, and Black Populations

	Largest Absolute Loss, 1980-90				Highest Percent Loss, 1980-90			
Rank Name	Total	NH-White	Black	Hispanic	Rank Name	Total	NH-White	Black	Hispanic

TOTAL

Rank Name	Total	NH-White	Black	Hispanic	Rank Name	Total	NH-White	Black	Hispanic
1. Chicago, IL	-208289	-242308	-105406	130419	1. Johnstown, PA	-21	-22	-7	11
2. Detroit, MI	-182575	-201197	21058	1206	2. Wheeling, WV-OH	-19	-19	-19	-51
3. Philadelphia, PA	-103986	-153082	-2303	36993	3. Gary-Hammond, IN	-18	-28	-10	-7
4. Cleveland, OH	-68206	-58418	-15942	5425	4. Youngstown-Warren, OH	-15	-20	-3	0
5. New Orleans, LA	-63171	-63063	-125	-1963	5. Huntington-Ashland,	-14	-14	-14	-20
6. Pittsburgh, PA	-59055	-55287	-6181	216	6. Steubenville-Weirton,	-13	-14	-10	-9
7. St. Louis, MO	-57494	-33310	-27074	-301	7. Parkersberg-Marietta	-13	-14	-11	-39
8. Gary-Hammond, IN	-50679	-34483	-12337	-2561	8. Niagara Falls, NY	-13	-17	6	3
9. Newark, NJ	-50226	-40591	-28316	25252	9. Detroit, MI	-13	-36	3	3
10. Baltimore, MD	-49314	-56063	4331	31	10. Pittsburgh, PA	-13	-16	-6	6
11. Memphis, TN	-35898	-67219	29058	-944	11. Benton Harbor, MI	-13	-53	-7	-12
12. Louisville, KY	-30169	-26818	-3973	-298	12. Cleveland, OH	-12	-19	-6	31
13. Buffalo, NY	-29747	-42203	5463	6630	13. Flint, MI	-12	-23	2	1
14. Youngstown-Warren, OH	-25540	-23667	-1427	-20	14. Pascagoula, MS	-12	-17	13	-37
15. Denver, CO	-24755	-39392	794	15034	15. Newark, NJ	-12	-31	-13	28

NON-HISPANIC WHITES

Rank Name	Total	NH-White	Black	Hispanic	Rank Name	Total	NH-White	Black	Hispanic
1. New York, NY	252644	-508413	318350	381224	1. Benton Harbor, MI	-13	-53	-7	-12
2. Chicago, IL	-208289	-242308	-105406	130419	2. Miami-Hialeah, FL	9	-38	18	34
3. Detroit, MI	-182575	-201197	21058	1206	3. Detroit, MI	-13	-36	3	3
4. Houston, TX	42342	-172320	20220	174588	4. Atlanta, GA	-6	-34	-3	150
5. Los Angeles-Long Beach	647687	-163919	3507	686851	5. Newark, NJ	-12	-31	-13	28
6. Philadelphia, PA	-103986	-153082	-2303	36993	6. Bergen-Passaic, NJ	2	-31	8	46
7. Boston-Lawrence-Salem	35143	-101029	41466	70288	7. Gary-Hammond, IN	-18	-28	-10	-7
8. Memphis, TN	-35898	-67219	29058	-944	8. New Orleans, LA	-11	-25	-10	-10
9. Milwaukee, WI	-1485	-66422	44439	14081	9. Flint, MI	-12	-23	0	1
10. Miama-Hialeah, FL	50774	-66356	16494	108605	10. Johnstown, PA	-21	-22	2	11
11. New Orleans, LA	-63171	-63063	-125	-1963	11. Trenton, NJ	-4	-22	-7	70
12. Cleveland, OH	-68206	-58418	-15942	5425	12. Birmingham, AL	-5	-22	4	-55

Table 2.5 (Continued)

	Largest Absolute Loss, 1980-90				Highest Percent Loss, 1980-90		
Rank Name	Total NH-White	Black	Hispanic	Rank Name	Total NH-White	Black	Hispanic
13. Baltimore, MD	-49314	4331	31	13. Kankakee, IL	-9	-20	17	107
14. Pittsburgh, PA	-59055	-6181	216	14. Jersey City, NJ	-2	-20	9	11
15. Minneapolis-St. Paul, MN	3941	26985	7190	15. Youngstown-Warren, OH	-15	-20	-3	0
BLACKS							
1. Chicago, IL	-208289	-242308	-105406	130419	1. Wheeling, WV-OH	-19	-19	-19	-51
2. Washington, DC-MD-VA	-1034	10003	-44118	29810	2. Huntington-Ashland,	-14	-14	-14	-20
3. Newark, NJ	-50226	-40591	-28316	25252	3. Newark, NJ	-12	-31	-13	28
4. St. Louis, MO	-57494	-33310	-27074	-301	4. Parkersberg-Marietta	-13	-14	-11	-39
5. Cleveland, OH	-68206	-58418	-15942	5425	5. St. Louis, MO	-9	-9	-10	-4
6. Atlanta, GA	-17705	-8661	-14380	2735	6. Gary-Hammond, IN	-18	-28	-10	-7
7. Gary-Hammond, IN	-50679	-34483	-12337	-2561	7. Steubenville-Weirton	-13	-14	-10	-9
8. San Francisco, CA	44985	-18043	-7375	17344	8. Washington, DC-MD-VA	0	3	-9	111
9. Pittsburgh, PA	-59055	-55287	-6181	216	9. Chicago, IL	-7	-17	-9	30
10. Louisville, KY	-30169	-26818	-3973	-298	10. San Francisco, CA	7	-5	-9	21
11. Chattanooga, TN	-17099	-15591	-2378	-321	11. Greeley, CO	14	8	-8	49
12. Philadelphia, PA	-103986	-153082	-2303	36993	12. Muncie, IN	-8	-8	-8	1
13. Dayton-Springfield	-23403	-21496	-1679	-458	13. Johnstown, PA	-21	-22	-7	11
14. Youngstown-Warren, OH	-25540	-23667	-1427	-20	14. Benton Harbor, MI	-13	-53	-7	-12
15. Pensacola, FL	546	1175	-980	120	15. Cleveland, OH	-12	-19	-6	31

Source: Compiled at the University of Michigan Population Studies Center from decennial censuses.

include several New Jersey areas (Atlantic City, Bergen-Passaic, Trenton, and Jersey City), all of which lost over 20 percent of their white populations yet gained Hispanics (and sometimes, blacks). Three large cities lost over one-third of their non-Hispanic white population between 1980 and 1990 (Miami—38 percent, Detroit—36 percent, and Newark—34 percent).

Conclusions about city population loss vary depending on the group of interest and whether the focus is on absolute or relative loss. One group of large Midwestern and Northeastern cities stands out, especially if the focus is on absolute loss: Chicago, Cleveland, Detroit, Gary, Newark, Philadelphia, and Pittsburgh. These cities have sustained population losses over several decades through suburbanization and regional restructuring. A second group represents cities in which heavy white population losses were more than offset by minority population gains (primarily Hispanics and Asians): Boston, Houston, Los Angeles, Miami, Minneapolis, and New York City. Those experiencing large percentage losses make up a third group containing the cities of small metropolitan areas in the heavy manufacturing-mining district of Ohio, Pennsylvania, and West Virginia.

MINORITY SUBURBANIZATION

Suburbanization Levels

Another major trend characterizing the 1980s was the increased suburbanization of minorities. Over the decade, the proportion of metropolitan residents living in the suburbs (suburbanization level) increased 5 percentage points for the combined minority population (from 34 to 39 percent) and only 2 points (from 65 to 67 percent) for non-Hispanic whites (Figure 2.5). Despite this increase for minorities, suburbanization levels among non-Hispanic whites continued to be much higher than those of all three minority groups in all regions and in most individual metropolitan areas. In 1990, for the United States as a whole, two-thirds (67 percent) of non-Hispanic whites lived in the suburbs, compared to 51 percent of Asians, 43 percent of Hispanics, and 32 percent of blacks. Asian and Hispanic suburbanization levels would be higher were it not for a tendency among recent immigrants to concentrate in central cities (Frey and Speare 1988).

Blacks are distinct; their suburbanization level remains much lower than those for other groups, even though it has increased by five percentage points in each of the last two decades. While the emergence of a bona-fide black middle class and the enactment of federal fair housing legislation in the 1960s spurred suburbanization among blacks, the black-white gap in suburbanization levels has changed very little (Fielding and Frey 1994).

However, the majority-minority difference in suburbanization level varies widely across metropolitan areas. In some areas, such as Los Angeles, even the level for blacks approaches that for non-Hispanic whites. In general, differences

Figure 2.5
Proportions Residing in Suburbs, 1980–1990: Metropolitan-Area Race and Ethnic Groups

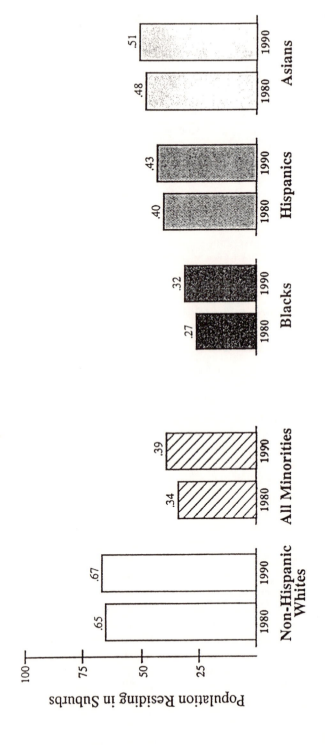

Proportions Residing in Suburbs - 1980 and 1990

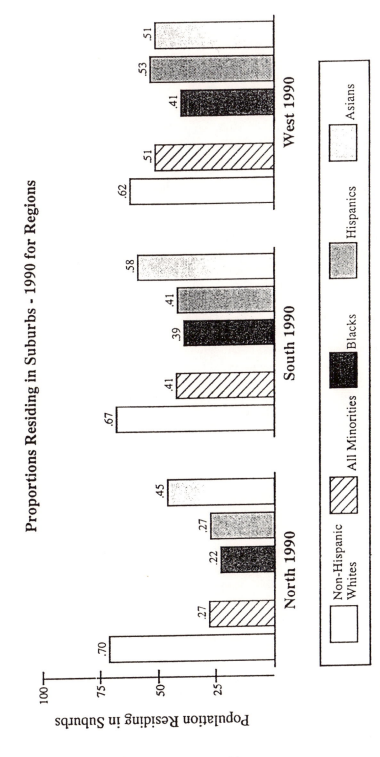

Proportions Residing in Suburbs - 1990 for Regions

North 1990

.70 Non-Hispanic Whites
.27 All Minorities
.22 Blacks
.27 Hispanics
.45 Asians

South 1990

.67 Non-Hispanic Whites
.41 All Minorities
.39 Blacks
.41 Hispanics
.58 Asians

West 1990

.62 Non-Hispanic Whites
.51 All Minorities
.41 Blacks
.53 Hispanics
.51 Asians

Population Residing in Suburbs: 100, 75, 50, 25

Legend:
Non-Hispanic Whites
All Minorities
Blacks
Hispanics
Asians

Source: Frey (1994a).

41

among areas can be traced to historical development patterns (Frey and Speare 1988), with majority-minority disparities being widest in larger metropolitan areas of the two northern regions and smallest in the West (see bottom panel of Figure 2.5). Blacks represent the extreme case. In the West, the black suburbanization level (41 percent) was only about 20 points lower than that for non-Hispanic whites, whereas in the North, the gap is nearly 50 percentage points (22 percent for blacks and 70 percent for non-Hispanic whites).

The continued majority-minority gap in suburbanization levels perpetuates the difference in racial-ethnic composition between cities and suburbs. The minority percentage of central city populations is generally much higher than those of their surrounding suburbs. This is less the case in Western metropolises, owing to the more sprawling, over-bounded central cities, but it is quite distinct in most Northern and Southern metropolitan areas. Eleven of the nation's largest central cities have populations comprised of "majority-minorities"—led by Miami (83 percent), Detroit (70 percent), and Atlanta (65 percent). None of the nation's suburban rings have minority shares that high, though the multiethnic suburban areas surrounding Miami and Los Angeles have approached "majority-minority" status.

Although city-suburb racial disparities deserve emphasis, it is also important to note that all three major minorities—blacks, Hispanics, and Asians—increased their suburbanization level in all regions of the country over the 1980s. How these changes affect population patterns *within* suburban rings plays out quite differently across metropolitan areas, depending on their mixes of minorities and historical growth patterns. Additional evidence from the 1990 census (not shown) provides some examples:

1. Older metropolitan areas, with suburbanizing blacks and new minority groups, showing further redistribution of whites to outer suburbs (e.g., New York and Philadelphia).

2. West and Southwest metropolitan areas, with multiracial mixes, exhibiting lower levels of neighborhood segregation during new, dynamic transition patterns as well as "majority-minority" suburban cities (e.g., Los Angeles).

3. Minority (largely black) growth and suburbanization in several Southern metropolitan areas (e.g., Atlanta).

4. Extreme patterns for individual areas: 1950s-style black city concentration and white suburban flight (e.g., Detroit). White city gains coupled with suburban dispersal of minorities (e.g., Washington, D.C.).

These scenarios illustrate several potential avenues for suburban racial change in the future. The relative changes in majority and minority populations in individual suburbs will have long-term effects on the economic, social, and political development of those communities.

Suburbanization by Socioeconomic Status

Historically, suburbanization was linked to upward mobility. That is, families with greater income levels, or higher education and socio-economic or occupational characteristics, were more likely to live in the suburbs than in the city. While this was true for the population as a whole, it was not until recently the case for blacks (Frey and Speare 1988; Fielding 1990). For the other minorities, Hispanics and Asians, the link is a bit stronger.

The graph in Figure 2.6a shows how suburbanization levels by education and race (for the population 25 years old and over) changed over the 1980s for the country as a whole. For the total population, the proportion in the suburbs remained stable for the two lowest education groups (less than 9 years and 9–11 years), while it increased slightly for the three highest groups. This pattern is somewhat misleading, however, because it characterizes none of the individual race or ethnic groups.

The pattern for whites is distinctive: The proportion of college-educated whites living in the suburbs actually declined between 1980 and 1990. This decline occurred in all regions and size categories of metropolitan areas, but it was most pronounced in the largest ones. Some of this decline can be explained by gentrification among highly educated whites, but most of it is attributable to white movement away from older, Northeast metropolitan areas to central cities in newer parts of the country. Because of de-suburbanization among highly educated whites over the last two decades, the class pattern for whites in 1990 is an inverted U-shape, with the college educated being even less likely than the least educated to live in the suburbs. This pattern contrasts sharply with those for the minority groups, all of which exhibit the traditional class-selective pattern of suburbanization.

Among blacks and Asians, the pattern of change in suburbanization over the 1980s reinforced this pattern with greater increases for the higher education categories. For black college graduates, vigorous suburbanization led to an increase of 7 percentage points (from 33 percent in 1980 to 40 percent in 1990) in the percent living in the suburbs. Although suburbanization level rises with education for Hispanics, increases in level over the 1980s were nearly even across education categories.

Because class patterns of metropolitan residence are strongly affected by the historical development of areas, they play out quite differently across regions, size categories, and metropolitan areas. To illustrate this, the 1980 and 1990 suburbanization levels by race and education level are shown in Figure 2.6b for three individual metropolitan areas—Dallas, Detroit, and Los Angeles.

In Dallas (first panel of Figure 2.6b), all groups experienced increases in suburbanization level over the 1980s. Within each race, the class pattern is similar to that for the country as a whole, with the college educated displaying the lowest level of suburbanization among whites and the highest level among each of the minority groups. This pattern is typical of large metropolitan areas

Figure 2.6a
Proportion in Suburbs by Race and Education, for Total United States, 1980 and 1990

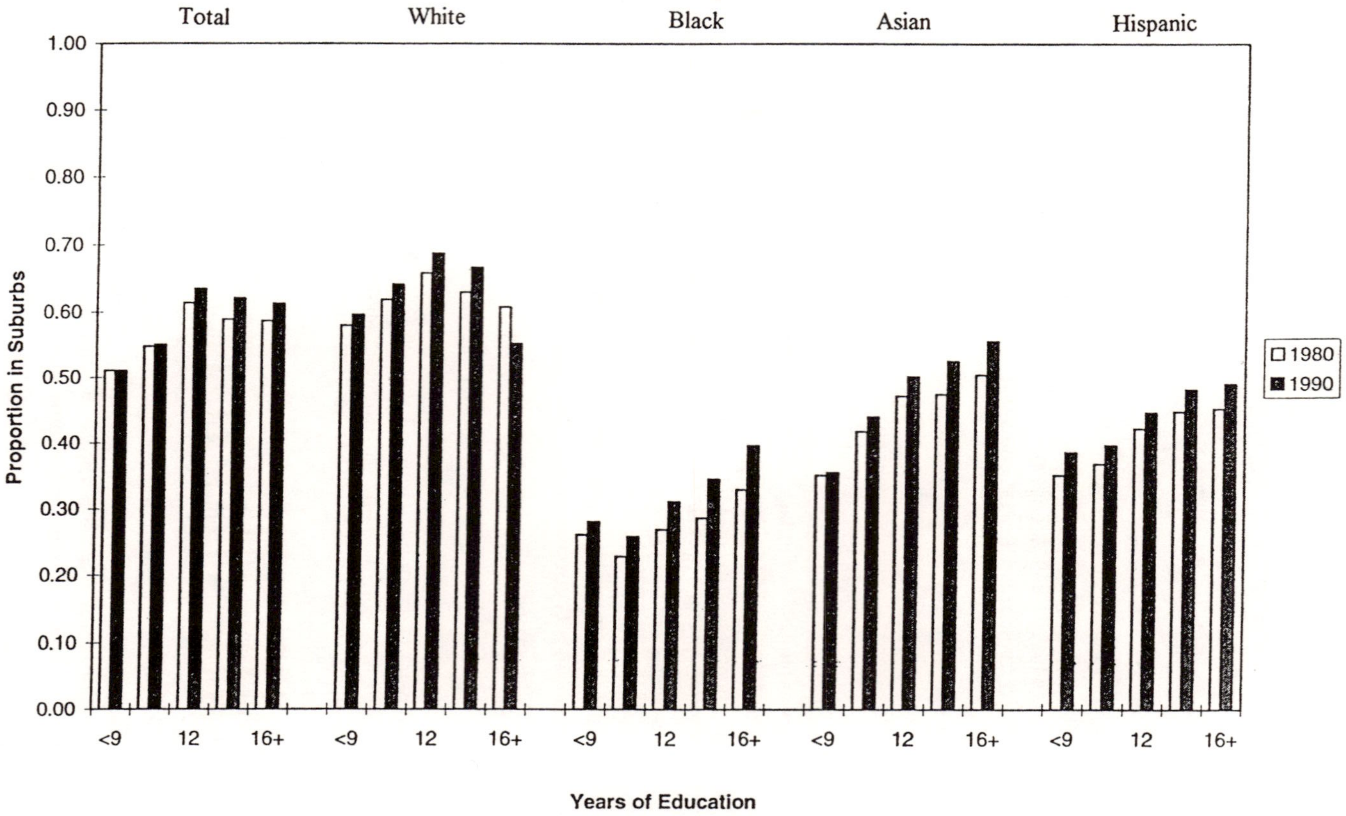

Years of Education

Proportion in Suburbs

Total   White   Black   Asian   Hispanic

1980
1990

Source: Compiled at the University of Michigan Population Studies Center from decennial censuses.

Figure 2.6b
Proportion in Suburbs by Race and Education, Selected Areas, 1980 and 1990

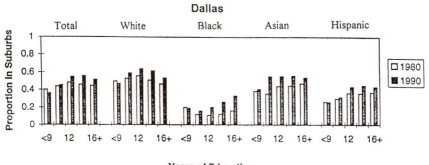

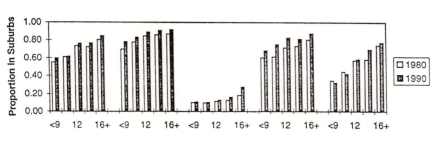

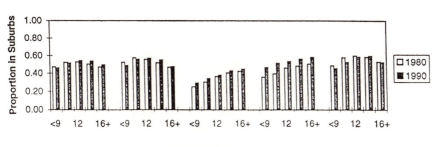

Source: Compiled at the University of Michigan Population Studies Center from decennial censuses.

in the South. The increase in suburbanization among college-educated blacks was dramatic; their level doubled from 16 percent in 1980 to 33 percent in 1990. The Dallas area attracted a large number of high-status black in-migrants over the 1980s, many of whom moved directly to the suburbs.

In Detroit, the disadvantage of blacks at the suburban level is glaring. Even among college graduates, the 1990 level for blacks is more than 60 percentage points less than that for whites (second panel of Figure 2.6b). As in Dallas, black college graduates in Detroit experienced significant suburbanization over the 1980s, exacerbating the sharp upturn in suburbanization level for the highest education category. Unlike for the nation as a whole, the suburbanization level for *whites* has increased with education. Very few whites with high educational attainment live in the city of the Detroit metropolitan area.

Two aspects of suburbanization patterns are unique in Los Angeles (third panel of Figure 2.6b): much narrower racial differentials than in other areas and negligible increases in suburbanization levels over the 1980–1990 decade for all groups except Asians. The traditional class-selective pattern characterizes blacks in 1990, and the level for black college graduates approaches that for other groups. Low and decreasing suburbanization levels among low-education whites (which include white Hispanics) and Hispanics can be traced to the heavy immigration of Hispanics to Los Angeles during the 1980s. Most new arrivals have low educational attainment and locate initially in the city.

POVERTY

Urban poverty has emerged as a major policy concern over the last decade. Rising poverty rates in central cities, as well as the increasing concentration of the poor population in specific areas within cities, have captured the attention of researchers and policy-makers (Wilson 1987; Ricketts and Sawhill 1988; Jargowsky and Bane 1991). This section focuses on poverty in cities and suburbs, covering the following issues: 1980–1990 trends in poverty rates and the growth of the poverty and non-poverty populations; the level of economic polarization between cities and suburbs; rates of female headship and poverty among female-headed households; and the poverty rates of children.

Several consistent themes run through this section: First, poverty conditions and trends vary widely across metropolitan areas and regions, generally mirroring area-specific economic conditions. While the poverty rate increased only slightly across all areas between 1980 and 1990, some cities (like Detroit and Houston) experienced large increases. Second, the poverty population is concentrated in the central cities of metropolitan areas and within cities, in specific high-poverty areas. Trends in the concentration of poverty follow those for poverty rates, with increases in similar cities and regions. Third, poverty conditions are worse among minorities (especially blacks and Hispanics), female-headed households, and children.

1980–1990 Trends

Poverty rates (the proportion of the population with incomes below the federal poverty line) for cities and suburbs in 1980 and 1990 appear in Table 2.6 for the total, black, and Hispanic populations. Beginning with the total population, the national poverty rate rose slightly for central cities, from 16.2 percent in 1980 to 18 percent in 1990. The rate in suburbs remained stable at 8 percent. These trends in rates reflect the differential growth rates of the poverty and non-poverty populations over the 1980s. In cities, the poverty population grew noticeably faster (18.4 percent) than the non-poverty population (4.1 percent), while for the suburbs, the differential was much smaller (poverty—17.3 percent and non-poverty—14.9 percent).

Focusing first on cities, the trends vary by region and size category. Among the four regions, only the Northeast showed no increase in its poverty rate. Here the poverty population actually declined slightly (−0.1 percent), while the non-poverty population increased (0.4 percent). The largest increase in city poverty rate took place in the Midwest, where the percent in poverty went from 15.5 percent in 1980 to 19.1 percent in 1990. Behind this change was a growth (16.5 percent) of the poverty population and a sizable decline (−9.6 percent) of the non-poverty population. Midwestern cities are still experiencing out-migration of higher-status persons. Cities in the South and West, on the other hand, experienced increases in both their poverty and non-poverty populations.

Change in city poverty rates between 1980 and 1990 was negatively related to size of metropolitan area, with the smallest areas experiencing the largest increase (3.1 percentage points). Like the Midwest region, cities in the small metropolitan category had a growing poverty population (16.7 percent) and a declining non-poverty population (−7.0 percent). In the medium and large metropolitan categories, both poverty and non-poverty populations grew, with the former growing faster, yielding increases in poverty rates.

The pattern of changes in poverty rates for suburbs is quite similar to that for cities, although the suburban changes are smaller in magnitude. One difference is for the South, where suburbs, unlike the cities, had a lower poverty rate in 1990 (10.2 percent) than in 1980 (10.4 percent). The ranking of regions and size categories by poverty rates is also different for the suburbs, probably reflecting higher poverty rates among the *rural* populations of some suburban rings. Southern and Western areas, as well as small metropolitan areas, show relatively high poverty rates in both decades. Small metropolitan areas are also distinct in having experienced a *decline* (−2.9 percent) in their suburban poverty populations.

Trends in city poverty rates for blacks over the 1980s mostly parallel those for the total population, but most of the changes are larger in magnitude. For example, the city poverty rate for blacks in the Northeast declined −3.5 percentage points in the Northeast and rose 5.7 points in the Midwest. In the suburbs, poverty rates declined in all regions except the Midwest and in large- and

Table 2.6
1980–1990 Trends in Poverty Rate and Population Growth by Race and Ethnicity for Regions and Metro Size Categories

	% Poverty City			% Poverty Suburb			Growth In Pov Pop		Growth In Non-Pov Pop	
	1990	1980	Diff	1990	1980	Diff	City	Suburb	City	Suburb
A. TOTAL										
REGIONAL TOTALS										
Northeast	19	19	0	6	7	-1	0	-5	0	7
Midwest	19	15	4	6	6	0	17	8	-10	2
South	19	17	2	10	10	0	23	25	7	28
West	15	13	2	10	9	1	40	34	19	24
U.S. TOTALS										
Large Met	18	17	1	7	7	0	18	30	8	25
Medium Met	17	15	2	9	9	0	21	11	2	7
Small Met	18	15	3	11	11	1	17	-3	-7	-9
Total	18	16	2	8	8	0	18	17	4	15
B. BLACKS										
REGIONAL TOTALS										
Northeast	27	31	-3	15	18	-3	-1	6	18	32
Midwest	35	29	6	19	17	2	18	40	-9	26
South	32	31	1	22	26	-4	15	14	7	41
West	25	25	0	17	18	-1	12	31	12	43

U.S. TOTALS										
Large Met	30	29	1	16	18	-2	11	38	8	56
Medium Met	33	31	2	24	26	-2	13	4	3	18
Small Met	37	33	4	30	30	0	15	-10	-4	-11
TOTAL	31	30	1	19	22	-3	12	18	6	38
C. HISPANICS										
REGIONAL TOTALS										
Northeast	34	37	-3	14	16	-2	22	41	38	66
Midwest	25	23	2	11	10	1	36	68	20	44
South	30	25	5	22	21	1	67	95	31	84
West	25	21	4	19	17	2	95	76	55	55
U.S. TOTALS										
Large Met	28	27	1	16	15	1	55	93	44	77
Medium Met	29	25	4	26	22	4	72	83	42	47
Small Met	31	27	4	27	25	2	22	7	-1	-5
TOTAL	29	26	2	19	18	1	56	78	40	62

Source: Compiled at the University of Michigan Population Studies Center from decennial censuses.

medium-sized metropolitan areas. These declines stem partly from class-selective suburbanization among blacks over the 1980s.

Poverty trends for Hispanics over the 1980s are quite similar to those for the total population, although increases in and absolute levels of poverty rates are higher for Hispanics. In the aggregate, Hispanic poverty increased 2.2 points (from 26.4 percent to 28.6 percent) for the cities and 1.4 points (from 17.7 percent to 19.1 percent) in the suburbs. Increases in the city poverty rate for Hispanics were largest in the South and West regions as opposed to the Midwest for the total population. The South and West contain the primary destinations for most new Hispanic immigrants, many of whom are poor. The city poverty rate for the Northeast, even after declining over the decade, was noticeably higher in 1990 than in the other regions, reflecting the concentration of Puerto Ricans there.

A sense of the changes in poverty indicators for the total population in the most distressed cities can be gained from looking at the rankings displayed in Table 2.7. Among the metropolitan areas in 1990 with the highest city poverty rates are two large cities (New Orleans and Detroit), three university towns (State College, Pennsylvania; Athens, Georgia; and Bloomington, Indiana) and three heavily Hispanic Texas border towns (Brownsville, Laredo, and McAllen). Many of these same cities also appear on the top list for greatest increases in poverty rates between 1980 and 1990. Poverty rates increased in areas with already high rates. Nearly all of the cities with large increases in poverty rates had growing poverty and declining non-poverty populations. Especially prevalent on this list are industrial, Midwestern cities (Flint, Jackson, and Detroit, Michigan; Youngstown, Ohio; and Johnstown, Pennsylvania) These cities continued to lose jobs over the 1980s, pushing some people into poverty and spurring others to migrate out of the city.

Focusing on absolute growth of poverty population produces a different top fifteen list—one headed by Los Angeles, which gained nearly 200,000 poor residents between 1980 and 1990. Among Hispanics the poverty population in the city of Los Angeles rose by 200,000, while among Asians it decreased by nearly 80,000. It should be noted, however, that Los Angeles also tops the list of growth in *non-poverty* population. Immigration dominated the population growth figures for Los Angeles in the 1980s. Other magnets for Hispanic immigration appearing on both lists include Phoenix, Fresno, San Diego, Anaheim, Fort Worth, Dallas, and San Antonio. Only four of the cities (Houston, Detroit, Milwaukee, and Minneapolis) on the top poverty gainers list actually had decreases in their non-poverty populations, yielding substantial increases in their poverty rates.

Similarly, most of the cities on the list of top gainers of non-poverty population make the top twenty-five list of poverty gainers. Four cities (New York, Norfolk, Raleigh-Durham, and Jacksonville, Florida) stand out as having increases primarily in their non-poverty populations and decreases in their poverty rates. Because of expanding corporate and high-technology sectors, New York

Table 2.7

Rankings of Poverty Measures and Population Growth by Poverty Status for the *Total* Population of Central Cities

Highest 1990 City Poverty Percentage

Rank Name	1990 % Pov.	1980-90 Change in % Pov.	Growth of Pov. Pop.	Growth of Non-Pov. Pop.
1. Benton Harbor, MI	58	19	1703	-3647
2. State College, PA	45	6	3100	601
3. Brownsville, TX	39	8	17598	453
4. Athens, GA	39	13	5876	-2042
5. Monroe, LA	38	8	3469	-5786
6. Laredo, TX	37	3	13835	16558
7. McAllen-Edinberg, TX	36	7	23284	17215
8. Augusta, GA-SC	33	3	211	-3620
9. Chico, CA	32	6	5596	7437
10. Blommington, IN	31	8	5775	2945
11. New Orleans, LA	31	5	8343	-74916
12. Flint, MI	31	14	15642	-35001
13. Detroit, MI	30	10	81197	-258069
14. Fort Pierce, FL	29	2	1456	1702
15. Bryan, TX	29	5	10072	12655

Greatest 1980-90 Increases in City Pov. Percentage

Rank Name	1990 % Pov.	1980-90 Change in % Pov.	Growth of Pov. Pop.	Growth of Non-Pov. Pop.
1. Benton Harbor, MI	58	19	1703	-3647
2. Flint, MI	31	14	15642	-35001
3. Athens, GA	39	13	5876	-2042
4. Houma-Thibodaux, LA	29	11	4149	-8272
5. Cumberland, MD-WV	26	11	2260	-4675
6. Johnstown, PA	27	10	1667	-9102
7. Detroit, MI	30	10	81197	-258069
8. Youngstown-Warren, OH	26	9	8541	-35134
9. Jackson, MI	25	9	2865	-5155
10. Merced, CA	25	8	7846	11439
11. Fresno, CA	24	8	49812	83644
12. Brownsville, TX	39	8	17598	453
13. Lake Charles, LA	24	8	4889	-9917
14. Monroe, LA	38	8	3469	-5786
15. Blommington, IN	31	8	5775	2945

Greatest Absolute Increase in Poverty Population

Rank Name	1990 % Pov.	1980-90 Change in % Pov.	Growth of Pov. Pop.	Growth of Non-Pov. Pop.
1. Los Ang.-Long Beach	18	2	198221	433249
2. Houston, TX	21	8	137441	-106021
3. Detroit, MI	30	10	81197	-258069
4. Phoenix, AZ	13	2	75224	324158
5. Dallas, TX	17	4	67707	93256
6. Milwaukee, WI	21	8	51111	-55187
7. Fresno, CA	24	8	49812	83644
8. Miami-Hialeah, FL	26	6	46814	1115
9. San Diego, CA	13	1	46325	249445
10. San Antonio, TX	23	2	45873	98819
11. El Paso, TX	25	4	39636	49218
12. Fort Worth-Arlington	14	2	35533	124858
13. Anaheim-Santa Ana	15	4	35079	97133
14. Minneapolis-St. Paul	16	5	34091	-27296
15. Tucson, AZ MSA	20	5	32152	39907

Greatest Absolute Increase in Non-Poverty Population

Rank Name	1990 % Pov.	1980-90 Change in % Pov.	Growth of Pov. Pop.	Growth of Non-Pov. Pop.
1. Los Ang.-Long Beach	18	2	198221	433249
2. Phoenix, AZ	13	2	75224	324158
3. San Diego, CA	13	1	46325	249445
4. New York, NY	19	-1	-6910	226058
5. Norfolk-Virginia Beach, V/	12	-2	-882	162259
6. San Jose, CA	9	1	20420	131699
7. Fort Worth-Arlington	14	2	35533	124858
8. Sacramento, CA	16	1	25783	103888
9. San Antonio, TX	23	2	45873	98819
10. Anaheim-Santa Ana.	15	4	35079	97133
11. Dallas, TX	17	4	67707	93256
12. Raleigh-Durham, NC	13	-2	8922	92462
13. Jacksonville, FL	13	-3	-4632	91829
14. Austin, TX	18	2	28476	91335
15. Fresno, CA	24	8	49812	83644

Source: Compiled at the University of Michigan Population Studies Center from decennial censuses.

and Raleigh-Durham both attracted many new white-collar residents during the 1980s.

Economic Polarization of Metropolitan Areas

Metropolitan areas are polarized by economic status, with poor people being more likely to live in cities and non-poor people to live in the suburbs. This polarization is reflected in higher poverty rates in cities than in suburbs, a condition that exists in nearly all U.S. metropolitan areas. Changes over time in this phenomenon are influenced by two factors, which could have either opposing or reinforcing effects: One factor involves the destination choices of poor and non-poor intrametropolitan movers and metropolitan in-migrants (whether native or immigrant). If poor movers tend to choose city destinations at the same time as non-poor movers choose the suburbs, metropolitan polarization would increase. The other factor concerns changes in the poverty status of non-movers. Economic conditions, such as the closing of a large factory in the city, could impact city residents disproportionately, thereby increasing city poverty rates relative to suburban rates.

Data relevant to level of metropolitan polarization (differing class compositions of cities and suburbs) in 1990 are provided in Table 2.8, which contains some of the same information as Table 2.7, but arranged differently. Poverty rates in cities are higher than in suburbs across all races, regions, and size categories. Nationally, 18 percent of the city population had incomes below the poverty line, compared with 8.1 percent for the suburbs. This polarization of metropolitan areas by poverty status is larger and more consistent than for other socio-economic indicators, such as education. For instance, in many metropolitan areas the proportion with a college education is higher in the city than in the suburbs (Frey 1993c).

The level of polarization by poverty status stems largely from variations in suburban poverty rates; city rates, though higher, vary within a narrower range. Nevertheless, cities do vary in their poverty levels because of their size, regional location, and racial composition. For example, Detroit's high poverty rate (30.2 percent) for the total city population is linked to both poor economic conditions and the large proportion of blacks, whose poverty rate is high.

Degree of polarization by poverty status tends to be greater in the industrial North than in the Sunbelt, as well as for the larger metropolitan areas. These differentials can be attributed to the generally higher suburban poverty levels in the South and West and in small metropolitan areas due to their larger rural, but suburban, populations. This pattern holds for the total population and for whites but sometimes plays out differently for the minority groups.

Polarization among blacks is highest in the Midwest but is also high in some large Southern metropolitan areas. Among the areas listed, Atlanta had the greatest difference in city and suburb poverty rates for blacks (19.4 percent). For Hispanics, the gap was largest in the Northeast, as typified by Philadelphia

Table 2.8
1990 Percent in Poverty, by Race and Ethnicity for Central City(ies) and Suburbs of Region and Metro Categories, and Selected Metro Areas

	Total			Whites			Blacks			Hispanics			Asians		
	City	Suburbs	Diff.	City	Suburbs	Diff.	City	Suburbs	Diff.	City	Suburbs	Diff.	City	Suburbs	Diff.
Selected Metro Areas															
New York	30	9	21	20	6	14	34	23	12	46	24	22	19	3	16
Philadelphia	31	6	25	14	4	10	41	20	21	57	18	38	38	9	28
Chicago	33	6	27	16	4	12	47	21	26	30	12	19	19	3	16
Detroit	44	9	35	30	8	23	48	27	21	44	13	31	41	7	34
Dallas-Ft. Worth	25	9	16	13	6	7	38	24	15	33	21	11	20	8	12
Atlanta	41	10	31	10	6	4	48	21	28	38	16	22	33	10	23
Los Angeles	27	17	10	19	13	6	37	24	12	34	23	11	21	13	9
Denver	27	9	18	19	7	11	39	31	8	41	18	22	33	12	21
REGION TOTALS															
Northeast	29	8	21	19	7	12	38	21	16	47	19	27	23	6	17
Midwest	28	8	20	16	7	9	49	27	22	31	14	17	35	6	29
South	28	14	14	16	10	6	44	29	15	38	28	10	21	9	11
West	22	14	8	15	10	4	36	24	12	32	25	7	24	13	12
U.S. TOTALS															
Large Met	28	10	18	16	7	9	42	23	19	36	21	16	23	10	14
Medium Met	25	12	13	16	10	7	44	32	13	38	33	5	27	11	17
Small Met	23	15	9	16	12	3	49	38	11	38	33	5	34	21	13
TOTAL	27	11	16	16	9	7	43	27	16	37	24	12	25	10	15

Source: Compiled at the University of Michigan Population Studies Center from decennial censuses.

where the difference was 32.2 percent. The relationship between polarization and metropolitan size is reversed for both Hispanics and Asians. Asians, in particular, showed a high city poverty rate (30.6 percent) and a large city-suburb difference (14 percent) in *small* metropolitan areas, reflecting the destinations of recent Southeast Asian immigrants.

In summary, poverty is not exclusively a problem of central cities, but in all regions, metropolitan-size categories, and nearly all metropolitan areas, it is *concentrated* in cities. That is, the city-suburb difference in poverty rate is consistently positive. Changes over the 1980s in polarization by poverty status varies widely across metropolitan areas, depending on the volume and destinations of immigrant and internal migrant streams, as well as differential changes in income levels of city and suburban residents. In some areas, both trends exert the same direction of impact, as in Detroit, where differential internal migration and difficult economic conditions both contributed to increasing concentration of poverty in the city. Economic conditions in New York yielded a decrease in the city poverty rate, probably caused by both improved incomes among residents and by high-status in-migration.

In addition to being concentrated in the central cities of metropolitan areas, the poverty population, especially among blacks, is concentrated *within* cities (Kasarda 1993a and 1993b; Jargowsky 1994). Certain areas of large cities have high poverty rates and also contain a disproportionate share of the poverty population. Both the number of high poverty tracts and the concentration of the poor in them increased over the 1980s. The pattern of increase during the 1980s was diffused across all regions and sizes of metropolitan areas, whereas for the 1970s, increases occurred mainly in the large areas of the Northeast and Midwest (Kasarda 1993a; Jargowsky 1994).

As was the case for cities overall, changes in the concentration of poverty *within* cities over the 1980s were tied to wider metropolitan economic conditions. Cities with poor or declining economies (like Detroit) often experienced increases in both city poverty rates and the concentration of poverty within the city. Those experiencing good economic fortune (like New York) often saw decreases in poverty rates and in poverty concentration over the decade.

Female-Headed Households, Children, and Poverty

One of the major concerns in the poverty literature is the rising number of female-headed households and their difficult economic situations (see for example, Garfinkel and McLanahan 1986; Wilson 1987). Poverty rates are high for female-headed households, with the consequences being especially severe for their children (Newberger, Melnicoe, and Newberger 1986; Danziger and Stern 1990; Danziger and Danziger 1993). Shown in Table 2.9 are statistics for urban areas in 1990 for the percent of female-headed households and the percent of children below the poverty line. These data provide a preliminary look at the complex issues concerning female-headed households, children, and poverty.

Table 2.9
1990 Percent in Poverty for Female-Headed Households and Children for Central Cities and Suburbs by Race, Region, and Metro Size Category

	Total			Whites			Blacks			Hispanics			Asians		
	City	Suburbs	Diff.	City	Suburbs	Diff.	City	Suburbs	Diff.	City	Suburbs	Diff.	City	Suburbs	Diff.
A. Female-Headed Households															
REGION TOTALS															
Northeast	36	16	19	26	14	12	38	27	11	56	34	22	30	18	12
Midwest	40	20	20	28	18	10	50	35	16	51	30	21	43	19	24
South	37	24	13	23	19	4	48	37	11	45	35	10	34	22	12
West	29	24	6	23	20	3	39	32	7	42	36	6	25	21	4
U.S. TOTALS															
Large Met	35	19	17	22	15	7	42	29	13	48	32	17	28	20	8
Medium Met	37	24	13	26	20	6	49	42	7	52	45	7	29	23	5
Small Met	39	30	8	30	26	4	56	50	5	53	49	4	44	36	9
TOTAL	36	21	15	25	18	7	45	34	11	49	36	14	29	21	8
B. Children															
REGION TOTALS															
Northeast	29	8	21	19	7	12	38	21	16	47	19	27	23	6	17
Midwest	28	8	20	16	7	9	49	27	22	31	14	17	35	6	29
South	28	14	14	16	10	6	44	29	15	38	28	10	21	9	11
West	22	14	8	15	10	4	36	24	12	32	25	7	24	13	12
U.S. TOTALS															
Large Met	28	10	18	16	7	9	42	23	19	36	21	16	23	10	14
Medium Met	25	12	13	16	10	7	44	32	13	38	33	5	27	11	17
Small Met	23	15	9	16	12	3	49	38	11	38	33	5	34	21	13
TOTAL	27	11	16	16	9	7	43	27	16	37	24	12	25	10	15

Source: Compiled at the University of Michigan Population Studies Center from decennial censuses.

Female-headed households exhibited higher rates of poverty than other house-holds in 1990. Nationally, their percentage in poverty for cities was 36.1 percent (see top panel of Table 2.9). Among regions, the poverty rate among female-headed households was lowest in the West (29.3 percent). However, patterns for the suburbs diverge, with rates for female-headed households being lowest in the Northeast and highest in the West. Consequently, the level of metropolitan polarization by poverty status (the difference between city and suburb rates) was very low in the West (5.7 percentage points). This finding is consistent with the results for overall poverty rates. That is, in the West, the poor population is much more evenly distributed between cities and suburbs than in other regions. The relationship between size of area and poverty is negative for female-headed households, whereas it was positive for the total population. Perhaps in small areas, women are less able to find employment sufficient to support their house-holds, thereby raising poverty rates among female-headed households. In large metropolitan areas, female-headed poverty is primarily concentrated in cities, rather than suburbs.

Among the four racial/ethnic groups, Hispanic female-headed households had the highest rates of poverty (49.2 percent nationally for cities), followed closely by blacks (45.1 percent). Levels were much lower for Asians (28.8 percent) and whites (24.8 percent). Within each race, patterns are quite consistent with those for the total population. Poverty rates for black female-headed households were especially high in the Midwest (city rate of 50.2 percent) and the South (47.5 percent). Black women in those regions have a difficult time earning enough money to support their dependents. The regional pattern is different for Hispan-ics. City poverty rates were highest in the Northeast (56.3 percent) for Hispanic female-headed households. Not only are there many female-headed Hispanic households in Northeastern cities, over half of them have incomes below the poverty line. Thus, one expects high rates of poverty among Hispanic children in the Northeast.

In general, patterns in the poverty rates of female-headed households parallel those for female-headship rates. That is, areas in which a large proportion of households are female-headed also tend to have high rates of poverty among those households. In the city of Detroit, for example (data not shown), 36 per-cent of all black households are female-headed, and of these, one-half have incomes below the poverty line. Both of these phenomena are related to general economic and social conditions, thus it is not surprising that they vary together.

Poverty rates for children, which are intimately linked to those for female-headed households, appear in the bottom panel of Table 2.9. In 1990, poverty among children was more severe in cities (26.6 percent) than in suburbs (16 percent). Regional patterns are similar to those discussed for the poverty of female-headed households. That is, the West was characterized by a low city rate (21.5 percent) and a high suburban rate (13.7 percent), while in the North-east and Midwest, the converse (high city and low suburban rates) was true. An analogous pattern appears for the metropolitan-size comparison with large areas being like the two Northern regions and small areas being like the West. The trends by region and for individual areas are partly driven by racial composition patterns. Blacks and Hispanics have much higher child poverty rates than whites. Because the cities of large metropolitan areas, especially those in the Northeast and Midwest, have large minority populations, their child poverty rates were high. Similarly, suburban child poverty rates in those same areas were relatively low partly because of the lack of minorities in their rings. In the South and West, where minorities are more evenly distributed within metropolitan areas, city and suburban poverty rates for children were much closer in 1990.

Unlike for female-headed households, child poverty in cities was higher for blacks (43.0 percent) than for Hispanics (36.8 percent). In addition, the poverty rate among city children for Asians (24.9 percent) is well above that for whites (16 percent). This finding for Asians probably reflects higher fertility and poverty rates of more recent immigrants from Southeast Asia. Among minorities, poverty rates for children follow the same patterns as those for female-headed households. For black children, city poverty was especially prevalent in the Midwest (48.6 percent) and the South (43.9 percent), and for Hispanics, it was especially high in the Northeast (46.5 percent).

As for the other populations studied, poverty rates for children in cities vary widely across metropolitan areas. Rankings of cities with the most distressed child populations appear in Table 2.10. For the total population, child poverty rates in 1990 ranged from a high of 70.5 percent in Benton Harbor, Michigan, to a low of 7.8 percent in Portsmouth, New Hampshire. Among the cities with the highest child poverty rates are three Texas border towns with large Hispanic populations (Brownsville, McAllen, and Laredo); New Orleans and two small Louisiana areas (Monroe and Alexandria); and three medium-to-large industrial, Midwestern cities (Flint, Detroit, and Cleveland). These cities also ranked high in poverty for the total population (Table 2.7).

The list of highest poverty rates for black children looks somewhat different than that for the total population. Many of the areas have very small black populations; these are not discussed. The others are all small metropolitan areas, mostly in the South (Houma and Monroe, Louisiana; Pascagoula, Mississippi; and Owensboro, Kentucky). Two Michigan cities on Lake Michigan (Benton Harbor and Muskegon) also make the list. Thus, the country's highest poverty *rates* among black children do not occur in the large cities of the Northeast and Midwest that are home to the largest underclass populations. These large cities have very large numbers of poor black children, but rates of poverty are higher for children in small Southern areas.

Unlike that for blacks, the list of cities with highest child poverty rates for Hispanic children does include some larger cities, all in the Northeast (Springfield, Massachusetts, Buffalo, and Hartford). Most Hispanics in these cities are of Puerto Rican origin. Also on the list are some smaller areas in New York and Pennsylvania, as well as several other scattered areas with small Hispanic populations.

Table 2.10
Rankings of Child Poverty Rate in Central Cities for the Total, Black, and Hispanic Populations

TOTAL			BLACK			HISPANIC		
	Highest 1990 City Poverty Rate			Highest 1990 City Poverty Rate			Highest 1990 City Poverty Rate	
Rank	Name	1990% In Poverty	Rank	Name	1990% In Poverty	Rank	Name	1990% In Poverty
1. Benton Harbor, MI		70	1 Eau Claire, WI		100	1 Cumberland, MD-WV		80
2. Monroe, LA		53	2 Provo-Orem, UT		100	2 Hagerstown, MD		77
3. Augusta, GA		50	3 Houma-Thibadaux, LA		75	3 York, PA		73
4. Brownsville-Harlingen, TX		50	4 Benton Harbor, MI		72	4 Monroe, LA		69
5. McAllen-Edinburg, TX		47	5 Cumberland, MD-WV		68	5 Erie, PA		69
6. Fort Pierce, FL		47	6 Owensboro, KY		67	6 Springfield, MA		66
7. Laredo, TX		46	7 Monroe, LA		67	7 Jamestown-Dunkirk, NY		66
8. New Orleans, LA		45	8 Williamsport, PA		66	8 Anderson, IN		65
9. Flint, MI		45	9 Vancouver, WA		66	9 Elmira, NY		63
10. Athens, GA		44	10 Johnstown, PA		65	10 Buffalo, NY		63
11. Detroit, MI		44	11 Casper, WY		65	11 New Bedford-Fall River, MA		61
12. Cumberland, MD-WV		44	12 Sioux City, IA-NE		65	12 Harrisburg-Lebanon, PA		60
13. Johnstown, PA		43	13 Medford, OR		64	13 Utica-Rome, NY		60
14. Cleveland, OH		43	14 Pascagoula, MS		64	14 Hartford-New Britain, CT		59
15. Alexandria, LA		42	15 Muskegon, MI		63	15 State College, PA		59

Source: Compiled at the University of Michigan Population Studies Center from decennial censuses.

CONCLUSION

Over the past decade, the growth and decline patterns of America's cities and broad urban regions have been transformed by changes in the global economy, as well as by new domestic social and economic trends. Regional and metropolitan-wide industrial restructuring has created new dynamics of growth and decline across the national landscape favoring areas that serve as corporate headquarters and advanced service centers, "knowledge-based" industries, and resort and recreation areas. This had led to a return to urban growth in several large metropolitan areas that had shown declines during the "de-industrialization" 1970s but has resulted in continued and, sometimes, accelerated stagnation in many other places that could not make the manufacturing-to-services transition, with economies still grounded in less-than-competitive industries.

Another important source of population growth is immigration. While the United States is a nation of immigrants and immigration from abroad has continued to reinvigorate the populations of our traditional "port-of-entry" areas, recent immigration to the United States is unique. Larger numbers and more racially and ethnically diverse origins have led to new challenges for "port-of-entry" regions that continue to gain from the vibrancy and vitality of new immigrants but also face increased demands on their social service systems. Moreover, migration data from the 1990 census make a clear distinction between areas gaining population largely from immigration and those gaining primarily from internal migration (Frey 1994b). These two migration components differ sharply on race-ethnicity, skill levels, and even age structures in the migrants they bring to their destination areas. The continued disparity across areas in these two sources of migration growth could well lead to racial and ethnic polarization *across* regions in the same way it has long been evident *within* metropolitan areas and central cities.

The demographic trends of the last decade have also underscored the indisputable dominance of the suburbs as the primary locus of activity for new urban economic development and growth of the nation's middle class white population. This trend has emphasized even further the plight of new immigrants, minorities, and poverty-stricken and low-skilled residents who continue to remain "trapped" in segregated cities, inner-suburban communities, and neighborhoods, as a consequence of housing discrimination and the outward relocation of appropriate employment opportunities. Patterns of concentrated poverty, especially among minorities, have accelerated in many Midwestern and Southern interior metropolitan areas that experienced economic declines during the 1980s. Increases in the poverty population are also evident in the central cities of large "port-of-entry" metropolitan areas. While minority and poverty concentration in central cities is evident in most parts of the country, it has come to be particularly acute in these interior and immigrant destination areas.

The urban demographic trends of the 1980s and 1990s have created both new opportunities and challenges. Sharper, more dynamic growth patterns have brought renewed population gains to revitalized economies in the nation's coastal regions, especially in the South Atlantic states and in the states surrounding California. Migrants attracted to these areas bring with them experience, college educations, and, among the elderly, significant disposable incomes. At the other extreme are many metropolitan areas located largely in the interior parts of the country that have suffered economic declines and selective out-migration of their younger and most well-educated populations. Within these areas, in particular, levels of minority segregation and concentrated poverty have been exacerbated as the traditional "stepping stones" to entry-level jobs and affordable housing have been taken away. Apart from these two contexts are the large multiethnic immigrant "port-of-entry" areas in California, Texas, and the greater regions surrounding New York, Miami, and Chicago where new demographic dynamics have just begun to emerge. Both skilled and unskilled immigrants are moving to these areas, but the preponderance of the latter has fueled an out-migration of native-born residents at the lower end of the socio-economic spectrum. Although poverty is not as concentrated in these areas as in older Midwest and Southern cities, poverty populations, fueled by immigration, are rising, and Asian and Hispanic residential patterns are becoming more segregated. Each of these dynamics of recent urban demographic change are associated with regional industrial restructuring, racial polarization, and varied patterns of poverty concentration. They will pose continuing challenges for federal and local policies aimed at bridging the divided opportunity potentials that are emerging both within and across regions.

REFERENCES

Barringer, Herbert R., Robert W. Gardner, and Michael J. Levin. 1993. *Asians and Pacific Islanders in the United States.* New York: Russell Sage Foundation.

Bean, Frank D. and Marta Tienda. 1987. *The Hispanic Population of the United States.* New York: Russell Sage Foundation.

Cervero, Robert. 1989. *America's Suburban Centers: The Land Use Transportation Link.* London: Unwin Hyman.

Danziger, Sandra K. and Sheldon Danziger. 1993. "Child Poverty and Public Policy: Toward a Comprehensive Antipoverty Agenda." *Daedalus* 122:57–82.

Danziger, Sheldon and Jonathan Stern. 1990. "The Causes and Consequences of Child Poverty in the United States." *Research Report.* No. 90-194. Ann Arbor: Population Studies Center, University of Michigan.

Day, Jennifer Cheeseman. 1993. "Population Projections of the United States, by Age, Sex, Race, and Hispanic Origin: 1992 to 2050." *Current Population Reports.* P-25-1104. Washington, D.C.: U.S. Bureau of the Census.

Fielding, Elaine L. 1990. "Black Suburbanization in the Mid-1980s: Trends and Differentials." *Working Paper.* No. 90-13. Madison: Center for Demography and Ecology, University of Wisconsin.

Fielding, Elaine L. and William H. Frey. 1994. "Black Suburbanization Over Three Decades: Progress or Continued Polarization?" Paper presented at the Annual Meetings of the Population Association of America, May.

Fix, Michael and Jeffrey S. Passel. 1994. *Immigration and Immigrants: Setting the Record Straight.* Washington, D.C.: Program for Research on Immigration Policy, The Urban Institute.

Frey, William H. 1987. "Migration and Depopulation of the Metropolis: Regional Restructuring or Rural Renaissance?" *American Sociological Review* 52:240–257.

————. 1992. "Metropolitan Redistribution of the U.S. Elderly: 1960–70, 1970–80, 1980–90." Pp. 123–142 in Andrej Rogers (ed.), *Elderly Migration and Population Redistribution: A Comparative Perspective.* London: Belhaven Press.

————. 1993a. "The New Urban Revival in the United States." *Urban Studies* 30:741–774.

————. 1993b. "Interstate Migration and Immigration for Whites and Minorities, 1985–90: The Emergence of Multi-ethnic States." *Research Report.* No. 93-297. Ann Arbor: Population Studies Center, The University of Michigan.

————. 1993c. "People in Places: Demographic Trends in Urban America." Pp. 3-1–3-106 in Jack Sommer and Donald A. Hicks (eds.), *Rediscovering Urban America: Perspectives on the 1980s.* Washington, D.C.: U.S. Department of Housing and Urban Development.

————. 1994a. "Minority Suburbanization and Continued 'White Flight' in U.S. Metropolitan Areas: Assessing Findings from the 1990 Census." *Research in Community Sociology* 4:15–42.

————. 1994b. "The New White Flight." *American Demographics* (April):40–48.

————. 1994c. "The New Geography of U.S. Population Shifts: Trends Toward Balkanization." Pp. 271–336 in Reynolds Farley (ed.), *Social and Economic Trends in the 1980s.* New York: Russell Sage Foundation.

Frey, William H. and Alden Speare, Jr. 1988. *Regional and Metropolitan Growth and Decline in the United States.* New York: Russell Sage Foundation.

————. 1992. "The Revival of Metropolitan Population Growth in the United States: An Assessment of Findings from the 1990 Census." *Population and Development Review* 18:129–146.

Garfinkel, Irwin and Sara McLanahan. 1986. *Single Mothers and Their Children: A New American Dilemma.* Washington, D.C.: The Urban Institute Press.

Jargowsky, Paul A. 1994. "Ghetto Poverty among Blacks in the 1980s." *Journal of Policy Analysis and Management* 13:288–310.

Jargowsky, Paul A. and Mary Jo Bane. 1991. "Ghetto Poverty in the United States, 1970 to 1980." Pp. 235–273 in Christopher Jencks and Paul E. Peterson (eds.), *The Urban Underclass.* Washington, D.C.: The Brookings Institution.

Kasarda, John D. 1988. "Jobs, Migration and Emerging Urban Mismatches." Pp. 148–198 in Margaret McGeary and Lawrence E. Lynn, Jr. (eds.), *Urban Change and Poverty.* Washington, D.C.: National Academy Press.

————. 1993a. "Industrial Restructuring and the Consequence of Changing Job Locations." Paper prepared for the 1990 Census Project Committee of the Russell Sage Foundation and the Social Science Research Council. Chapel Hill, N.C.: Kenan Institute of Private Enterprise, University of North Carolina.

————. 1993b. "Inner-City Concentrated Poverty and Neighborhood Distress: 1970 to 1980." *Housing Policy Debate* 4:253–302.

Newberger, C., L. Melnicoe, and E. Newberger. 1986. *The American Family in Crisis: Implications for Children.* Chicago: Year Book Medical Publishers, Inc.

Noyelle, Thierry J. and Thomas M. Stanback, Jr. 1984. *The Economic Transformation of American Cities.* Totowa, N.J.: Roman and Allanheld.

Ricketts, Erol R. and Isabel V. Sawhill. 1988. "Defining and Measuring the Underclass." *Journal of Policy Analysis and Measurement* 7:316–325.

Stanback, Thomas M., Jr. 1991. *The New Suburbanization: Challenge to the Central City.* Boulder, Colo.: Westview Press.

Taeuber, Cynthia M. 1992. "Sixty-five Plus in America." *U.S. Bureau of the Census Current Population Reports: Special Studies.* Washington, D.C.: U.S. Government Printing Office.

Wilson, William J. 1987. *The Truly Disadvantaged.* Chicago: University of Chicago Press.

3

Age and Race in the United States: The 1980s and Beyond

DONALD W. BOGIE

In examining the structure of the U.S. population, the distribution of people by age and race is of primary importance. When the U.S. census was first conducted in 1790, both of these variables were prominently incorporated into the data collection and reporting process. Age and race continue to be an important part of the decennial census, with more extensive information being reported and refinements being made in order to better understand how these demographic variables affect the structure of the U.S. society.

Knowledge of the age structure of a population is important whether for economic enterprise, community organizations, or for governmental entities. Contemporary market research, for example, is dependent on information relating to the age distribution of the population. The proportion of individuals of working age, and the number of younger and older persons, is central to civic planners and legislators to adequately address people's needs. The extent to which future needs and goals of the larger society will be met is contingent on the number of persons at various stages in the life cycle. Similarly, the racial and ethnic composition of the population defines the fundamental character of American society.

Age is an important social factor, in that it directly affects individual needs, desires, and daily activities. On a more general level, the age distribution influences the character and orientation of the entire social system. Race is central to self-identity and continues to have a major effect on social relationships and the configuration of American institutions.

This chapter begins with a discussion of various features of the age distribution of the U.S. population, including long-term changes in the median age,

Table 3.1

Median Age of the U.S. Population, 1850–1990, and Projected Median Age, 2000–2050

Year	Median Age	Year	Median Age
1850	18.9	1980	30.0
1900	22.9	1990	32.9
1910	24.1	2000	35.5
1920	25.3	2010	37.3
1930	26.5	2020	37.7
1940	29.0	2030	38.6
1950	30.2	2040	39.1
1960	29.5	2050	39.0
1970	28.1		

Sources: U.S. Bureau of the Census (1975), p. 19; U.S. Bureau of the Census (1983a), p. 23; U.S. Bureau of the Census (1992), p. 13; U.S. Bureau of the Census (1993b), pp. 26, 38, 42, 46, 50, 54. Projected values for 2000–2050 are derived from middle series population projections.

variations in age composition according to sex, race, and place of residence, and projected changes through the first half of the twenty-first century. The discussions of the racial and ethnic composition of the population will focus on current patterns and projected changes over the next several decades.

CHANGES IN THE U.S. AGE STRUCTURE

The United States has changed from a nation that once was predominantly a young population to a population that is advancing toward middle age. In the census of 1820 (the first census in which the median age was reported for whites and blacks), the median age was 16.7 (U.S. Bureau of the Census 1975, p. 19). This median age indicated both the youthful age of those who were immigrating to the United States in large numbers at that time and the high birth rates and low life expectancy that were characteristic of the early 1800s. Three decades later, in 1850, the median age had increased to 18.9. It was not until 1870 that the median age rose above 20, and by 1900, the median age was 22.9 years (Table 3.1; U.S. Bureau of the Census 1975, p. 19).

The median age for the U.S. had increased to 30.2 by 1950, but then declined during the next two decades, largely as a result of the large birth cohorts during the 1946–1964 baby-boom period. A post–World War II low of 28.1 median years was recorded in 1970. Since that time, however, the advancing median age has resumed, increasing the national median to 30 years in 1980 and to 32.9 years in 1990 (see Table 3.1). The 2.9 year increase experienced during the 1980s represents the largest increment ever recorded over a ten-year period, and it can be attributed to the baby boomers, most of whom were 30 years of age or over by 1990.

When the median age is examined for various subgroups within the population, some noteworthy variations emerge. For example, in 1990, females were older than males (34.1 years versus 31.7) and whites were significantly older than blacks (34.4 and 28.1). Hispanics, of which 22.4 million were enumerated in the 1990 census, are the youngest (median age 25.5) of any major racial/ethnic group within the population. White females, at 35.6 years, are the oldest, and the median age rises to 36.1 when Hispanics are excluded from that category[1] (U.S. Bureau of the Census 1992, pp. 17–18). These variations reflect a number of interrelated factors, including variations in life expectancy, differential fertility rates, and migration patterns.

The median age of the rural population is older than the urban population (34.1 versus 32.5). Within the rural category, the highest median age (35) is associated with persons living in places of less than 1,000 population (U.S. Bureau of the Census 1992, p. 19). Nonmetropolitan residents tend to be older than metropolitan dwellers (33.8 versus 32.6).[2] Within metropolitan areas, central city residents (31.6) are almost two years younger than those who reside outside the central core (33.3) and, in urbanized areas, residents of the central city are more youthful (31.5 years) than those residing in the urban fringe (33.3 years)[3] (U.S. Bureau of the Census 1992, pp. 19, 21). Although none of these age variations are statistically significant, the data suggest differential tendencies for different segments of the population, part of which can be explained by birth rates, social mobility, and migration patterns.

The median age of residents of the Northeast in 1990 was 34.2. Midwestern residents were older (32.9) than those residing in the South (32.7), while the West had the youngest population (31.8 years)[4] (U.S. Bureau of the Census 1992, p. 321). The lower median age recorded in the West may be explained by the fact that the Western United States continues to be the destination for a large number of youthful migrants, including many immigrants. These two factors largely explain why the growth rate for the West (22.3 percent) exceeded that of all other regions during the 1980s (U.S. Bureau of the Census 1983a, p. 62; U.S. Bureau of the Census 1992, p. 321).

In 1990, two states in the West, namely Utah (26.3) and Alaska (29.4), recorded the lowest median ages. Texas, the third most populous state, was third at 30.7 years (U.S. Bureau of the Census 1992, p. 321). Both Texas and Alaska attract youthful migrants, while the high birth rate that is associated with the predominantly Mormon population of Utah is a factor in the low median age of that state. On the other hand, the in-migration of older persons explains why Florida had the oldest population in 1990 (36.3 years). West Virginia, which experienced significant out-migration during the 1980s, was the second oldest (35.4 years), followed by Pennsylvania (35 years) (U.S. Bureau of the Census 1992, p. 321).

Population projections suggest that the U.S. median age will continue to increase well into the twenty-first century. Birth rates are projected to remain near their present levels, and the large birth cohorts of the post–World War II years will grow older. According to middle series projections, the median age of the

Table 3.2

Distribution of the U.S. Population According to Selected Age Categories, 1980–1990

Age Category	Percent of Total Population/ Number, 1980[a]	Percent of Total Population/ Number, 1990[a]	Percent/Numerical Change in Population 1980–1990[a]
Under 5	7.2 (16,348)	7.4 (18,354)	12.3 (2,006)
5–17	20.9 (47,407)	18.2 (45,250)	− 4.5 (−2,157)
18–24	13.3 (30,022)	10.8 (26,738)	−10.9 (−3,284)
25–44	27.7 (62,717)	32.5 (80,755)	28.8 (18,038)
45–64	19.6 (44,503)	18.6 (46,371)	4.2 (1,868)
65+	11.3 (25,549)	12.6 (31,242)	22.3 (5,692)
Total	100.0 (226,546)	100.0 (248,710)	9.8 (22,164)

[a]Numbers are reported in 1,000s. Computations are based on unrounded data.
Sources: U.S. Bureau of the Census (1983a), p. 27; U.S. Bureau of the Census (1992), p. 19.

United States will increase to 39.1 by 2040 and then decrease to 39 years in 2050 (see Table 3.1).

The data pertaining to median age, however, reflect only one dimension of recent change in the age distribution. In the following section, separate groupings within the total configuration will be examined to further evaluate the changes that lie behind what Sheppard and Rix (1977) refer to as the "graying of America."

Growth of the Elderly Population

There are considerably more persons aged 65 years and over in the U.S. population than those between aged 13–19. The 31.2 million people 65+ comprised 12.6 percent of the U.S. population, while the 24.3 million teenagers represented 9.8 percent (U.S. Bureau of the Census 1992, p. 19). As the data shown in Table 3.2 indicate, except for the under age 5 category, the younger age groups declined proportionately during the 1980s. Beginning with the young adults category, however, increases were recorded.

The most dramatic change in the U.S. age structure during the 1980s was the 29 percent increase in the 25–44 age category (Table 3.2). This finding, of course, reflects the movement of the baby-boom generation (those born between 1946 and 1964) into their young-adult and middle-adult years. Approximately 75 million people were born during the 1946–1964 period and, just as their numbers enhanced school enrollment during the 1950s and 1960s, their large numbers now affect employment and occupational opportunities.

Equally dramatic is the growth in the elderly population. Longer life expectancy is responsible for the increased number of persons aged 65+, a number that grew from 25.5 million in 1980 to 31.2 million in 1990, for a 22 percent increase (Table 3.2). However, the greatest proportional increase of any age group during the last decade was among those aged 85+, an age category that rose by 37.5 percent. Approximately 840,000 persons, the majority of whom are female, were added to this population sector during the 1980s (U.S. Bureau of the Census 1983a, p. 27; U.S. Bureau of the Census 1992, p. 19).

Although the data in Table 3.2 indicate a decline of 4.5 percent in the 5–17 age group during the 1980s, this decrease was actually concentrated among the 14–17 age category. There were approximately 3 million fewer persons of high school age in 1990 than in 1980, a decline of 18.3 percent, while the elementary school-age population increased by 811,000, or 2.6 percent, during the same period (U.S. Bureau of the Census 1983a, p. 27; U.S. Bureau of the Census 1992, p. 19). The numerical decline among those aged 18–24 (3.3 million) was slightly greater than that for high school-age individuals.

The growth in the under 5 and the 5–13 age groups reflects an increase in the number of births beginning in the early 1980s. The school-age population may continue to grow well into the next century as the projected numbers to be presented in a later section will show.

Some variations in the sex ratios within the age distribution are noteworthy. Given the uneven sex ratio at birth (i.e., about 105 males born for every 100 females), it is not surprising that in 1990 a larger proportion of males (26.9 percent) than females (24.3 percent) are under age 18. Differences in life expectancies (79.1 for females and 72.2 for males in 1991) account for a larger percentage of females than males age 65+ (14.7 and 10.4 percent, respectively) (U.S. Bureau of the Census 1992, pp. 19–20; U.S. Bureau of the Census 1993a, p. 3).

A larger proportion of school-age children under 18 resides in rural areas than in urban areas (27.3 percent versus 25.0 percent), while a slightly larger percentage of persons of working age reside in urban settings (62.4 percent aged 18–64 versus 60.2 percent). A similar pattern is found for residents of nonmetropolitan areas, while a higher proportion of persons under age 18 reside in nonmetropolitan settings (26.6 percent) than in metropolitan areas (25.3 percent). A larger percentage of working-age persons, however, are in metropolitan counties (62.8 percent as opposed to 58.6). There is also a higher proportion of persons aged 65+ (15 percent) residing in nonmetropolitan than in metropolitan areas (12 percent). However, no meaningful variation is found in the age distribution when the population is divided into the under 18, 18–64, and 65+ age groupings. This is true both for urbanized areas relative to residence in the central city versus urban fringe residents, and for metropolitan central cities and those residing outside the central city. The only exception is a slightly higher proportion of elderly persons residing in the urban core of the central city (U.S. Bureau of the Census 1992, pp. 20, 22).

The most notable variation in the age distribution examined thus far is associated with race and ethnicity. A markedly smaller proportion of whites are found in the under 18 age category (23.9 percent in 1990) than blacks (32 percent); American Indians, Eskimos, and Aleuts (35.6 percent); Asians and

Pacific Islanders (28.6 percent); or Hispanics (34.7 percent). The white population also is significantly older, as indicated by the proportion aged 65+ (13.9 percent for whites compared to 8.4 percent for blacks; 5.8 percent for American Indians, Eskimos, and Aleuts; 6.2 percent for Asians and Pacific Islanders; and 5.2 percent for those of Hispanic origin). When whites of Hispanic origin are removed from the white category, the proportion of whites aged 65+ rises another one-half percentage point to 14.4 (U.S. Bureau of the Census 1992, p. 24).

Similar to the population living within the urban and metropolitan areas, differences in age distribution among the four U.S. census regions are minimal. The only notable variations in 1990 were the lower proportion of persons under age 18 in the Northeast (23.4 percent versus 25.8 to 26.7 in the other regions), and the lower percentage of persons aged 65+ in the West (10.9 percent as opposed to 12.6 to 13.8 in the other regions) (U.S. Bureau of the Census 1992, pp. 86, 150, 214, 278).

Changes that occurred in regional age distributions during the 1980s, however, are much more dramatic, although somewhat reflective of the variations just noted. Precipitated primarily by an influx of migrants, which involved primarily younger people, the West and South registered increases in the under 18 population (16.1 and 1.7 percent, respectively) while the Northeast and Midwest experienced declines of 8.9 percent and 7.7 percent. Although the population aged 18–64 grew in all four regions of the United States, the growth in the Midwest (3 percent) and the Northeast (6.4 percent) was significantly less than the rate of increase in the South (16.5 percent) and the West (23.1 percent). The highest growth rates for all four regions during the 1980s were associated with the elderly. While the population aged 65+ grew by 15.2 percent in the Northeast and by 15.8 percent in the Midwest, the growth rate was 26.3 percent in the South and 34.3 percent in the West (U.S. Bureau of the Census 1983a, p. 62; U.S. Bureau of the Census 1992, pp. 85, 149, 213, 277).

Aging in the Twenty-First Century

Major demographic shifts are neither inconsequential nor short-lived. Once set in motion, population changes can, and often do, have relevance far into the future. Precipitated by the increased fertility levels from the late 1940s through the early 1960s, the large birth cohorts of the post-war years will continue to manifest a considerable effect on the age structure.

Projections into the twenty-first century indicate a continuing increase in the elderly population (Figure 3.1). Those aged 65+, a group that numbered approximately 31 million in 1990, are projected to almost triple in size, according to the Census Bureau's middle series projections, to 80.1 million by the year 2050. One in every five Americans is expected to be aged 65 or older by 2050, an increase from the one in eight that was recorded in 1990 (U.S. Bureau of the Census 1992, p. 19; U.S. Bureau of the Census 1993b, pp. 50, 54). A steady

Figure 3.1
Percent of the U.S. Population Aged 65+ and 75+, 1950–2050

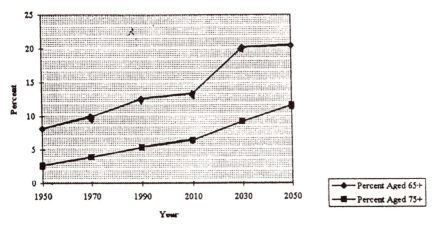

Sources: U.S. Bureau of the Census (1983a), p. 42; U.S. Bureau of the Census (1992), p. 19; U.S. Bureau of the Census (1993b), pp. 38, 46, 54. Projected values for 2010–2050 are computed from middle series population projections.

size increase is expected to occur in the elderly population throughout the first four decades of the next century as the proportion aged 65+ increases from a projected 12.8 percent in the year 2000 to 20.7 percent in 2040. Only in 2050, as the last of the baby boomers reach advanced years, is the proportion of elderly in the population projected to decline slightly to 20.4 percent (Table 3.3).

The Non-elderly Population

The data shown in Table 3.3 indicate the absence of a dramatic change in the younger age groups in the U.S. population for the first half of the twenty-first century. Preschoolers (under the age of 5) are projected to remain at approximately 7 percent of the total population, although their numbers will increase by nearly 6 million. While the school-age population is expected to drop from 19 percent of the total population in 2000 to 17.1 percent by the year 2020, this proportion is projected to remain basically constant from 2020 through 2050. Still, the 5–17 age group is expected to grow by 14 million persons between the years 2000–2050, according to the middle series projections. Although the range in variation for those of college age is limited to just 1 percentage point over the next fifty years, the proportion in the young adult category is projected to decline from 30.2 percent of the population in 2000 to 25.9 percent during the first decade of the twenty-first century, a pattern that can be traced directly to the aging of the large birth cohorts of the 1946–1964 era. These proportions should remain at about that same level through the first half of the twenty-first century. Both groups, however, are expected to register a significant numerical

Table 3.3

Projected Change in the Age Distribution of the U.S. Population, 2000–2050

A.   Percent of Total Population

Year

Age Category	2000	2010	2020	2030	2040	2050
Under 5	7.0	6.7	6.7	6.5	6.5	6.5
5-17	19.0	17.8	17.1	17.2	16.9	16.9
18-24	9.4	10.1	9.3	9.1	9.3	9.1
25-44	30.2	25.9	25.5	25.3	24.6	24.8
45-64	21.7	26.2	24.9	21.8	22.1	22.3
65+	12.8	13.3	16.4	20.1	20.7	20.4
Total	100.0	100.0	100.0	100.0	100.0	100.0

B.   Percent Change in Population

Year

Age Category	2000-2010	2010-2020	2020-2030	2030-2040	2040-2050
Under 5	3.0	9.7	3.3	5.7	5.9
5-17	2.4	4.1	8.1	4.1	5.7
18-24	16.6	0.8	4.4	8.5	3.5
25-44	-6.6	6.9	6.5	3.0	6.5
45-64	31.4	3.2	-5.9	7.3	6.5
65+	13.5	33.0	31.5	9.7	4.0
Total	8.8	8.5	7.4	6.1	5.5

Source: U.S. Bureau of the Census (1993b), pp. xvi, xvii. The data reported herein are based on middle series population projections.

increase between 2000 and 2050, 9.8 million in the 18–24 age group and 13.8 million for those aged 25–44.

The 45–64 group is projected to grow by one-third (or by nearly 19 million persons) during the first decade of the next century alone, reaching 26.2 percent of the total population in 2010. By 2030, the proportion is expected to recede to 21.8 percent or essentially the same percentage that is projected for the year 2000. A 6 percent loss (4.8 million persons) is anticipated for this age group during the 2020s as the last of the baby boomers move into the 65+ age category.

In the year 2011, the first members of the large post–World War II cohorts will reach age 65. As a result, the number aged 65+ is expected to increase by approximately one-third between 2010 and 2020. A similar increase (i.e., 31.5 percent) is anticipated during the following decade, before the rise in the number of elderly persons begins to moderate during the 2030s. As a result of proportional changes in the other age groups, however, the 65+ population will remain at approximately 20 percent of the total population in the year 2050.

Overall, the age structure will reflect a pattern of stationary growth into the twenty-first century that is characteristic of demographically mature nations (see Figure 3.2). The base of the 1990 age-sex pyramid will have narrowed further, and the aberration caused by the large number of births during the 1946–1964

Figure 3.2
Age-Sex Pyramids for the U.S. Population, 1990, 2010, 2030, and 2050

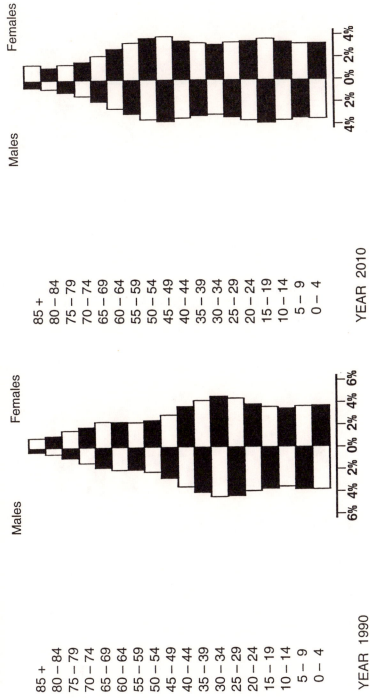

Figure 3.2 (Continued)

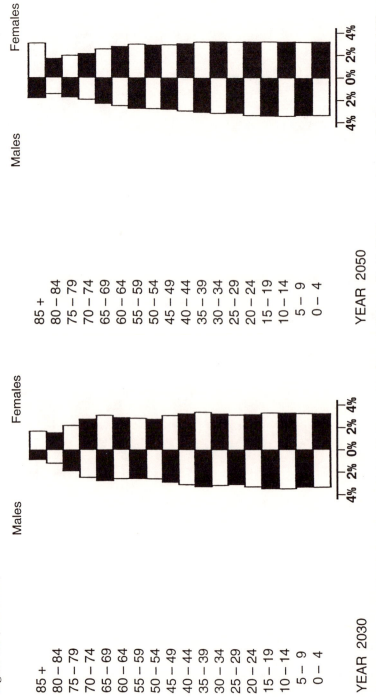

Males | Females

85 +
80 – 84
75 – 79
70 – 74
65 – 69
60 – 64
55 – 59
50 – 54
45 – 49
40 – 44
35 – 39
30 – 34
25 – 29
20 – 24
15 – 19
10 – 14
5 – 9
0 – 4

YEAR 2030   YEAR 2050

Sources: U.S. Bureau of the Census (1992), pp. 19–20; U.S. Bureau of the Census (1993b), pp. 38, 46, 54. The projected age-sex distributions for 2010–2050 are based on middle series population projections.

period will have largely lost its visibility by 2030. However, the large numbers of females in the 85+ age group in 2050 will represent the survivors of demographic and biological events that occurred nearly 100 years before.

RACIAL AND ETHNIC CHANGES

When the first U.S. Census was conducted in 1790, the population was classified into four major race-sex categories: free white males, free white females, other free persons (such as American Indians eligible for taxation, free blacks, and persons of other races), and slaves. This classification scheme reflected the prevailing social arrangements of the U.S. population, as well as social arrangements within the American society. Since that time, the classification of racial and ethnic groups has been altered many times, reflecting the changing composition and diversity of the U.S. population, social and political movements, and federal policy changes.

Formerly based on the observations of census enumerators, assignment to a race or ethnic category is currently based entirely on self-identification. According to Federal Statistical Directive Number 15, issued by the Office of Management and Budget in 1978, a five-category race classification is to be utilized by all governmental agencies: white; black; American Indian, Eskimo, or Aleut; Asian or Pacific Islander; and other. The first four categories are what may be termed non-scientific categories, while the fifth category is reflective of race, ethnic origin, and other factors influencing self-classification. Separate data reported by the Bureau of the Census for specific groupings among Native Americans, Asians, and Pacific Islanders are based on nativity, national origin, or ancestry.[5] In addition, the 1990 census questionnaire contained a separate question on Spanish/Hispanic origin, as it has since 1970. While the present system of classification is not without limitations, Americans appear to be reasonably consistent in stating their racial and/or ethnic identification. Post-enumeration surveys indicate a relatively high degree of agreement with responses from the census questionnaire (Lott 1993).

Changes in racial composition occur in a diverse, changing society. As shown in Table 3.4, whites declined in proportion to the population from the 83.1 percent recorded in 1980 to 80.3 percent in 1990, while the proportions of blacks, Native Americans, Asians, and Pacific Islanders increased. Persons of Hispanic origin also increased in size from 6.4 percent in 1980 to 9 percent in 1990. About 20 percent of the U.S. population is non-white, while approximately 25 percent is non-white or white-Hispanic.

Chinese and Filipinos (3.1 million) account for approximately 42 percent of all Asians and Pacific Islanders in the United States. In total, the six major groupings within the Asian/Pacific Islander category (see Table 3.4) total 6.1 million people, comprising 84.3 percent of the total Asian population. Sixty percent of the Hispanics in the United States are of Mexican origin. Puerto Ricans and Cubans number 3.8 million, or 16.9 percent of persons of Hispanic

Table 3.4

Distribution of the U.S. Population, by Race and Hispanic Origin, 1980–1990

Race/Hispanic Origin	Percent of Total Population/ Number, 1980[a]		Percent of Total Population/ Number, 1990[a]		Percent and Numerical Change in Population, 1980–1990[a]	
White	83.1	(188,372)	80.3	(199,686)	6.0	(11,314)
Non-Hispanic Origin	79.6	(180,256)	75.6	(188,128)	4.4	(7,872)
Black	11.7	(26,495)	12.1	(29,986)	13.2	(3,491)
American Indian/ Eskimo/Aleut	0.6	(1,420)	0.8	(1,959)	37.9	(539)
Asian/Pacific Islander[b]	1.5	(3,500)	2.9	(7,274)	107.8	(3,773)
Chinese	0.4	(806)	0.7	(1,645)	104.1	(839)
Filipino	0.3	(775)	0.6	(1,407)	81.6	(632)
Japanese	0.3	(701)	0.3	(848)	20.9	(147)
Asian Indian	0.2	(362)	0.3	(815)	125.6	(454)
Korean	0.2	(355)	0.3	(799)	125.3	(444)
Vietnamese	0.1	(262)	0.2	(615)	134.8	(353)
Other Race[c]	3.0	(6,758)	3.9	(9,805)	45.1	(3,047)
Hispanic Origin[d]	6.4	(14,609)	9.0	(22,354)	53.0	(7,745)
Mexican	3.9	(8,740)	5.4	(13,496)	54.4	(4,755)
Puerto Rican	0.9	(2,014)	1.1	(2,728)	35.4	(714)
Cuban	0.4	(803)	0.4	(1,044)	30.0	(241)
Other Hispanic	1.3	(3,051)	2.0	(5,086)	66.7	(2,035)
All Persons	100.0	(226,546)	0100.0	(248,710)	9.8	(22,164)

[a]Numbers are reported in 1,000s.

[b]The 1980 total for Asians and Pacific Islanders, along with the totals for the specific groups that comprise this category, are not completely comparable to the 1990 counts because of differences in questionnaire items pertaining to race and variations in coding procedures between 1980 and 1990. For additional information see U.S. Bureau of the Census (1991), *1990 Census of Population, Summary Population and Housing Characteristics,* CP-1-2 (Washington, D.C.: U.S. Government Printing Office), p. B-13.

[c]In this table, as well as Tables 3.6 and 3.7, "other race" encompasses all persons not included in the "white," "black," "American Indian, Eskimo, or Aleut," and "Asian or Pacific Islander" race categories. This includes persons who identified themselves as "multiracial," "multiethnic," "mixed," "interracial," or members of a Spanish/Hispanic origin group in the census questionnaire item regarding race.

[d]Persons of Hispanic origin may be of any race.

Sources: U.S. Bureau of the Census (1983a), p. 21; U.S. Bureau of the Census (1992), p. 3; U.S. Bureau of the Census (1993c), table 18.

background, while the remaining 5.1 million originate from other geographical locations. Hispanics may be of any race. According to the 1990 census, 51.7 percent were white, while 42.7 percent were classified as "other." The remainder (5.5 percent) were classified as either blacks, Native Americans, or Asians and Pacific Islanders (U.S. Bureau of the Census 1992, p. 3).

As noted, the rate of growth is greater for non-whites than for whites. As shown in Table 3.4, the number of Asians and Pacific Islanders increased by 107.8 percent during the 1980s, compared to a 4.4 percent growth for non-Hispanic whites. Persons of Hispanic origin increased by 53 percent, Native Americans grew by 37.9 percent, and blacks by 13.2 percent. Every group within the Asian and Pacific Islanders category experienced high rates of increase dur-

Table 3.5
Ten Leading Sources of Immigrants to the United States, by Country of Birth, 1981–1990

Country	Number (1,000s)	Percent of All Immigrants
Mexico	1,653.3	22.5
Philippines	495.3	6.7
Vietnam	401.4	5.5
Mainland China/Taiwan	388.8	5.3
Korea	338.8	4.6
India	261.9	3.6
Dominican Republic	251.8	3.4
El Salvador	214.6	2.9
Jamaica	213.8	2.9
Cuba	159.2	2.2
Total--All Countries	7,338.1	100.0

Source: U.S. Bureau of the Census (1993c), table 8.

ing the last decade, with the Vietnamese, Asian Indians, and Koreans making highest proportional gains. Mexican growth was the highest among all Hispanic groups during the 1980s.

Minority groups are characterized by more youthful populations; hence, their high growth rate can be explained in part by the larger proportion of persons in their reproductive years. The highest rates of migration into the United States are also associated with the increases recorded in these same groups. The ten countries from which the largest number of immigrants arrived during the 1980s accounted for three-fifths of all the documented immigrants entering the United States during the 1982–1990 period (see Table 3.5). These are Hispanic (Mexico, Dominican Republic, El Salvador, and Cuba), Asian (Philippines, Vietnam, Mainland China/Taiwan, Korea, and India), or black (Jamaica).

In addition to high fertility levels, it is generally acknowledged that one major reason for the high growth rate in the Native American population is the increased likelihood that persons of American Indian heritage are now identifying themselves as such. American Indians increased in size nearly 40 percent during the 1980s, a figure that is four times greater than the general increase for the U.S. population (U.S. Bureau of the Census 1983a, pp. 19 and 50; U.S. Bureau of the Census 1992, pp. 1, 3).

Although it is informative to examine the racial and ethnic composition of the United States, important trends occurring in various regions may be masked. In the following section, changes in the racial and ethnic composition at the regional level over the past decade will be examined.

Regional Differences in Racial Composition

Whites comprise more than 80 percent of the total population located in the Northeast and the Midwest regions. Still, the white population decreased in size in both the South and West (see Table 3.6). When whites of Hispanic origin are removed from the white category, more than one-fourth of the population located in the South, one-third in the West, and more than one-fifth in the Northeast is composed of other racial and ethnic groups. The highest proportion of blacks among the four regions (52.8 percent) is still located in the South (U.S. Bureau of the Census 1992, pp. 323–324). Native Americans and Asians and Pacific Islanders, on the other hand, are more likely to reside in the West. Indeed, 47.6 percent of all American Indians, Eskimos, and Aleuts reside in Western states, as do 55.7 percent of the Asians and Pacific Islanders (U.S. Bureau of the Census 1992, pp. 323–324).

The white population decreased in all four major geographical regions during the 1980s (Table 3.6). These declines ranged from a 1.5 percentage decrease in the Midwest to a 5 percentage points decrease in Western states. Blacks experienced a modest increase in all regions of the country except in the South where the percentage remained unchanged; Asians and Pacific Islanders and persons of Hispanic origin recorded increases in all four regions.

In-migration during the 1980s facilitated the growth in the number of non-Hispanic whites residing in the South (5.3 million) and the West (3.5 million). However, non-Hispanic whites declined in the Northeast (−628,763) and the Midwest (−334,844). All other major racial and ethnic groups recorded increases in each region of the country, with Asians and Pacific Islanders having the largest gains. The largest numerical gains were by Southern blacks (1.8 million), Asians and Pacific Islanders (2 million), Hispanics (3.9 million), and Native Americans (approximately 213,000) living in the West (U.S. Bureau of the Census 1983a, pp. 53, 55; U.S. Bureau of the Census 1992, pp. 323–324).

Rural areas, according to the 1990 census, were more than 90 percent white, while the percentage of whites residing in urban areas was 76.9. Blacks, who comprised 14 percent of the urban population in 1990, represent the second largest group of urban dwellers. With the exception of Native Americans, all of the major racial/ethnic groups are highly urbanized. Asians and Pacific Islanders are most likely to be urban residents (95.3 percent in 1990), followed by Hispanics (91.4 percent), blacks (87.2 percent), whites (72 percent), and Native Americans (56.3 percent) (U.S. Bureau of the Census 1992, p. 3).

Whites constitute the largest proportion of central city and suburban fringe populations. Among the 1990 fringe population, 79.8 percent was white non-Hispanic; slightly more than 59 percent of central city populations was white non-Hispanic. Blacks are the second most represented group both in central cities and in fringe areas (22 percent and 7.8 percent, respectively). More than 56.3 percent of all whites residing in urbanized areas live in the fringe area, while three-fourths of urban blacks reside in the central city. Nearly two-thirds of all

Table 3.6
Distribution of the U.S. Population by Race, Hispanic Origin, and Region, 1980 and 1990

	Region									
	Northeast		Midwest		South		West		U.S.	
Race/Hispanic Origin	1980	1990	1980	1990	1980	1990	1980	1990	1980	1990
White	86.1	82.8	88.7	87.2	78.2	76.8	80.8	75.8	83.1	80.3
Non-Hispanic Origin	83.4	79.4	87.5	85.8	74.3	71.8	73.5	66.7	79.6	75.6
Black	9.9	11.0	9.1	9.6	18.6	18.5	5.2	5.4	11.7	12.1
American Indian, Eskimo, and Aleut[a]	0.2	0.2	0.4	0.6	0.5	0.7	1.7	1.8	0.6	0.8
Asian and Pacific Islander	1.1	2.6	0.7	1.3	0.6	1.3	4.8	7.7	1.5	2.9
Other Race	2.7	3.3	1.2	1.4	2.0	2.8	7.5	9.4	3.0	3.9
Hispanic Origin	5.3	7.4	2.2	2.9	5.9	7.9	14.5	19.1	6.4	9.0

[a]See footnote b, Table 3.4.
Source: U.S. Bureau of the Census (1983a), pp. 20, 21, 53, 55; U.S. Bureau of the Census (1992), pp. 323–324.

Hispanics, three-fifths of all Native Americans, and more than one-half of all Asians and Pacific Islanders also reside in the central city (U.S. Bureau of the Census 1992, p. 3).

A similar residential pattern holds for metropolitan areas and central cities. Eighty-seven percent of the 1990 nonmetropolitan population was comprised of whites, while the percentage for metropolitan areas was 78.3. Similarly, 86.5 percent of the population living outside the central city was white, compared to 66.1 percent of all central city dwellers (U.S. Bureau of the Census 1992, p. 7).

Blacks are more highly represented in metropolitan areas[6] than they are in non-metropolitan areas and are more likely to live in the central city than in fringe areas. Blacks totaled 13 percent of the metropolitan area population in 1990, and 9 percent of all persons living in nonmetropolitan areas. Likewise, they comprised 22.1 percent of the population of central cities, but only 6.9 percent of the metropolitan population that was living outside central cities. A similar pattern is observed for Asians and Pacific Islanders and Hispanics (U.S. Bureau of the Census 1992, p. 7).

Mississippi has the highest concentration of blacks (35.6 percent), followed by Louisiana (30.8 percent), South Carolina (29.8 percent), Georgia (27 percent), and Alabama (25.3 percent). The Mountain states and the New England states have the lowest proportions. American Indians, Eskimos, and Aleuts are most highly represented in Alaska (15.6 percent) and New Mexico (8.9 percent); Asians and Pacific Islanders in Hawaii (61.8 percent) and California (9.6 percent); and Hispanics in New Mexico (38.2 percent), California (25.8 percent), and Texas (25.5 percent). Hawaii has the most varied racial mixture where one-third of the population is white, 62 percent is Asian and Pacific Islander, 7.3 percent is Hispanic, and 2.5 percent is black. California is also characterized by racial and ethnic diversity, where whites represent approximately 70 percent of the total population followed by Hispanics (25.8 percent), Asians and Pacific Islanders (9.6 percent), and blacks (7.4 percent) (U.S. Bureau of the Census 1992, pp. 324–329).

Social and Economic Characteristics

With the exception of Asians and Pacific Islanders, minorities do not compare well with the white population in terms of educational attainment, employment, income levels, and family stability. The data presented in Table 3.7 indicate that blacks, Native Americans, and Hispanics fare considerably worse on selected social and economic indicators. Black households with children under age 18, for example, are three times more likely than whites to be headed by one parent. Only about one-half of all Hispanics aged 25+ are high school graduates or more, whereas approximately 80 percent of all non-Hispanic whites are high school graduates. Unemployment rates for minority groups other than Asians and Pacific Islanders are at least two times higher than that of whites, while median family income levels for these same groups range from 58.5 percent

Table 3.7
Selected Characteristics of the U.S. Population According to Race and Hispanic Origin

Race/Hispanic Origin	Percent Single Parent Families[a]		Percent High School Graduates[b]		Percent Unemployed[c]		Median Family Income ($)[d]		Percent Persons Below Poverty	
	1980	1990	1980	1990	1980	1990	1979[d]	1989	1979	1989
White	14.4	17.6	68.8	77.9	5.8	5.2	35,586	37,152	9.4	9.8
Non-Hispanic Origin	14.1	17.1	69.6	79.1	5.7	5.0	35,892	37,628	8.9	9.2
Black	45.8	53.2	51.2	63.1	11.8	12.9	21,517	22,429	29.9	29.5
American Indian Eskimo/Aleut	28.5	36.6	55.5	65.5	13.2	14.4	23,440	21,750	27.5	30.9
Asian and Pacific Islander	11.5	13.1	74.8	77.5	4.7	5.3	38,794	41,251	13.1	14.1
Other Race	26.2	30.3	37.9	43.4	10.2	11.4	22,638	22,949	27.2	28.2
Hispanic Origin	23.5	28.6	44.0	49.8	8.9	10.4	25,128	25,064	23.5	25.3
All Persons	18.7	22.8	66.5	75.2	6.5	6.3	34,018	35,225	12.4	13.1

[a]With own children under 18 years of age.
[b]Persons 25 years old and over.
[c]Civilian labor force 16 years old and over.
[d]Reported in 1989 dollars.

Sources: U.S. Bureau of the Census (1983b), pp. 69, 71–72, 78–79, 93–94, 97–98, 99–100, 111–114, 116, 118–119, 125–126, 157–159, 161–165, 167–168; U.S. Bureau of the Census (1993d), pp. 41–42, 44, 48–49.

(Native Americans) to 67.5 percent (Hispanics) of whites. Poverty rates highlight a similar pattern. Blacks and Native Americans are three times more likely than whites to be at or below the poverty level, while Hispanics are 2.6 times more likely than whites to be poor. Asians and Pacific Islanders compare most favorably to whites. As shown in Table 3.7, a smaller proportion of Asian and Pacific Islander families with children under the age of 18 than white families are headed by single parents. The median family income of Asian and Pacific Islander families is 111 percent that of white families.

Other than the percentage of the adult population graduating from high school, only limited improvement occurred during the 1980s (see Table 3.7). While unemployment decreased, the poverty rate declined only 0.4 percentage points for blacks, and income levels (after adjustment for inflation) increased for all groups except Native Americans and Hispanics. Otherwise, each group's relative position declined during the 1980s. The proportion of single-parent households, for example, increased for all five groups and, for the general population, they increased from 18.7 percent in 1980 to 22.8 in 1990.

The differences when comparing whites with other groups in the proportion of single-parent families increased during the 1980s as did the percentage of persons unemployed. Income differentials remained the same for blacks, while declining slightly for Native Americans and Hispanics. The differences in poverty rates between whites and each of the other groups, except for blacks, increased. Blacks and Native Americans gained relative to whites in the percentage of adults with high school diplomas. For Hispanics, the education difference increased.

In 1980, a 31.4 percentage point differential was shown between black families (45.8 percent) and white families (14.4 percent) headed by single parents. By 1990, however, this difference increased to 35.6 percentage points. The percentage point differential for unemployment was 6 in 1980, increasing to 7.7 in 1990. Median family income levels for blacks, as a percentage of white income, remained unchanged (60.5 percent versus 60.4 percent), as did the proportion living below the poverty level (20.5 percentage points in 1979 versus 19.7 in 1989). Only in the area of education, from a difference of 17.6 percentage points in 1980 to 14.8 in 1990, did blacks increase.

The Next American Minority

Over the next fifty years, a decline in the portion of the white population is projected (Table 3.8). While non-Hispanic whites are expected to be the dominant category in 2050, with 52.5 percent of the population, it is also anticipated that major gains will be registered by Asians/Pacific Islanders and Hispanics. Asians/Pacific Islanders will increase from less than 1 out of every 23 Americans in the year 2000 to 1 of every 10 by 2050, while Hispanics will increase from 11.3 percent of the population in 2000 to 22.5 percent in 2050. Non-Hispanic blacks are projected to increase slightly from 12.2 percent of the total population

Table 3.8
Projected Change in the Distribution of the U.S. Population by Race and Hispanic Origin, 2000–2050

A. Percent of Total Population

Year

Race/Hispanic Origin	2000	2010	2020	2030	2040	2050
White	81.9	80.0	78.2	76.4	74.6	72.8
Non-Hispanic	71.6	67.7	63.9	60.1	56.3	52.5
Black	12.8	13.4	13.9	14.5	15.1	15.7
Non-Hispanic	12.2	12.6	13.0	13.4	13.9	14.4
American Indian Eskimo, and Aleut	0.9	0.9	0.9	1.0	1.0	1.1
Non-Hispanic	0.7	0.8	0.8	0.8	0.9	0.9
Asian and Pacific Islander	4.4	5.7	7.0	8.1	9.3	10.3
Non-Hispanic	4.1	5.4	6.5	7.7	8.7	9.7
Hispanic Origin	11.3	13.5	15.7	17.9	20.2	22.5

B. Percent Change in Population

Year

Race/Hispanic Origin	2000-2010	2010-2020	2020-2030	2030-2040	2040-2050
White	6.2	6.0	5.0	3.7	3.0
Non-Hispanic	2.8	2.4	1.1	-0.6	-1.6
Black	13.4	12.9	11.4	10.5	10.1
Non-Hispanic	12.4	11.9	10.5	9.7	9.4
American Indian Eskimo, And Aleut	14.2	13.6	12.4	12.1	11.6
Non-Hispanic	13.7	13.1	12.1	12.0	11.7
Asian and Pacific Islander	41.8	31.8	25.7	21.1	17.5
Non-Hispanic	42.0	31.8	25.6	20.9	17.4
Hispanic Origin	30.0	26.4	22.6	19.6	17.2

Source: U.S. Bureau of the Census (1993b), p. xxii. Data reported are based on middle series population projections.

at the beginning of the twenty-first century to 14.4 percent in 2050, but the proportions of American Indians, Eskimos, and Aleuts will remain unchanged. Each of these projections is based on the Census Bureau's middle projections.

The white non-Hispanic group is the slowest growing sector of the population, a process that is evidenced by the projected rate of change over the next fifty years. Modest increases are expected for non-Hispanic whites until 2030, with slight declines anticipated during the next two decades. The rates of increase will be greater for all other racial and ethnic categories, especially for Asians and Pacific Islanders and persons of Hispanic origin. Growth rates for these two groups will be especially large at the beginning of the century.

The future growth of Asians/Pacific Islanders and Hispanics assumes a continuation of high rates of immigration into the United States. As the data presented in Table 3.5 suggest, these groups currently account for the majority of U.S. immigrants. Most immigrants are youthful and of childbearing ages. Thus, growth is anticipated. High fertility rates associated with Hispanics remain an important part of the projection model.

SUMMARY AND CONCLUSION

The two major themes of this chapter are (1) that the U.S. population is growing older and (2) that this population is becoming more racially diverse. Both of these trends will precipitate widespread changes in the American society, altering the manner in which individual perceptions and identities are constructed, as well as the way in which many institutions are configured. An increasing number of elderly persons will channel the society in new directions. At the same time, new and vexing concerns relating to housing, medical care, and other human needs will develop. The growth of this elderly population will also place additional financial strain on social service and governmental entitlement programs such as Social Security and Medicare. Development of a more racially diverse society will present unique challenges in human relations. Such challenges may require change in existing institutional arrangements to further accommodate this increased number of individuals who represent different cultural perspectives.

As a whole, Americans are moving into their middle years. That is, the average age is increasing. While the United States was once a very young population (one-half of all Americans were less than 23 years of age at the beginning of the twentieth century), the median age at the time of the 1990 census was 33. By the year 2040, the median age will approach 40. The inevitable movement of the baby-boom generation through the stages of the life cycle, along with a decline in fertility rates, indicates that a larger proportion of the population than ever before will be moving into the elderly age group. There are already considerably more persons aged 65+ in the U.S. population than teenagers. By the year 2050, this elderly group is expected to increase from 31 million to more than 80 million people; approximately one in every five Americans will be aged 65+.

There is considerable variation in age among the population. In general, females are older than males, whites older than blacks, and rural residents older than their urban counterparts. Within the rural sector of the population, residents of small communities (i.e., less than 1,000) exhibit the highest median age. Similarly, nonmetropolitan residents tend to be older than metropolitan dwellers and those living in the Northeast area of the United States are older than those residing in other regions, especially the West, which is characterized by the youngest population. These variations reflect a number of basic demographic phenomena, including variations in fertility levels, differential migration patterns, and differences in life expectancy.

Although each of the major racial groups in the U.S. population is growing in size, the rate of increase is much greater for non-whites, such as blacks, Asians and Pacific Islanders, Native Americans, and Hispanic Americans. Whites are declining in size proportionate to these other groups, decreasing from 83 percent of the total population in 1980 to 80 percent in 1990. One-fourth of the U.S. population is now either non-white or white-Hispanic. Substantial population increases in Asians and Pacific Islanders (108 percent) and Hispanics (+53 percent) during the 1980s suggest that by 2050, white non-Hispanics will comprise only one-half of the U.S. population. Hispanics are expected to total 23 percent of the total population, while Asians and Pacific Islanders will be about 10 percent.

With the exception of Native Americans, racial minorities are heavily concentrated in urban and metropolitan communities, and they are most likely to live in central cities. Ninety-five percent of all Asians and Pacific Islanders live in urban areas, as do 91 percent of all Hispanics, 87 percent of all blacks, 72 percent of whites, and 56 percent of Native Americans. Similar proportions are observed for metropolitan areas.

Blacks, Native Americans, and Hispanics all fare considerably worse than do white Americans on major social and economic indicators such as educational attainment, employment, income levels, and family stability. Asians and Pacific Islanders are the only group that compares favorably to whites on these indices. Other than for educational attainment, none of these groups (including whites) registered much improvement during the 1980s. Furthermore, all groups—with the exception of Asians and Pacific Islanders—either lost ground to whites or made virtually no progress in closing the gap.

This chapter has examined recent changes in the age and race distribution of the U.S. population. It has also provided information concerning projected trends in age and race over the next several decades. While the general course of the future will be shaped by trends that have already been set in motion, unexpected events are certain to occur over the next fifty years. However, two of the major challenges of the twenty-first century will relate to meeting the needs of an aging population and the extent to which an increasingly culturally diverse population will strive toward toleration and cooperative interaction.

NOTES

The author gratefully acknowledges the assistance of Doris H. Moffett and Cheryl E. Bogie in the preparation of this report.

1. Data pertaining to other races (or persons who are not white, black, American Indian, Eskimo, Aleut, or Asian/Pacific Islander) are reported in several of the tables that appear in this report. These data are not discussed in the text of the report, however, since most of the persons who comprise that category are of Spanish origin and are included under the more clearly defined ''Hispanic'' classification.

2. Metropolitan areas, as defined by the Federal Office of Management and Budget, must contain either a place with a population of 50,000 or more or a Census Bureau-

defined urbanized area and a total metropolitan area population of 100,000 or more,
except in New England where the threshold is 75,000. The remainder of the county is
also included in the metropolitan area plus one or more contiguous counties if certain
criteria are met. In New England, however, metropolitan areas are composed of cities
and towns rather than whole counties.

3. An urbanized area, according to the Bureau of the Census, is comprised of one or
more places and the adjacent territory (or urban fringe) in which total 50,000 or more
persons reside.

4. The Midwest region for which data will be reported in this report was referred to
as the North Central region in the 1980 and earlier censuses.

5. Native American is generally used in this report to refer to American Indians,
Eskimos, and Aleuts.

6. There were 284 metropolitan areas at the time of the 1990 census.

REFERENCES

Lott, Juanita T. 1993. "Do United States Racial/Ethnic Categories Still Fit?" *Population
Today* 21:6–7, 9.

Sheppard, Harold L. and Sara E. Rix. 1977. *The Graying of Working America: The
Coming Crisis in Retirement Age Policy.* New York: The Free Press.

U.S. Bureau of the Census. 1975. *Historical Statistics of the United States: Colonial
Times to 1970.* Parts 1 and 2. Washington, D.C.: U.S. Government Printing Office.

———. 1983a. *1980 Census of Population. Characteristics of the Population.* Vol. 1,
Chap. B (Part 1), *General Population Characteristics.* Washington, D.C.: U.S.
Government Printing Office.

———. 1983b. *1980 Census of Population. Characteristics of the Population.* Vol. 1,
Chap. C (Part 1), "General Social and Economic Characteristics." Washington,
D.C.: U.S. Government Printing Office.

———. 1992. *1990 Census of Population. General Population Characteristics.* CP-1-1.
Washington, D.C.: U.S. Government Printing Office.

———. 1993a. "Population Profile of the United States: 1993." *Current Population
Reports.* Series P-23, No. 185. Washington, D.C.: U.S. Government Printing Office.

———. 1993b. "Population Projections of the United States, by Age, Sex, Race, and
Hispanic Origin: 1993 to 2050." *Current Population Reports.* Series P-25, No.
1104. Washington, D.C.: U.S. Government Printing Office.

———. 1993c. *Statistical Abstract of the United States: 1993.* CD-ABSTR-93. Washington, D.C.: Data User Services Division.

———. 1993d. *1990 Census of Population. Social and Economic Characteristics.* CP-
2-1. Washington, D.C.: U.S. Government Printing Office.

4

Fertility Trends in the United States

DUDLEY L. POSTON, JR. AND HONG DAN

INTRODUCTION

This chapter focuses on the changing patterns of fertility in the United States in recent decades. American women in 1990 were having just about 2 children each. This rather low fertility rate, however, is a relatively new phenomenon in the United States. In the course of U.S. history, the level of fertility has on average been higher than those of any of the European countries at comparable stages of development. Indeed, when the first census was conducted in the United States in 1790, the fertility rate exceeded 8 children per woman (Weeks 1989, p. 39).

Fertility began to decline in the middle and latter part of the nineteenth century, so that by the 1980s, American women were having roughly 1.8 children each, which is fertility below the replacement level. It will thus serve well to examine fertility trends in the United States since the country's founding; this will help develop an understanding of its dynamics over the past two centuries. Such an undertaking will be accomplished within the context of a discussion of the demographic transition; that is, the movement or transition of the United States from a regime of high birth and death rates to one of low birth and death rates.

After discussing the course of the demographic transition in the United States, we will then review some of the primary factors responsible for the transition. Prominent in our review will be considerations of urbanization, technology, and the changing roles of women. We will then consider the various bases upon which fertility currently varies in the United States. The analysis of "differential fertility'' will focus primarily on such characteristics as residence, religion, race/ethnicity, and socio-economic status. However, fertility conceptualization and measurement are important topics to consider prior to the substantive presentation of fertility trends.

THE CONCEPTUALIZATION AND MEASUREMENT OF FERTILITY

The Concepts of Fertility and Fecundity

Fertility refers to the number of children a population of women actually produces in a specific period of time, such as a year or a lifetime. The concept of fertility may be distinguished from that of *fecundity,* which refers to the physical and physiological ability to produce children. Fertility and fecundity reflect different characteristics of a population: the former refers to the actual production of children and the latter to the biological potential for producing children. Given that women's reproductive years are in the approximate age range of 15 to 49, there is a theoretical limit of about 45 births per woman because the time intervals between successive births must be about nine months or so. In actuality, few women ever have as many as 20 children, let alone 45, owing to a number of additional biological constraints and demographic factors (for a discussion of these factors, see Bongaarts [1975]).

The population with the highest fertility in recorded history is the Hutterites, a contemporary sect living in small communities on the border of the United States and Canada. Married Hutterite women were reported in the 1930s to have a fertility rate of about 12 children each (Coale and Treadway 1986, p. 34). Bongaarts (1975, p. 289) notes that ''although Hutterite fertility is very high compared with that of many other human populations, it is surprisingly low from the point of view of biological reproductive efficiency.'' Because a population's level of fertility is to an important extent determined by biological and social factors, few women have the maximum number of children possible.

Measures of Fertility

Fertility may be measured in several different ways, and each measure has its own weaknesses and strengths. This chapter will discuss four of the more popular measures. Each requires data on the number of children born in an area over a certain period of time, usually a year (the numerator) and data on the number of persons exposed to the risk of fertility occurring to them (the denominator). The rates are based on the following general formula:

$$Rate = \frac{B}{PR} k \qquad\qquad 1$$

where B is the number of events, in this case births, occurring in an area in a particular time period, usually 1 year; PR is the number of persons exposed to the risk of the event of a birth occurring to them during the time period; and k is a constant, usually 1,000.

When B is divided by $PR,$ and the resulting fraction multiplied by $k,$ the result indicates the rate at which births occur to every k persons (for example, 1,000 persons) over the course of the time period studied. Greater accuracy is achieved as the denominator is increasingly restricted to those persons in the population who are actually exposed to the particular event of a birth; this population is known as "the population at risk."

Crude Birth Rate (CBR) is the number of live births in a given year per 1,000 persons in the midyear population. It is expressed as:

$$CBR = \frac{B}{P} k \qquad 2$$

where B is the number of births occurring in the population in a given year; P is the size of the population at the midpoint of the year; and k is a constant of 1,000.

The CBR represents the number of births occurring in a population over a given time interval, usually 1 year, per 1,000 members of the population. For example, in the United States in 1990, there were 4,158,212 births; the midyear population of the United States in 1990 was 249,924,000. The CBR for the United States in 1990 is hence calculated as:

$$CBR = \frac{4,158,212}{249,924,000} \times 1,000 = 16.6 \qquad 3$$

The CBR for the United States for 1990 is 16.6, meaning that in the U.S. in 1990, there were 16.6 births for every 1,000 persons in the population. Laypersons use the CBR more frequently than any of the fertility measures, but it is one of the least accurate. The denominator does not really indicate the population that is exposed to the risk of having a birth because all males, prepuberty females, women past the childbearing ages, and females who cannot have children are included in the CBR's denominator. Owing to this inadequacy, the CBR is indeed crude, and should be used with caution.

General Fertility Rate (GFR) records the childbearing behavior of a population actually exposed to the risk of the event of a birth. The GFR is the number of births in a given year per 1,000 women in the childbearing ages. It is calculated as follows:

$$GFR = \frac{B}{P_{f(15-49)}} k \qquad 4$$

Table 4.1
Age-Specific Fertility Rates, United States, 1990

Age Group (1)	Live Births to Women of Specified Age (2)	Number of Women of Specified Age (3)	ASFR (4)
15-19	533,483	8,651,317	61.7
20-24	1,093,730	9,344,716	117.0
25-29	1,277,108	10,617,109	120.3
30-34	886,063	10,985,954	80.7
35-39	317,583	10,060,874	31.6
40-44	48,607	8,923,802	5.4
45-49	1,638	7,061,976	0.2

$$\text{Total Fertility Rate (TFR)} = \Sigma(\text{ASFR}) * 5$$
$$= 416.9 * 5$$
$$= 2084.5$$

Sources: National Center for Health Statistics (1993); U.S. Bureau of the Census (1991b).

where B is the number of births occurring in the population over a given year; $P_{f(15-49)}$ is the number of females between the ages of 15 and 49 in the population at midyear; and k is a constant of 1,000.

The GFR may be interpreted as the number of births in the population in a given year per 1,000 women in the childbearing years. (The definition of the childbearing years occasionally varies. The United Nations recommends the interval of 15 to 49 because it covers the complete range of potential ages during which childbearing may occur. In contrast, the United States National Center for Health Statistics recommends the interval of 15 to 44, "because in the United States there is almost no childbearing after age 44" [Hobbs and Bogue 1993, p. 10-2]; for instance, it turns out that in the state of Texas in 1990, there were only 135 babies born to women in the age group of 45–49 [Texas Department of Health 1990, p. 77]. Therefore, when using GFRs, one should make certain the denominators refer to the same age interval.) The GFR is more representative of the area's true level of fertility than the CBR. Its principal limitation is that it does not consider differences in the age distribution of women 15 to 49 among different populations. This is an important consideration owing to the fact that fecundity and fertility vary by age, declining for the most part as the women of childbearing age become older (Bongaarts and Potter 1983).

Table 4.1 provides the data needed to calculate the GFR for the United States in 1990. Formula (4) above indicates that the GFR requires data on the number of births (the numerator) and the number of women of childbearing age (the denominator). The number of births in the United States in 1990 is obtained by summing the seven figures in Column 2 of Table 4.1, for a value of 4,158,212.

The number of women in the childbearing ages in the United States in 1990 is obtained by summing the figures in Column 3, for a value of 65,645,748. Following Formula (4), the number of births (4,158,212) is divided by the number of women in the childbearing ages (65,645,748), and the quotient is multiplied by k of 1,000. The result is 63.3, which means that for every 1,000 women between the ages of 15 and 49 living in the United States in 1990, there were 63.3 births.

Age-Specific Fertility Rate (ASFR) offers one satisfactory solution to the shortcoming that the GFR does not take into account the fact that fertility varies by age. An ASFR is the annual number of births per 1,000 women of a specific age or age group. ASFRs are typically calculated for each of the seven, five-year age groups of women in the following childbearing years: 15–19, 20–24, 25–29, 30–34, 35–39, 40–44, and 45–49. As mentioned, most births occur to women between the ages of 15 and 49. When births occur to women younger than age 15, those births are usually included among the births ascribed to women aged 15–19. Similarly, when births occur to women older than age 49, those births are included among the births ascribed to women aged 45–49. In Texas in 1990, for instance, there were 952 births to women younger than age 15; these 952 births were included among the births to women 15–19. In Texas in 1990, there were no births to women above the age of 49 (Texas Department of Health 1990, p. 77). Other states likely have similar patterns.

The general formula for the age-specific fertility rate for age group a is as follows:

$$ASFR_a = \frac{B_a}{P_{f(a)}} k \qquad\qquad 5$$

where B_a is the number of births in the population over a given year to women in age group a (where a is one of seven, five-year age groups, 15–19, 20–24, ... 45–49); $P_{f(a)}$ is the number of women in age group a in the population at midyear; and k is a constant of 1,000.

Table 4.1 contains data on the number of births in the population of the United States in 1990 by age of mother. Column 4 of the table presents the age-specific fertility rates for each of the seven age groups; these rates show clearly that fertility varies by age. For example, in the United States in 1990 (Table 4.1) there were more than 120 births per 1,000 women aged 25–29. For the age group 40–44, however, there were slightly more than 5 births per 1,000 women. Younger women in the childbearing ages have more children than older women in the childbearing ages, and the data in Table 4.1 affirm this fact.

The ASFRs are particularly useful in indicating the pattern and extent of the age differential in childbearing; they also comprise the raw materials for the last measure to be discussed below.

Total Fertility Rate (TFR) is a summary measure of fertility often employed by demographers, rather than a schedule of seven age-specific rates to reflect the fertility performance of a population. The TFR is an estimate of the lifetime fertility of a population; it is not affected by the age composition of the child-bearing population, as is the GFR. The TFR is the average number of live births that would be born to a cohort of 1,000 women during their lifetime if they all went through their childbearing years (ages 15–49) exposed to the age-specific fertility rates in effect in a population in a given year. The formula for the TFR is as follows:

$$TFR = \sum(ASFR_a)\, t \qquad\qquad 6$$

where $ASFR_a$ is the age-specific fertility rate for each of n age groups of women in the childbearing years; t is the width of the age interval of the age groups; hence, if the age groups are the frequently used seven, five-year age groups of 15–19, 20–24, . . . 45–49, then the width of these age groups, or t, is 5.

To compute this rate for a population at a particular time, one sums the age-specific fertility rates and then multiplies the sum by the width of the age group interval, t. The calculation of the TFR for the United States in 1990 is given in Table 4.1. Looking at the TFR calculations in the bottom of the table, it is seen that the sum of the seven ASFRs is 416.9; this figure is multiplied by 5, yielding a TFR of 2084.5. This number means that if 1,000 women went through their childbearing years exposed to the age-specific fertility rates of United States women in effect in 1990, they would bear 2,084 babies, or about 2.08 each.

The TFR is generally regarded as the best single cross-sectional measure of fertility, because it is rather closely restricted to the childbearing population and is not influenced by differences in age structure. Thus TFRs of different countries may be compared. However, when the TFR is calculated with cross-sectional data, as in the above example, it must be interpreted as a cross-sectional, not as a cohort, measure of fertility.

U.S. FERTILITY TRENDS AND SOCIETAL CHANGE

Trends

The United States population has increased from about 4 million in 1790, the date of the country's first census, to an estimated 256 million in 1992. Rapid growth occurred during the years of the 1800s and the early 1900s while the United States was experiencing the transition from high to low birth and death rates. The high growth rates resulted from a major imbalance between fertility and mortality, resulting in significant increases in population size. In the early decades of the nineteenth century, fertility rates in the United States were still somewhat high. The crude birth rate for the United States at the time of its first census in 1790 was 55 per 1,000 population (Westoff 1986, p. 555), which suggests that American women were having about eight or nine children each

(Select Committee on Population 1978). This was a level of fertility higher than the levels of many European countries at that time and was higher than those of most developing countries today. Assuming a death rate in the United States in 1790 of 28 per 1,000, and implying a 2.7 percent rate of natural increase, this would mean that if these birth and death rates were maintained, the population of the United States would double every twenty-five years, leading to a population of 1 billion people by the year 1990 (Gill, Glazer, and Thernstrom 1992, p. 42). It is known that this population explosion did not occur because birth rates did not remain high. Indeed, the population of the United States in 1992 was about one-fourth what it would have been had this population explosion occurred.

U.S. fertility rates began to decline in the late 1700s. By 1900, the CBR had reached 32; and during the years of the Great Depression, it fell to 21 (Figure 4.1). The reduction of the fertility rate in the United States is believed, on the one hand, to be a response to declines in mortality. Since 1900, U.S. death rates have been declining steadily, with the major exception being a significant increase in 1918 because of the flu epidemic (Crosby 1989) (see Figure 4.1). The death rates were reduced and, as a consequence, children obtained a better chance than before of surviving to adulthood. There was hence less of a motivation for parents to have many children, because fewer were needed for the same number to survive. On the other hand, additional factors that certainly had an influence in the reduction of fertility include the following: industrialization, accompanied by an improvement in living conditions; delay in age at first marriage; and the greater tendency to use birth control within marriage. With respect to birth control, it is noted that after World War I, the condom was a popular choice for contraception in the United States and, along with withdrawal and abstinence, is thought to have played a significant role in the reduction of fertility during the Depression years (Weeks 1989, p. 141).

After World War II, the birth rate began to rise and continued to increase through the late 1940s and the 1950s, reaching a high of 25 in 1957. The TFR for that year was 3,700 (or an average of 3.7 children per woman), a very significant increase from the TFR of approximately 2,400 in 1940 (U.S. Bureau of the Census 1975). These increases resulted in a tremendous addition in the number of births added to the U.S. population each year. To illustrate, in the year 1957 when the TFR reached a high of 3.7, more than 4.3 million births were added to the U.S. population, as compared to the annual average of 2.7 million births for the period of 1909 through 1945 (Population Reference Bureau Staff 1982, p. 7). This sharp reversal, from declining to increasing fertility, is referred to popularly as the baby boom, and children born during this period are known as baby boomers.

The baby boom lasted for about twelve years, and in 1958 the birth rate began to decline. By 1964, the TFR had fallen to 3,200, by 1970 to 2,480, and by 1976 to 1,740. Since then, the TFR has increased ever so slightly year by year, so that in 1990, it was just above the level of 2,000. The declines in the fertility

Figure 4.1
Crude Birth and Death Rates, United States, 1820–1991

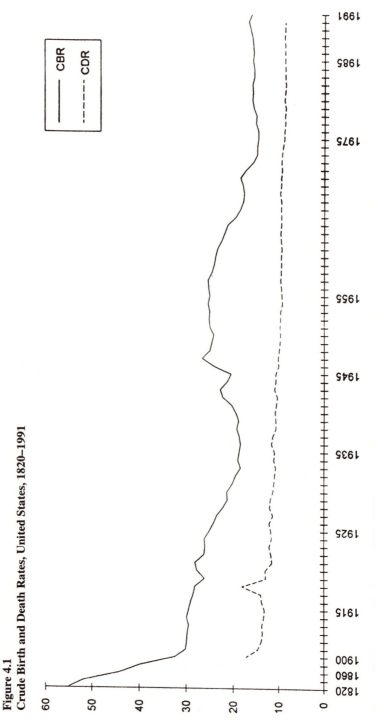

Sources: U.S. Bureau of the Census (1975, 1992b); National Center for Health Statistics (1991a, 1991b); Population Reference Bureau (1991).

rate at the conclusion of the baby boom may be explained by several factors. First, a relatively larger number of babies were born in the 1920s than during the Depression years, and they all reached childbearing age in the mid-1940s and early 1950s; this higher proportion of women in the childbearing ages resulted in a larger number of births. Second, following World War II, there were significant decreases in the proportion of women remaining single, in the average age at first marriage, and in the intervals following marriage and first and later births; these factors, which were due, in part, to the economic prosperity occurring after World War II, resulted in more children being born. Third, during this period there were also births to couples who had delayed having children during the Depression and the wartime years. Finally, there was a resurgence after the war of normative factors favoring marriage, fertility, households, and wives not working outside the home. All of these provided cultural support for having larger numbers of children than might have been the case otherwise (Population Reference Bureau Staff 1982, pp. 7–8).

As shown in Figure 4.1, the U.S. birth rate did not remain high but began to fall sharply after 1958, reaching a low of 15 in 1976; meanwhile, the TFR fell to below replacement levels in the early 1970s. Babies born in the 1960s and early to mid-1970s are members of the baby bust generation, because they were born during a period when fertility rates were low. These lower birth rates may be accounted for, in part, by the slow economic growth and greater competition for jobs, because the baby boomers then entering adulthood were larger in number than their predecessors. Many American women, as a consequence, delayed their marriages and childbearing. The 1960s were also marked by the introduction of highly efficient contraception into the mass market; the oral contraceptive first appeared in the early 1960s and the IUD in 1965, and the U.S. Supreme Court issued its ruling in 1973 permitting abortion. All these events resulted in a normative climate allowing childbearing to be a matter of choice more so than it had ever been in the past. Pregnancy and childbearing were no longer inevitable for women, and motherhood was placed in competition with other social roles that could be assumed by women (Bumpass 1973, pp. 67–68; Poston and Browning 1980, p. 229).

As a result of the baby bust, the United States returned to its long-run fertility decline. However, after the mid-1970s, American fertility climbed slightly, and a baby boomlet followed. As seen in Figure 4.1, the birth rate rose from 15 in 1976 to about 17 in 1990; during this same period, the TFR increased from 1.7 in 1976 to 2 in 1989. The number of annual births rose from 3.1 million in the mid-1970s to 4.2 million in 1990, and there was an increase in the number of childbearing women from over 48 million in 1970 to over 65 million in 1990 (National Center for Health Statistics 1991a; U.S. Bureau of the Census 1992b). The baby boomlet was influenced, in part, by women in their early 30s having births, many of which had probably been delayed. Indeed the age-specific birth rate for women aged 30–34 has been increasing ever so slightly since 1975 (National Center for Health Statistics 1991a; U.S. Bureau of the Census 1992a).

American fertility has thus been rising ever so slightly in recent years; this has been most obvious in the late 1980s. Previously, the total fertility rate in the United States mostly maintained a level at or about 1.8; by 1990, it reached 2.08 (National Center for Health Statistics 1991a, 1993; U.S. Bureau of the Census 1992b). Corresponding to this change, the absolute number of births in the United States each year increased, and in the late 1980s, it reached the highest level it ever had since 1964. In every year between 1989 and 1991, more than 4 million babies were born in the United States. As more and more young women enter the childbearing ages, especially when the babies of the baby boomers reached adulthood by the end of this century, U.S. fertility could well rise slightly above replacement levels, other things equal.

Overall, however, we predict that in the 1990s and into the next century, U.S. fertility will likely remain low. One fact influencing this belief is the postponement of marriage. To illustrate, in 1970, only 36 percent of women aged 20–24 had never married, but by 1991 the percentage of never-married women had risen to 64 percent (the corresponding figures for males are 54 percent in 1970 and 80 percent in 1991). In 1991, the median age at first marriage was as high as it had been in decades: 24.1 for females, and 26.3 for males (U.S. Bureau of the Census 1992a). These factors, coupled with increasing educational and labor force opportunities for women, the availability of more effective contraception, and legal abortion, should all act against dramatic increases in fertility in the years ahead.

As noted, in the past 200 years, the United States has gone through a demographic transition; that is, it has experienced a long-term downward trend in fertility accompanied by a sharp decline in mortality. Other Western countries have also experienced this transition, except that their declines began much earlier, their death rates had further to decline than those of the United States, and their postwar baby booms tended to be shorter and less pronounced. Fertility has been declining in the United States, at least since 1810, and were it not for the sustained baby boom that occurred in this century, current levels of fertility would now be much below replacement. What are the principal kinds of social and economic changes that have occurred in the United States that may be associated with these changing patterns of fertility? Three major factors deserving attention are the transformation of society into an urban and industrial society, technological changes, and the changing role and status of women. All three have had important influences on the fertility declines in the United States, as discussed below.

Societal Change

In the past 200 years or so, the United States has gone through a transition from a rural-agricultural society to an urban-industrial one. In the early nineteenth century, 90 percent of the U.S. population lived in rural areas, and 80 percent were actually engaged in agriculture. At the end of the nineteenth century, the rural component of the population had declined to about 40 percent, and less than 40 percent of the labor force was engaged in agriculture. By the late 1980s, those rates had fallen to 27 and 2 percent, respectively (Gill et al. 1992, pp. 44–45).

This transition certainly had an impact on the desires of parents to have children. In an agricultural and rural setting, children are viewed as a form of security and job assistance; they are expected to provide sustenance and support to their parents in their latter years, and they serve as extra workers in the family agricultural enterprise. The shifts from a rural to an urban setting and from an agricultural to an industrial workforce tend to make it economically disadvantageous for many families to have more than a few children. For one thing, rearing children in urban areas tends to be more expensive than in rural areas. The urbanization process, therefore, is certainly an influential agent of fertility change but not the only one. Another important agent is technological change.

The Industrial Revolution in England in the 1800s had a major influence on the social fabric of other European countries, as well as on that of the United States. As Gill and his associates (1992, p. 45) have observed, the breakthroughs associated with the revolution "had begun to have a major impact on the United States by the 1840s and dominated much of our social and economic life in the remainder of the nineteenth and twentieth centuries." There were important effects of technological change on efforts to limit family size. One aspect of industrialization that should be considered in this context was the development of health technology and general improvements in the level of living, both of which lowered infant and child mortality. As a consequence, parents soon discovered that they no longer needed to have many children for a few to survive. Child labor laws and compulsory education mandates further reduced the economic advantages of having many children. Additional considerations within the global concepts of industrialization and urbanization are increased women's participation in the labor force (discussed in more detail below) and the changing role of the family. The increasing importance of urbanization significantly affects the family by altering its role in production. For instance, compared to rural families, the urban family is less often the unit of production, and the value of children is considerably lessened. At the same time, urban families need to meet considerably higher demands for consumption by their children, especially with regard to education and recreation. These and associated changes greatly reduce the economic value of children and increase their cost (Gill et al. 1992, p. 45).

Modernization also resulted in changes in industry and increases in formal education, and these changes together resulted in differences in the role and status of women. On the one hand, more jobs were created in the white collar and service sectors than in the other industrial sectors, thus expanding the number of job opportunities for women. On the other hand, mass education led to more and more women becoming better educated than in previous generations, resulting in greater chances for them to compete for jobs in the labor force. The number of women in the labor force thus tended to increase tremendously, so that today the dual-earner family has become the norm, and not the exception. These and numerous other changes that occur as a society becomes modernized have a cumulative impact on the birth rate. In the words of Gill and his associates (1992, p. 46),

these changes have tended to raise the opportunity costs of having children. The more opportunities women have to use money for desirable purposes and to earn money through relatively desirable jobs and ultimately full-fledged careers, the more it costs them to have children.

The individual response to these changes is the decision to have fewer children.

Compared to 7 or 8 children per woman in the 1800s, U.S. fertility has been much lower in this century. To a great extent, the socio-economic development that occurred during the transition from a rural to an urban society, industrialization, and the changing roles of women largely accounted for this change. On the other hand, noneconomic forces may also have been at work. For instance, it's known that individualism has become a somewhat dominant value in American society since the 1970s when more and more young people ''set financial success as a major life goal'' (Bumpass 1990, p. 492; Easterlin and Crimmons 1988). American fertility rates were most likely affected by the growing need of individual self-fulfillment, which was often related to marital disruption, cohabitation, the postponement of marriage, and increasing numbers of women in the labor force. In this sense, family and parenthood are becoming less attractive to some subpopulations in the society. In fact, many of today's parents tend to spend less time with their children and families; their jobs are likely very rewarding to them and may well account for their concerns.

Fertility Differentials

The preceding paragraphs outlined some of the key societal changes in the United States that have led to declines in the birth rate. Implied in this discussion is that there is no single factor or effect that causes the birth rate to decline. There are several influences that need to be taken into consideration; only a few of them are covered in this chapter. Although fertility has declined in the United States today to below replacement levels, it still varies considerably among many population subgroups in the United States. In this last section of the chapter, the authors consider the topic of fertility differentials. Among which groups in the United States today does one find major differences in fertility? This question will be answered in the remaining paragraphs.

An important characteristic associated with fertility differences among groups is region of residence. In the United States, birth rates tend to be higher in the West and the South than in the Northeast and Midwest. This difference is due in part to the large numbers of Mormons (who reside in Utah and Idaho) and

Hispanics (who reside in the Southwestern states, especially Texas and California). Also, rural women tend to have larger families than urban women, and a larger proportion of the West and South is rural than is the case in the Northeast and Midwest. An interesting example of the higher fertility rates of rural compared to urban women is that in 1990, farm women aged 25–34 had 1,732 births per 1,000, while the rate of nonfarm women was only 1,339 per 1,000 women (U.S. Bureau of the Census 1991a).

There is one long-standing fertility differential in the United States that has almost disappeared: the difference in family size between Catholic and non-Catholic women. This differential began to narrow in the third and fourth decades of this century but then widened during the baby-boom years. By the mid-1970s, however, the rates of the two groups were nearly identical. Despite the Catholic Church's proscription against the use of contraception, for the past two decades more than three-quarters of Catholic couples in the United States report using artificial contraception methods, which, by the way, is a proportion just slightly less than that of non-Catholic women (Population Reference Bureau Staff 1982; Poston 1990). Moreover, according to data from the National Survey of Family Growth, the TFR in 1982 for married Catholic women was 1.96, compared to 1.92 for married Protestant women (Pratt et al. 1984, p. 8). Although there still are differences between Catholics and non-Catholics in areas such as voluntary and involuntary childlessness (Poston 1990), the fertility behavior of Catholic women today is much more similar to that of non-Catholic women than it is dissimilar.

Although all the race and ethnic groups in the United States participated in the baby boom and baby bust, differences remain to this day in their birth rates. American women now have a TFR of slightly under 2. However, among white women, the TFR is about 1.8; it is somewhat higher for Asians (2.2) and blacks (2.3), and higher still for Hispanic women (3) (Bouvier 1991, p. 33). The question is: Why do black and Hispanic women have higher birth rates than white women? Although this differential is due in part to differentials in socio-economic status, another factor is the tendency for black and Hispanic women to have their children at a younger age than white women (Kammeyer and Ginn 1986, p. 197). The fertility differential between the race and ethnic groups of the United States today is narrower than it was a couple of decades ago: To illustrate, in 1960, the total fertility rate of whites was 3.5, versus 4.5 for blacks. Nevertheless, this remains as a very real fertility differential, and one that is not expected to converge in the near future.

Fertility differences are also closely associated with education and income. There is an inverse relationship between education and fertility; that is, more educated women tend to have fewer children than less educated women. To illustrate, in June 1992, among women in the age group 25–34, those with one or more years of college reported having 1,027 births, while those with four years of high school reported having 1,536 births (U.S. Bureau of the Census 1993). Since college educated women are more likely than women without college to have entree into, and to be able to establish, work careers outside the home, it is not surprising that on average they tend to have fewer children.

The birth rate also varies among the U.S. population by income. Westoff (1986, p. 558) indicated that in 1985, women with yearly family incomes above $35,000 had half the fertility rate of women with family incomes of less than $10,000. This fact also explains part of the fertility differential examined earlier by race and ethnic status. Blacks and Hispanics have decidedly lower average annual incomes than whites, with somewhat higher birth rates.

CONCLUSION

This chapter has examined the patterns of fertility change in the United States in recent decades. It noted that American women today are having just about 2 children each, a number just below that needed to replace the population. However, such a low fertility rate is a somewhat new phenomenon in the United States. When the first census was taken in the United States in 1790, the fertility rate exceeded 8 children per woman. During the next 200 years, the level of fertility has on average been higher than that of any of the European countries at comparable stages of development. Tracing fertility trends is informative in that fertility began to decline in the middle and latter part of the nineteenth century, so that by the early 1990s, American women were having about 2 children each.

There is little doubt that in the long run, fertility in America will likely fall below the replacement level, and remain there. For one thing, major social forces in society, such as socio-economic development, support a low fertility rate. Nevertheless, between now and the year 2000, the birth rate will probably rise slightly. At least two reasons may be considered. As previously noted, in the early 1990s, the number of annual births was mostly due to the increasing number of childbearing women. In the late 1990s and into the next century, this number will be even larger since the babies of the baby boomers will be in the childbearing ages; their impacts on fertility will be large even if they only give birth to 2 babies each.

Another factor to be considered is the growth of the minority population in American society, especially Hispanics and blacks. These minorities have maintained higher fertility rates than whites, mainly because of the earlier ages at which they begin childbearing (Bouvier and Poston 1993). Their influence on fertility is greater than their representation in the population. For instance, minorities today account for about one-quarter of the U.S. population, but in 1989 they contributed more than one-third of the 4 million U.S. births (O'Hare 1992, p. 15). Future changes in U.S. fertility will depend largely on the fertility of the minority populations.

American fertility in the immediate and the distant future is not expected to fall to the extraordinarily low levels of 1.3 and 1.4 that were seen in many European countries in the mid-1980s (van de Kaa 1987; Population Reference

Bureau 1991). An average TFR at or slightly above 2 is expected. The continuation of current contraceptive practices and marital patterns, along with increases in the numbers of women in the labor force, should be sufficient to maintain a fertility rate of this level, which for all intents and purposes, may still be characterized as low.

REFERENCES

Bongaarts, John. 1975. "Why High Birth Rates Are So Low." *Population and Development Review* 1:289–296.

Bongaarts, John and Robert G. Potter. 1983. *Fertility, Biology, and Behavior: An Analysis of the Proximate Determinants.* New York: Academic Press.

Bouvier, Leon. 1991. *Peaceful Invasions: Immigration and Changing America.* Washington, D.C.: Center for Immigration Studies.

Bouvier, Leon and Dudley L. Poston, Jr. 1993. *Thirty Million Texans?* Washington, D.C.: Center for Immigration Studies.

Bumpass, Larry L. 1973. "Is Low Fertility Here to Stay?" *Family Planning Perspectives* 5:67–71.

———. 1990. "What's Happening to the Family? Interactions Between Demographic and Institutional Changes." *Demography* 27 (November):483–498.

Coale, Ansley J. and Roy Treadway. 1986. "A Summary of the Changing Distribution of Overall Fertility, Marital Fertility, and the Proportion Married in the Provinces of Europe." Pp. 31–181 in Ansley J. Coale and Susan Cotts Watkins (eds.), *The Decline of Fertility in Europe.* Princeton, N.J.: Princeton University Press.

Crosby, Alfred. 1989. *America's Forgotten Pandemic: The Influenza of 1918.* New York: Cambridge University Press.

Easterlin, Richard A. and Eileen M. Crimmons. 1988. "Recent Social Trends: Changes in Personal Aspirations of American Youth." *Sociology and Social Research* 72: 217–223.

Gill, Richard T., Nathan Glazer, and Stephan A. Thernstrom. 1992. *Our Changing Population.* Englewood Cliffs, N.J.: Prentice-Hall.

Hobbs, Frank and Donald J. Bogue. 1993. "The Methodology of Period (Fixed Time) Fertility Measurement." Pp. 10-1–10-10 in Donald J. Bogue, Eduardo E. Arriaga, and Douglas L. Anderton (eds.), *Readings in Population Research Methodology, Vol. 3: Fertility Research.* Chicago: Social Development Center.

Kammeyer, Kenneth C.W. and Helen Ginn. 1986. *An Introduction to Population.* Chicago: The Dorsey Press.

National Center for Health Statistics. 1991a. *Vital Statistics of the United States, 1988. Vol. 1. Natality.* Washington, D.C.: U.S. Government Printing Office.

———. 1991b. *Vital Statistics of the United States, 1988. Vol. 2. Mortality.* Washington, D.C.: U.S. Government Printing Office.

———. 1993. "Advance Report of Final Natality Statistics, 1990." *Monthly Vital Statistics Report* 41, no. 9(S):42.

O'Hare, William P. 1992. "America's Minorities—The Demographics of Diversity." *Population Bulletin* 47, no. 4 (December):2–45.

Population Reference Bureau. 1991. *World Population Data Sheet 1991.* Washington, D.C.: Population Reference Bureau.

Population Reference Bureau Staff and Guest Experts. 1982. "U.S. Population: Where We Are; Where We're Going." *Population Bulletin* 37 (June):2–50.

Poston, Dudley L., Jr. 1990. "Voluntary and Involuntary Childlessness Among Catholic and Non-Catholic Women: Are the Patterns Converging?" *Social Biology* 37: 251–265.

Poston, Dudley L., Jr. and Harley L. Browning. 1980. "Four Case Studies: Mexico, India, China, United States." Pp. 215–232 in Rochelle N. Shain and Carl J. Pauerstein (eds.), *Fertility Control: Biologic and Behavioral Aspects.* Hagerstown, Md.: Harper & Row.

Pratt, William F., William D. Mosher, Christine A. Bachrach, and Marjorie C. Horn. 1984. "Understanding U.S. Fertility: Findings from the National Survey of Family Growth, Cycle III." *Population Bulletin* 39 (December):3–40.

Select Committee on Population, U.S. House of Representatives. 1978. *World Population: Myths and Realities.* Washington, D.C.: U.S. Government Printing Office.

Texas Department of Health. 1990. *Texas Vital Statistics, 1990 Annual Report.* Austin: Texas Department of Health.

U.S. Bureau of the Census. 1975. *Historical Statistics of the United States.* Washington, D.C.: U.S. Government Printing Office.

———. 1991a. "Fertility of American Women: June, 1990." *Current Population Reports.* Series P-20, No. 454. Washington, D.C.: U.S. Government Printing Office.

———. 1991b. *1990 Census of Population: Texas, General Population Characteristics.* Washington, D.C.: U.S. Government Printing Office.

———. 1992a. "Marital Status and Living Arrangements: March, 1991." *Current Population Reports.* Series P-20, No. 461. Washington, D.C.: U.S. Government Printing Office.

———. 1992b. *Statistical Abstract of the United States 1992.* Washington, D.C.: U.S. Government Printing Office.

———. 1993. "Fertility of American Women: June, 1992." *Current Population Reports.* Series P-20, No. 470. Washington, D.C.: U.S. Government Printing Office.

van de Kaa, Dirk J. 1987. "Europe's Second Demographic Transition." *Population Bulletin* 42 (March).

Weeks, John R. 1989. *Population: An Introduction to Concepts and Issues* (4th ed.). Belmont, Calif.: Wadsworth.

Westoff, Charles F. 1986. "Fertility in the United States." *Science* 234:554–559.

5

Public Health and Mortality: Public Health in the 1980s

DAVID W. COOMBS AND STUART A. CAPPER

INTRODUCTION

The task of the public health system is disease prevention. Prevention is defined as "activities that reduce the incidence, prevalence, and burden of disease and injury, and enhance (or preserve) health by improving physical, social, and mental well-being." Basic prevention activities are classified as:

health promotion—activities that promote personal health behaviors to maintain good health (e.g., nutrition programs);

health protection—activities that change the social or physical environment in order to restrict personal exposure to known risk factors (e.g., highway safety programs); and

clinical health services—activities such as counseling or screening—delivered in a clinical setting to prevent the onset or progression of specific diseases (i.e., vaccinations) (USDHHS 1991b).

State and local public health agencies form the vanguard of the system to carry out these activities.

The current perception among many academics and health care professionals is that the U.S. public health system is in disarray (Institute of Medicine 1988a). This perception also is increasing among the lay public and business community. For example, a feature article published in *Business Week* magazine states in part:

For many decades, an intricate web of federal and local agencies have protected public health through such efforts as keeping water supplies safe, immunizing children, and tracking new epidemics. The current crisis (in public health) is the result of a confluence of factors ("Public Health Is in a Bad Way" 1992, p. 103).

Among the "confluence of factors" specifically mentioned by *Business Week* are (1) the resurgence of infectious diseases, (2) rapidly growing expenditures on therapeutic medicine, (3) decreasing state government revenues, and (4) decreasing access to health care. The main objective of this chapter is to assess the public's health in the United States and to discuss some of the factors affecting public health service delivery during the past decade.

The sections that follow will (1) briefly describe federal, state, and local public health systems and their functions, (2) delineate how the systems and their environment have changed during the past decade, and (3) examine major changes in the health status of the American people during the 1980s and the responses of the public health system.

FEDERAL, STATE, AND LOCAL PUBLIC HEALTH SYSTEMS

The federal government is the largest single source of financial support for public health services. Although several federal agencies participate, including the U.S. Department of Agriculture through nutrition programs (e.g., Food Stamps and the supplemental food program for Women, Infants, and Children [WIC]), the primary focus of federal activities is in the U.S. Department of Health and Human Services (USDHHS). Each of the five divisions of the USDHHS plays a role in public health, essentially through financial support of activities at the state and local levels. One of these, the United States Public Health Service, (USPHS), has the most direct and focused role (Health Care Financing Review 1990).

Over $17.5 billion was expended in the United States for all governmental public health services in 1989 (U.S. Bureau of the Census 1991, p. 95). Approximately $9.5 billion was spent by state and territorial health agencies; however, 37 percent of state expenditures was derived from federal sources in 1989 (Public Health Foundation 1991a, p. 4).

Every state and U.S. territory has a designated State Health Agency (SHA) responsible for public health services within its jurisdiction. Although these agencies share some commonalities, there are significant differences in responsibilities, organization, functions, and financing. The data reported in Table 5.1 documents the number and percentage of SHAs actually designated to carry out these basic functions.

While every SHA is the designated public health authority in its state, only 8 percent of these agencies function as the state mental health authority, less than one-half (43 percent) are the official state health planning body, and less

Table 5.1
Responsibilities of State Health Agencies (SHAs)

	SHAs (N=51)	
Responsibilities	n	(%)
State Public Health Authority	51	(100)
Institutional Licensing Agency	41	(80)
Institutional Certifying Authority for Federal Reimbursement	40	(78)
State Agency for Children with Special Health Care Needs	39	(77)
State Health Planning and Development Agency	22	(43)
State Institutions/Hospitals	16	(31)
Lead Environmental Agency in the State	15	(29)
State Professions Licensing Agency	10	(20)
Medicaid Single State Agency	5	(10)
State Mental Health Authority	4	(8)

Source: F. Mullan and J. Smith, *Characteristics of State and Local Health Agencies* (Baltimore: Johns Hopkins School of Hygiene and Public Health, 1988), as cited in Centers for Disease Control (1991), p. 10.

than one-third (29 percent) are the lead environmental health agency. Because of these significant differences in responsibilities, it is difficult to compare public health funding levels among the states. However, it is possible to discuss how the states distribute funding among the various activities and how total funding has changed during the past decade.

As previously cited, in 1989, expenditures by state and territorial public health agencies totaled $9.5 billion. Of this amount, approximately $3.7 billion, or 39 percent, went for noninstitutional personal health services. However, if the nearly 22 percent of total expenditures allocated for the WIC program is included, the total expenditures for noninstitutional personal health services exceeds 60 percent of total expenditures. Although only 31 percent of the SHAs take responsibility for state provided institutional health services, the third largest category of expenditures is for such services. When institutional services are included in the personal health services category, over 75 percent of all state and territorial public health expenditures went for the provision of personal health services (Public Health Foundation 1991a; Public Health Foundation 1991b, figure 13).

Table 5.2
Local Health Departments

Source of Funds	Percent
Federal Funds	16
State Funds	28
Local Funds	34
Fees and Reimbursements	15
Source Unknown	8

Source: Public Health Foundation (1991b), figure 7.

In noninflation-adjusted dollars, total expenditures of SHAs grew from $4.5 billion in 1980 to approximately $9.7 billion in 1989 (NCHS 1991, p. 284). Although such growth may appear dramatic, when examined in the context of the rapid increase in total U.S. health care expenditures, the ability of increasing SHA expenditures to produce more or better services is not clear.

During the 1980s, the medical care component of the consumer price index (CPI) rose much more rapidly than the composite CPI (NCHS 1991, p. 270). Public health was subject to the same rapidly rising health care cost structure as the rest of the U.S. health care system. Thus, the availability of some public health services has been constrained due to rapidly rising costs of and fast-growing demands for such services. Increasing demands have been brought on by such factors as new infectious disease epidemics, growing numbers of individuals without health insurance, and greater numbers of children in poverty.

Local Public Health Agencies

Although most of the money allocated for public health services flows through state level agencies, the "front lines" of public health practice are the nation's nearly 3,000 local public health agencies (LPHAs). "Local" generally means located within a county and responsible for its population. However, this is not universally true. A recent study indicates that the jurisdictions of LPHAs are distributed as follows: county, 72 percent; town/township, 11 percent; city, 7 percent; city-county, 6 percent; and multicounty, 4 percent (Centers for Disease Control 1991, p. 3).

In fiscal year 1989, LPHA expenditures totaled $4.1 billion. Of this total, $1.8 billion was in the form of intergovernmental transfers from SHAs. These inter-governmental transfers were partially state funds and partially federal funds. Table 5.2 presents the percentage breakdown of sources of funds for LPHAs.

The activities and services of LPHAs also show considerable variation. One useful way to categorize local health service delivery is by the three groups of essential public health services identified by the Institute of Medicine (1988a):

Assessment—regular and systematic collection, assembly, analysis, and dissemination of information on the health of the community.

Policy Development—promotion of the use of the scientific knowledge base of public health in governmental decision-making that affects the health status of the population.

Assurance—activities that determine and guarantee (assure) a set of high-priority personal and community health services. Assessment, policy development, and assurance activities, reported by respondent LPHAs in a 1989 survey, are summarized in Table 5.3.

In general, comprehensiveness of services provided by a LPHA is a function of the size of the population served. As the population served increases in size, so does the comprehensiveness of the health services provided. Sixty-five percent of LPHAs serve jurisdictions with less than a 50,000 population.

The overall picture is of a large multilayered complex of governmental organizations with relatively little standardization of services. Federal, state, and local community resources flow throughout these organizations and provide a highly variable set of disease prevention and health promotion services. These public health systems, accounting for only 3 percent of total health care spending in the United States, are considered underfunded by many public health professionals, given the scope and the amount of disease prevention and health promotion work they attempt.

In the next section of this chapter, the authors will discuss two questions: First, looking back on the 1980s, they will evaluate the success of these public health systems in terms of their expressed goals and differences in the health status of the American people. Second, they will identify major changes to the public health environment during the 1980s.

THE STATUS OF THE PUBLIC'S HEALTH IN THE 1980s

In 1979, the Surgeon General of the United States Public Health Service published *Healthy People 2000*, the first comprehensive report on the health of the American people (USDHEW 1979). Broad goals to reduce premature death and disability in the 1980s were defined for five major age-related life stages. Within each life stage the goals were framed in terms of fifteen priority health areas. These areas included disease control as well as behavioral changes with respect to substance abuse, eating habits, and smoking. Unanticipated problems such as the AIDS epidemic not withstanding, these goals and priority areas were used as benchmarks to measure changes in the health status of the American people between 1980 and 1990.

In 1980, the U.S. Office for Health Promotion and Disease Prevention coor-

Table 5.3
Activities Reported by 2,269 Local Public Health Agencies, 1990

Activities	LPHAs Reporting Activities	
	n	(%)
Assessment		
A. Data Collection/Analysis		
1. Reportable Diseases	1,978	(87)
2. Vital Records and Statistics	1,440	(64)
3. Morbidity Data	1,114	(49)
4. Behavioral Risk Assessment	752	(33)
B. Epidemiology/Surveillance		
1. Communicable Diseases	2,072	(91)
2. Chronic Diseases	1,235	(54)
Policy Development		
A. Health Code Development and Enforcement	1,330	(59)
B. Health Planning	1,299	(57)
C. Priority Setting	1,166	(51)
Assurance		
A. Inspection		
1. Food and Milk Control	1,639	(72)
2. Recreational Facility Safety/Quality	1,233	(54)
3. Health Facility Safety/Quality	1,063	(47)
4. Other Facility Safety/Quality	722	(32)
B. Licensing		
1. Other Facilities	1,621	(71)
2. Health Facilities	489	(22)
C. Health Education	1,679	(74)

Table 5.3 (Continued)

Activities	LPHAs Reporting Activities n	(%)
D. Environmental		
1. Sewage Disposal Systems	1,785	(79)
2. Individual Water Supply Safety	1,742	(77)
3. Vector and Animal Control	1,582	(70)
4. Water Pollution	1,353	(60)
5. Public Water Supply Safety	1,311	(58)
6. Solid Waste Management	1,252	(55)
7. Hazardous Waste Management	1,048	(46)
8. Air Quality	739	(33)
9. Occupational Health and Safety	526	(23)
10. Radiation Control	472	(21)
11. Noise Pollution	458	(20)
E. Personal Health Services		
1. Immunizations	2,089	(92)
2. Child Health	1,903	(84)
3. Tuberculosis	1,826	(81)
4. Sexually Transmitted Diseases	1,650	(73)
5. Chronic Diseases	1,570	(69)
6. WIC	1,564	(69)
7. Family Planning	1,347	(59)
8. Prenatal Care	1,339	(59)
9. AIDS Testing and Counseling	1,294	(57)
10. Home Health Care	1,139	(50)
11. Handicapped Children	1,062	(47)
12. Laboratory Services	983	(43)
13. Dental Health	851	(38)
14. Primary Care	501	(22)

Table 5.3 (Continued)

	LPHAs Reporting Activities	
Activities	n	(%)
15. Obstetrical Care	459	(20)
16. Drug Abuse	389	(17)
17. Alcohol Abuse	351	(16)
18. Mental Health	319	(14)
19. Emergency Medical Service	293	(13)
20. Long-term Care Facilities	143	(6)
21. Hospitals	64	(3)

Source: National Association of County Health Officials (1990), as cited in Centers for Disease Control (1991), pp. 21–22.

dinated a conference of experts charged with developing measurable objectives to assess progress in achieving the life-stage goals. Two hundred and twenty-six specific objectives to be achieved by the year 1990 were elaborated by the panel. These objectives included cause-specific target reductions in mortality, morbidity, and the magnitude of risk factors; improvements in disease, injury, and risk factor surveillance; and greater public and professional awareness of major health problems. For each specific objective, conservative assumptions were made about the possible effects of new regulations, technology, and the political climate (USDHHS 1981). For example, a conservative 1990 national infant mortality rate of 9 per 1,000 births was sought, acknowledging that Japan, some West European countries, and certain localities in the United States had already achieved lower rates (USDHHS 1981). Table 5.4 summarizes progress actually made for each life-stage goal in 1989.

By 1989, the goal of a 20 percent lower death rate for children (ages 1 to 14) was exceeded. Although targeted mortality reductions for infants and adults 25 to 64 years were not achieved, differences between expected and actual death rates were not great (see Table 5.4). However, the nation remained well short of the 20 percent mortality reduction projected for adolescents and young adults.

Data for cause-specific mortality show that significant declines from heart disease and stroke had occurred between 1980 and 1989, along with very modest decreases for unintentional injuries and homicide among young males (see Figure 5.1). However, the U.S. Public Health Service (USPHS 1992) recently reported a 22 percent increase in homicide among young men, especially among younger blacks.

The decline in death rates for heart disease and stroke throughout the 1980s explain much of the overall decline in mortality for adults. It is possible that these downward trends reflect decreases in exposure to major risk factors for

Table 5.4
Progress toward 1990 Life-Stage Goals, 1989

Life Stage	1990 Target[a]	1989 Status
Infants (< 1 year)	35% lower death rate	31% lower
Children (1 to 14 years)	20% lower death rate	23% lower
Adolescents/Young Adults (15 to 24 years)	20% lower death rate	13% lower
Adults (25 to 64 years)	25% lower death rate	23% lower
Older Adults (> 64 years)	20% fewer days of restricted activity	14% fewer

[a]Relative to baseline (1977) data.
Source: Adapted from U.S. Department of Health and Human Services (1991a), pp. 102–106.

heart disease, such as cigarette smoking and dietary fat consumption, as well as a better understanding and control of high blood pressure. However, it is difficult to separate the contribution of better medical care from behavioral changes.

The modest decline in injury death rates masks a fairly significant decline in motor vehicle-related death rates, especially for persons ages 1–24 for whom unintentional injuries is the leading cause of death (USDHHS 1991a). This development is principally a result of more frequent seat belt use, child restraint laws, lower driving speeds, and possibly less driving under the influence of alcohol (USDHHS 1991a).

The stagnation with respect to cancer mortality also masks changes in specific cancers; cervical cancer has declined since the 1950s while breast cancer has not declined (Sutherland, Persky, and Brody 1990). Lung cancer deaths in-

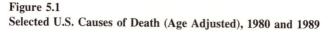

Figure 5.1
Selected U.S. Causes of Death (Age Adjusted), 1980 and 1989

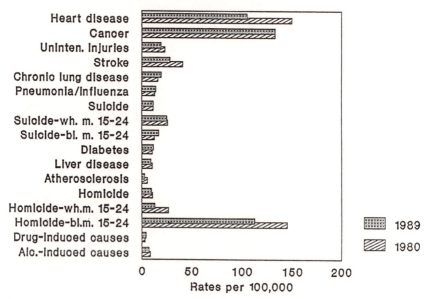

Source: Adapted from U.S. Department of Health and Human Services, Public Health Service (1991b), p. 3.

creased among women, but declined among men, especially males below the age of 50. The fact that cancer has replaced heart disease as the leading cause of death for adults 35 to 64 years of age may derive from declines in heart disease as well as other cerebrovascular diseases (Sutherland, Persky, and Brody 1990; USDHHS 1991a). Finally, the emergence of HIV infection during the 1980s has created a host of new health concerns as discussed below.

With respect to the 226 specific objectives, *Health United States and Prevention Profile* details estimates of progress in each priority area as of 1990 (USDHHS 1991a). In general, approximately one-third of the 226 targets used to measure these objectives were "achieved"; another one-third made some progress; 11 percent were considered worse than in 1980; and 23 percent could not be evaluated because the data are unavailable.

In *Health United States and Prevention Profile,* the federal government does not offer specific reasons for why little or no progress was made in certain areas, except to observe that objective setting of this magnitude and complexity was new; in many instances objectives were set without benefit of accurate data or were based on idealistic expectations (USDHHS 1991a). It is noteworthy that in some areas where little progress was achieved, politically sensitive and value-laden behaviors are involved. Thus, progress toward family planning objectives may have been difficult because of opposition to many interventions proposed.

The 1980 objectives to reduce sexually transmitted diseases did not include the HIV infection because this disease was unrecognized until 1981.

Although all of these serious public health issues cannot be discussed in detail, two were chosen to illustrate the problems confronting public health practice during the 1980s: infant mortality and the AIDS epidemic.

The Case of Infant Mortality

The infant mortality rate is widely considered to be a good indicator of the overall healthfulness of a society. Statistically defined as the annual number of deaths under 1 year of age per 1,000 live births, infant death rates in the United States have been relatively high; only the former Union of Soviet Socialist Republics had a higher rate among advanced countries (USDHHS 1991a). A review of trends in those countries for 1983–1988 show that the average annual percent decline of 2.2 in U.S. infant mortality rates was comparatively small. Figure 5.2 indicates that the U.S. infant death rate dropped approximately 32 percent between 1977 and 1989. Provisional data for 1990 estimate a rate of 9.1 percent, a figure equal to the 1990 goal of 9 percent (USDHHS 1990; NCHS 1992). Nevertheless, 9 deaths per 1,000 live births means that approximately 40,000 infants died in the United States during the year 1990 (Novello 1991).

Figure 5.2 shows the death rate for black infants declined more in absolute terms than the rate for white infants (by 5.8 percent compared to 4.1 percent). However, the percentage decline was greater for whites than blacks (34 and 24 percent respectively). Thus, black babies remain more than twice as likely to die during the first year of life than white babies. Moreover, the rate for blacks did not appreciably decrease after 1984.

Infant death rates result from a complex series of interrelated medical, behavioral, economic, and political/regulatory factors. Deaths of infants usually occur because of an unfavorable pregnancy outcome, such as low birth weight (less than 2,500 grams) or maternal complications. The principal reasons for such deaths are inadequate prenatal care, unanticipated or unwanted pregnancy among teenagers, smoking, alcohol or other drug use, and poor nutrition (USDHHS 1991b). Behind these factors are socio-economic impediments to prenatal and perinatal care, as well as attitudes and beliefs rooted in poverty and a lack of education. These conditions are especially notable among disadvantaged groups and in geographic areas characterized by high levels of poverty such as inner cities, Appalachia, South Texas, and the rural Blackbelt areas of the South (Rosenblatt 1989).

Organized public health efforts to lower the rate of infant mortality are complicated by such structural and behavioral problems characterizing both individuals and the health care delivery system. Fundamental social problems, such as poverty and a lack of education, have been slow to resolve in the United States, so that public health efforts have focused on improving access to prenatal care (Klerman 1991). However, even this straightforward approach involves in-

Figure 5.2
Infant Mortality Rates, 1977–1989, According to Race of Mother

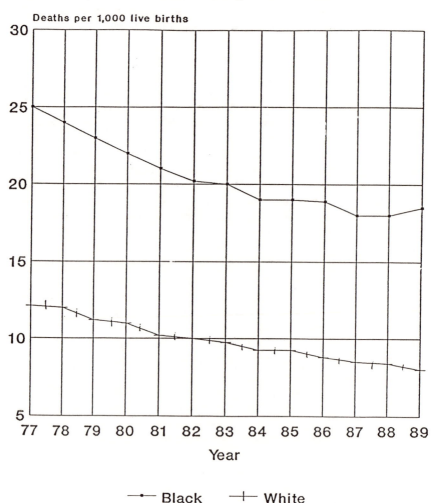

Deaths per 1,000 live births

Source: U.S. Department of Health and Human Services, Public Health Service (1991a), p. 16.

creased expenditures and politically sensitive actions that have been opposed at local, state, and federal levels. Thus, the proportion of pregnant women who do not receive prenatal care until the third trimester rose from 5.1 to 6.4 percent between 1980 and 1989 (USDHHS 1991a).

However, a major change in policy occurred in 1988 when Medicaid programs expanded and qualification limits for pregnant women and children up to age 6 rose from 100 percent of federally defined poverty income to 133 percent.

This change increased access to health services and created the expectation of meeting the objective of *Healthy People 2000* that 90 percent (or more) of pregnant women will be receiving prenatal care in the first trimester by year 2000. (USDHHS 1990; Lee, Soffel, and Luft 1992). In addition, the expansion of federal nutritional and food supplemental programs is expected to improve the nutritional levels of mothers and infants. However, as former U.S. Surgeon General Antonia Novello noted, about one-half of the nation's poor infants and children are still not covered by Medicaid (Novello 1991). Many pregnant women, especially teenagers, remain uninformed about the need for early prenatal care, do not know where such care can be obtained, are unaware of or cannot obtain family support services, and, in some cases, are not sufficiently motivated to take advantage of these services (Institute of Medicine 1988b; Samuelson 1992). The Institute of Medicine suggested that public prenatal care become more "user-friendly" by adjusting hours to working women's needs and providing transportation to clinics and child care centers.

One federal initiative used to address these concerns is the Healthy Start program, which is to reduce and eliminate barriers to prenatal care. In 1985, Massachusetts was one of the first of several states to implement this program, which focused on removing financial barriers for non-Medicaid eligible women. However, preliminary results suggest the program has been unable to increase participation in prenatal care or to improve birth outcomes (Haas et al. 1993). This finding suggests that the program needs to address lack of education or information about prenatal care, the increasing numbers of adolescent pregnancies, and monetary and logistical barriers.

The response to unwanted teenage pregnancies has been primarily through public health family planning programs. However, program expansions were delayed during the 1980s due to the federal government's shift from categorical to block grants, which allow each state to allocate monies among programs as they choose. This policy change led to significant funding reductions for family planning in some states (Klerman 1991; Samuelson 1992). In addition, the federal government restricted the number of family planning consultations per patient during the 1980s. Such changes in policy may have increased the number of unexpected and unwanted children born to women ill-equipped to deal with pregnancy or child rearing. It should be noted, however, that the percentage of births to unmarried women was rising before 1980, having increased from 10.7 in 1970, to 18.4 in 1980, and to 27.1 in 1989 (USDHHS 1991a).

The Case of the AIDS Epidemic

The development of the AIDS epidemic in the 1980s is perhaps the best known and most publicized public health event of the century. The epidemic has caused changes in spending priorities for health care in general and especially for public health. A statistical overview of AIDS incidence through 1991 is provided in Table 5.5.

Table 5.5
Number of AIDS Cases Reported by Age, Sex, and Race for 1981–1991, 1981–1993, and 1991

	Total Cases 1981-91	Cases 1981-1983	Cases 1991	Percent Distrib 1991
Total	199,516	2,920	43,672	100.0
Age:				
Under 5 years old	2,656	44	514	1.2
5-12 years old	623	2	144	0.3
13-29 years old	39,547	655	7,858	18.0
30-39 years old	91,571	1,338	19,931	45.6
40-49 years old	44,675	625	10,645	24.4
50-59 years old	14,438	221	3,242	7.4
60 years and over	6,006	35	1,338	3.1
Sex:				
Male	178,033	2,704	37,995	87.0
Female	21,483	216	5,677	13.0
Race/ethnic group:				
White	110,343	1,647	22,209	50.9
Black	59,975	826	14,548	33.3
Hispanic	27,159	436	6,399	14.7
Other/unknown	2,039	11	516	1.2

Source: U.S. Bureau of the Census (1992), p. 125.

The increase in documented AIDS cases from 1981 on is well known. Less well known is the disproportionate numbers of blacks and Hispanics infected with the AIDS virus. By 1991, AIDS had become the nation's ninth leading cause of death, claiming the lives of an estimated 152,000 Americans (USPHS 1993). About 60 percent of people known to have AIDS acquired the disease through homosexual contact, 21.2 percent through IV drug use, 6.5 percent through both drug use and homosexual activity, 4.3 percent through heterosexual contact (mostly through sex with an IV drug user), and 2.2 percent from blood transfusions. The remaining 6 percent were attributed to hemophilia, immigrants from the Caribbean or Africa, or to undetermined causes (USDHHS 1991a). Among whites, and to a lesser degree Hispanics, homosexual contact has been the dominant mode of transmission, while IV drug use was most prevalent among blacks.

The AIDS epidemic was first recognized during 1981–1982, and by 1987 enormous resources were being dedicated to identifying transmission modes, risk factors, and a cure. In the latter half of the 1980s, the numbers of AIDS cases among women, infants, and small children also began to increase (USDHHS 1990). About 75 percent of these victims were minorities, with the source of transmission for women most often through IV drug use or hetero-sexual sexual contact; young children usually acquired the AIDS virus in utero (USDHHS 1990). It has been widely feared that AIDS would become epidemic in the heterosexual population. This has not yet occurred in the United States, in part, because heterosexual modes of transmission are less efficient. However, as Choi and Wermuth (1991) note, most heterosexual AIDS victims are IV drug users or the sex partners of drug users who do not regularly use condoms. This obviously creates a potential for the spread of AIDS. Moreover, according to the 1989 data, most individuals are infected five to ten years prior to the onset of symptoms. Thus, by the year 2000, a different magnitude and distribution across population groups may be found.

As of 1992, almost $17 billion had been spent by federal agencies against HIV infection and AIDS (USPHS 1993). The federal budget for HIV/AIDS for 1993 was $4.9 billion—52 percent of which was for treatment; 27 percent for biomedical, behavioral, and health services research; and 11 percent for risk assessment, prevention activities, and personal income support (USPHS 1992).

No cure or preventive vaccine for AIDS is currently available, although drug therapies have been developed to retard progression of the disease and the con-version from asymptomatic HIV infection to clinical AIDS. For this reason, prevention programs focusing on behavior change have gradually assumed a role seldom observed in disease control efforts. Freudenberg (1990) concluded that AIDS prevention programs have effectively increased public knowledge about the disease and risk behaviors. Although less information is available about actual behavior changes, there have been significant changes in sexual behaviors by urban gay men and in drug-taking practices among drug users (Schilling et al. 1989; Freudenberg 1990; Watters et al. 1990; Guydish, Golden, and Hembry 1991). Whether these new behaviors can be maintained over time is debatable (Sorensen 1991; Guydish, Golden, and Hembry 1991).

Organizers of a conference on AIDS education at Rutgers University noted that prevention efforts to increase the practice of safe sex have been least suc-cessful among young adult heterosexuals despite increases in knowledge (Bie-miller 1992; Gladwell 1992). Schilling (1989) and Choi and Wermuth (1991) also note that IV drug users are more disposed to clean needles with bleach or to restrict needle sharing rather than to practice safe sex. The U.S. General Accounting Office's (GAO) report on AIDS prevention also states that IV drug users are the least likely of all high-risk groups to receive counseling or HIV testing or take advantage of these services when available (GAO 1991).

Finally, there is evidence that crack cocaine users do not practice safe sex and thus are also at high risk for HIV infections (Sorensen 1991). All of this suggests that AIDS prevention efforts in the 1990s should emphasize changing the high-risk behaviors of drug users and younger, sexually active heterosexuals, as well as the support of effective programs to reduce drug use.

Social Class and Health

The relationship between socio-economic status (SES) and health in general or almost any particular health problem is one of the best documented areas in the field of health behavior (see, for example, Antonovsky 1967; Kitigawa and Hauser 1973; Kaplan et al. 1987; Marmot, Kogevinas, and Elston 1987; Wilkinson 1992). In general, the higher the SES, the longer the life expectancy and the better the health status.

SES has been linked to health problems ranging from infant mortality to homicide, injuries, and chronic diseases. More recently, research efforts are directed to relationships between health and such mediators as nutrition, sanitation, access to medical care, insurance, high-risk employment, access to information, racial/ethnic differences, educational levels, and dangerous living conditions (Keil et. al. 1992; Nelson 1992). It is possible that formal education is actually the pivotal element that best mediates the effects of the other factors on health. Mechanic (1989), for example, notes the strong relationship between educational levels, health behaviors, and morbidity or mortality irrespective of income. Although the specific path from education to health behavior and health outcomes has not been established, Mechanic (1989) and Grossman and Joyce (1989) believe that education may significantly affect other behavioral characteristics, including child rearing practices, parental interest, coping skills or resourcefulness, self-esteem, access to health care and new knowledge, attitudes that motivate better preventive practices, and self-care. If true, these findings provide another argument for increased investment in education, especially head start programs, and educational reform that would significantly improve formal education for the disadvantaged.

Another analysis suggests that as SES declines, so do personal resources for coping with physical and social demands (Kaplan et al. 1987). These resources range from income or education to positive social support and personal coping skills. However, it seems that any one of these characteristics may compensate for the absence of others, so that low income can, for instance, be offset by strong social support. Thus, it is suggested that effective social service programs, such as meals on wheels and home health aids, can compensate for low SES and thereby improve health outcomes.

Health Care Access

Currently, major efforts to improve health for lower SES groups are focused on providing access to quality health care for 30 to 40 million uninsured Americans. The number of such persons increased through the mid-1980s due to the transfer of jobs to the service sector and the erosion of Medicaid coverage provided by most states (Lee, Soffel, and Luft 1992). In addition, there is another large group of people who are considered "under-insured," in that they face financial ruin in the event of catastrophic illnesses (APHA 1990).

This situation has been partially ameliorated by legislation that requires states to expand Medicaid coverage for children and adolescents. However, a variety of much broader changes are currently being discussed. These range from instituting single-payer comprehensive universal health care to less ambitious plans that would provide health insurance through mandated employer coverage or through a special tax on employers who do not provide employee health insurance. The unemployed and poor would receive government funds to buy coverage in HMO-type organizations, and Medicaid would be eliminated. Because these options are potentially more costly than the present system, the essential issue is how to "enhance financial access for large numbers while *contracting* the yearly outlays being devoted to or diverted into health care systems" (Bridgers 1992, p. 7).

This difficult issue is the central focus of the health care reform debate by policy-makers at all levels. Comprehensive reform in the United States almost always occurs in stages over many years (e.g., poverty amelioration since the Great Depression). A similar series of incremental changes seems improbable during the 1990s, given current beliefs that the U.S. health care system is in a crisis that endangers not only the quality of care for millions but also places the economic vitality of the country at risk. While the range of benefits may be reduced, basic health care coverage will likely be broadened to include underserved groups.

SOCIAL CHANGE THEORY AND HEALTH BEHAVIOR

It is well known that patterns of behavior constantly change, because behavior is embedded in larger social systems that are themselves ever changing. This complex arrangement produces change in ways that are not easy to comprehend or predict. Yet, explaining and predicting social change is the most important task of social scientists. Macro-level sociological models describe how relationships among major social institutions may predictably change with concomitant variation in arrangements of components, actors, methods of governance, and social control. Thus, demographic changes, such as an increasing proportion of elderly persons in a population, are linked to changes in health care delivery systems through mediating changes in the political and economic power of the elderly as well as more subtle changes involving work and kinship relationships. Policy changes based on valid macro-level models might then predictably involve innovations such as reimbursable, preventive health care programs to delay the onset of chronic diseases (Fries 1980; Pickett and Bridgers 1987).

Other perhaps more abstract models of society draw on historical processes to explain these institutional and behavioral changes. Cockerham, Abel, and

Luschen (1993) explain the shift in the United States from virtually complete dependence on physicians to increasing lay person utilization of scientific health-related knowledge by using Max Weber's ideas about the emergence of rational decision-making to control the environment. Thus, ever increasing numbers of people in modern society are educated and trained to seek out pertinent information in order to make informed decisions on their health and well-being with or without professional assistance.

Toffler (1990) similarly describes how the diffusion of technical and scientific information has enabled educated people to gain the knowledge and skills to better control their personal environment. This is an interesting countertrend to what Bidwell (1991) described, arguing that contemporary life experiences may be equated with the loss of personal autonomy.

Similarly, social scientists have described how ''fitness,'' as maintained by healthy lifestyles and self-help, has become the social norm in the United States and elsewhere (Crawford 1984; Glassner 1988). This trend apparently first became noticeable during the 1960s and increased as more information about the relationship between behavior and health became available. Crawford and Glassner point out that the key reinforcing corollary to the new health norm is the belief that fitness or good health is more a matter of individual action and self-control than medical care or policy. In the view of some health behaviorists, the current challenge is to better establish the health norm and its associated behaviors among lower SES groups.

Changing Individual Health Behavior

Because research on health behavior is usually at the community level, micro-theoretical models based on social psychology are most commonly used to explain or predict changes in health-related behaviors. Examples of social psychological models include Rogers's (1983) diffusion of innovations theory, Bandura's (1986) social learning theory, Ajzen and Fishbein's (1980) theory of reasoned action, and the health belief model advocated by Hochbaum (1958) and Green (1984). These theories focus on psychosocial processes through which specific behavioral changes can be introduced, advocated, and communicated, and then be accepted or rejected. With the exception of Rogers, these health behavior analysts do not emphasize macro- or societal-level influences; rather, they focus on how individuals process health-related messages and attempt to discover the determinants of individual acceptance or rejection of these messages. It is, of course, recognized that micro-level processes are affected at the macro-level; thus, for example, health messages that are understood and accepted may not be acted upon, because the individual does not have the resources to do so (e.g., he/she is unemployed or without health insurance).

Another case in point is that significant changes in health-related attitudes and behaviors over the last thirty years are the outcome of interrelated social changes at many levels, ranging from new government policies to the new health norms

(Rosenstock 1991). The radical shift in social attitudes about smoking and the proliferation of health claims in food product advertising are two indicators of the power of health communications (McGinnis 1990). Despite these successes, however, the USPHS estimates that better techniques to change high-risk behaviors could have prevented 40 to 70 percent of the premature deaths that occurred in 1990 (Arkin 1990).

These findings raise two important issues: (1) how best to make information available, persuasive, and interesting to those in need and (2) how to induce or encourage behavior changes in those individuals who fail to act on information, however convincing it might be. It is known, for example, that minority and low-income populations are least likely to attempt or maintain behavior change without considerable environmental support from significant others or health care professionals (Mason 1989). Theoretical models indicate that this may be due to beliefs that chronic diseases, such as cancer and diabetes, are beyond personal control and a matter of fate and/or heredity, so that changing behavior becomes irrelevant (White and Maloney 1990). Garber (1989) raises the possibility that the "time preference" factor discussed by Fuchs (1982) may contribute to these beliefs. That is, people who discount future costs and benefits tend to do so because they are of a long-term, seemingly unpredictable nature.

Whatever criteria behavioral theories emphasize, effective health education and promotion programs require multifaceted strategies involving health care professionals, teachers, clergy and community leaders, politicians, and other interested citizens. A broad range of techniques exist, ranging from media-based social marketing to self-help and counseling approaches. Some of these techniques have been professionally designed and tested. Others have been implemented by public health practitioners and members of voluntary organizations to meet the needs of aroused constituents. Most of the latter are not theoretical, have not been evaluated, and are seldom replicated.

Changing the Social Environment

A different macro-level approach to behavior change rewards healthy behaviors and restricts unhealthy, antisocial behaviors by imposing additional costs as a matter of policy. This is done through a variety of mechanisms ranging from economic incentives and disincentives, such as increased taxes, to explicit legal restrictions on behavior. Other examples of this approach include public smoking laws and programs to reduce injuries such as enactment of seat belt laws, lower speed limits, and child proof, low quantity aspirin bottles (Robertson 1978 and 1992). Most specific policy initiatives of this type are the result of political mobilization and media advocacy carried out by coalitions of interest groups (Wallack 1991).

Despite the potential effectiveness and relative efficiency of environmental or structural changes, these can be difficult to enact or implement in the United States because of opposition from powerful, vested interest groups such as the

National Rifle Association and the tobacco industry. As Robertson (1992) points out, interest groups not only block restrictive new policies but also reduce new standards to the minimum so that effects are minimal.

Howard Leichter's *Free to Be Foolish* (1991) provides an interesting description of the debate between public health regulators and those who would emphasize education and individual, voluntary change.

Health Policy in the 1990s

Because of the changing nature of public health problems during the 1980s and the response of health and social service agencies, new, creative prevention programs are needed for the 1990s. The USPHS, local state governments, and private groups have put together an ambitious set of health promotion and disease prevention objectives for the year 2000 (USDHHS 1991b). *Healthy People 2000* addresses twenty-two topic areas compared to fifteen listed for the 1980s. New areas include educational and community-based programs, clinical preventive services, family planning, cancer prevention, HIV infection, and food and drug safety. Specific objectives concentrate on behavioral changes in nutrition, exercise, sexual activity, smoking, alcohol and drug use, and safety in schools to be implemented as well within senior centers, worksites, churches, health maintenance organizations, and communities at large (USDHHS 1991b).

It is possible that budget constraints will focus resources on more specific objectives identified to hold the greatest potential for gains in morbidity reductions, and especially morbidity compression, or delaying the initial onset of disease and disability as long as possible so that health care costs, typically highest at the end of the life span, are compressed into shorter periods and are thus lower (Fries, Green, and Levine 1989). Also likely to receive special consideration are the health care needs of special interest groups. These latter include minority and women's health issues, HIV prevention, Alzheimer's disease, and other health problems of older Americans (Bowles and Robinson 1989).

Widespread public agreement exists on broadly defined health needs, but acrimonious disagreement develops over how these needs are to be satisfied. Thus, most people agree on the need for effective family planning, but they disagree on the means to achieve this goal. Hence, family planning is often, to use Robertson's (1992) words, "reduced to the minimum."

More importantly, national health policies for disease prevention and health care will need to be integrated into the type of national health care system that emerges during the 1990s (Bridgers 1992.) Such policies would hopefully include the recommendation made by the Association of Schools of Public Health that a federal trust fund for prevention education and practice be established using 1 percent of the available Medicare funds (Rosenfeld and Heaton 1991).

The final section of this chapter looks at the 1990s and beyond; it assesses major barriers representative of those that the public health system will confront in attempting to protect the public from known health hazards and in promoting healthy lifestyles to prevent unnecessary disease, disability, and premature death.

FOUR MAJOR TRENDS IN THE PUBLIC HEALTH ENVIRONMENT

The Resurgence of Infectious Diseases

In 1900, the leading causes of death in the United States were tuberculosis, pneumonia, diarrheal diseases, and enteritis. In 1946, the leading causes of death were heart disease, cancer, and injuries. This continues to be the case in 1990. For many, the war on infectious diseases has been won and public health efforts have been directed at chronic diseases.

The AIDS epidemic may be the beginning of a trend that will again focus public concern on the importance of communicable disease control. In addition to new infectious pathogens such as HIV, previously controlled agents such as the tubercle bacillus may be becoming resistant to modern antibiotic interventions. Moreover, vaccination rates for children ages 1 to 4 appeared to decrease during the 1980s. Forty percent of white children in this age group were not immunized, while the rate for nonwhites may approach 60 percent for some preventable diseases (NCHS 1991).

Increasing Poverty among the Nation's Children

The age distribution of U.S. citizens living in poverty is changing, and the relationship between poverty and race is most pronounced among young children. In 1990, 44 percent of black children and 40 percent of Hispanic children under 18 years of age were living at or below the poverty level (U.S. Bureau of the Census 1992, p. 473). By comparison, 14 percent of white children were living at or below that level. This trend takes on additional import given the facts that the numbers of children in poverty increased during the 1980s, in spite of improved economic conditions from 1985–1990, and the populations of black, Hispanic, and other minority children in the United States are growing more rapidly than the white population (Rosenbaum 1990).

If the public health goals for the year 2000 are to be met, these trends in poverty need to be dramatically reversed. A nation's future depends on the health status of its children. Poverty, health, educational achievement, and economic growth are interrelated: poverty and health in the short term; health and education in the middle term; education and economic status in the long term. Increasing poverty among U.S. families may lead to declining health status and even greater poverty in the future.

Decreasing Access to Health Care Services

Insurance status is one significant factor that affects access to health care. One recent study demonstrated that during the decade of the 1980s, employer-sponsored health insurance declined significantly for low-income workers (Kronick 1991). This, coupled with the increasing cost of health care in general, suggests that access to health services may continue to diminish. This downward trend will be especially problematic for certain population groups, including the working poor and the elderly.

During 1987, over 10 percent of the U.S. population was without health insurance for the entire year. Use of health services by these individuals was much lower than for individuals whose health needs were covered by some insurance. When the insured used health services, the proportion of the cost paid out-of-pocket was much higher (Lefkowitz and Monheit 1991). Even when health insurance is available, high out-of-pocket expenses prevent some individuals from seeking treatment and very likely decrease the consumption of important preventive services. Low-income children have triple the rate of delayed immunizations as children of families in other income categories (Starfield and Newacheck 1990).

Increasing Deficits in Government Funding

Public health services are subsidized by the federal government. However, recent trends, such as those described above and the aging of the American population, suggest that public health systems will be pressured to expand present services and encouraged to create new services. But the ability of the federal government to fund such services decreases as the national budget deficit increases. How prevention and health promotion activities will be funded in the 1990s remains one of the most important questions for public health policy officials.

This situation affects a significant number of Americans and should be a matter of great practical concern to social scientists who work in health-related research and service areas. If new public policy dictates a significant shift in emphases from biomedical activities to prevention, then the future may be bright even with funding reductions. Currently, there is growing interest among both health professionals and the public to make this type of policy change.

REFERENCES

Ajzen, Icek and Martin Fishbein. 1980. *Understanding Attitudes and Predicting Social Behavior.* Englewood Cliffs, N.J.: Prentice-Hall.

American Public Health Association (APHA). 1990. *A National Health Program for Us All.* Washington, D.C.: APHA.

Antonovosky, Aaron. 1967. "Social Class, Life Expectancy, and Overall Mortality." *Milbank Quarterly* 45:31–73.

Arkin, Elaine B. 1990. "Opportunities for Improving the Nation's Health Through Collaboration with the Mass Media." *Public Health Reports* 105:219–223.

Bandura, Albert. 1986. *Social Foundations of Thought and Action.* Englewood Cliffs, N.J.: Prentice-Hall.

Bidwell, C.E. 1991. "Opening Remarks." Pp. 189–198 in J. Coleman and P. Bourdieu (eds.), *Social Theory for a Changing Society.* Boulder, Colo.: Westview Press.

Biemiller, L. 1992. "Student-Health Experts Try Broad Approach in Combatting AIDS." *Chronicle of Higher Education* (September):A41–43.

Bowles, Jacqueline and William A. Robinson. 1989. "PHS Grants for Minority Group HIV Infection Education and Prevention." *Public Health Reports* 104:552–559.

Bridgers, William F. 1992. *Concatenation: Gridlock, Brownout, Meltdown, Recovery— The Rocky Road to Health Care Reform?* Delta Omega Lecture, School of Public Health, University of Alabama at Birmingham.

Centers for Disease Control (CDC). 1991. *Profile of State and Territorial Public Health Systems: United States 1990.* Atlanta: CDC.

Choi, Kyung-Hee and Laurie A. Wermuth. 1991. "Unsafe Sex and Behavior Change." Pp. 43–61 in James L. Sorensen, Laurie A. Wermuth, David R. Gibson, Kyung-Hee Choi, Joseph R. Guydish, and Stephen L. Batki (eds.), *Preventing AIDS in Drug Users and Their Sexual Partners.* New York: Guilford Press.

Cockerham, William C., Thomas Abel, and Gunther Luschen. 1993. "Max Weber Formal Rationality and Health Lifestyles." Unpublished Manuscript.

Crawford, R. 1984. "A Cultural Account of Health: Control, Release and the Social Body." Pp. 60–106 in J. McKinley (ed.), *Issues in the Political Economy of Health Care.* New York: Tavistock.

Freudenberg, N. 1990. "AIDS Prevention in the United States: Lessons from the First Decade." *International Journal of Health Services* 29:589–599.

Fries, James F. 1980. "Aging, Natural Death and the Compression of Morbidity." *New England Journal of Medicine* 303:130–135.

Fries, James F., Lawrence W. Green, and Sol Levine. 1989. "Health Promotion and the Compression of Morbidity." *Lancet* 314:481–483.

Fuchs, Victor R. 1982. "Time Preference and Health: An Exploratory Study." Pp. 93–120 in Victor R. Fuchs (ed.), *Economic Aspects of Health.* Chicago: University of Chicago Press.

Garber, Alan M. 1989. "Pursuing the Links Between Socioeconomic Factors and Health: Critique, Policy Implications and Directions for Future Research." Pp. 271–315 in John P. Bunker, Deanna S. Gomby, and Barbara H. Kehrer (eds.), *Pathways to Health: The Role of Social Factors.* Menlo Park, Calif.: Henry J. Kaiser Family Foundation.

Gladwell, M. 1992. "The Message on Safe Sex Just Isn't Getting Through." *Washington Post National Weekly* (May):38–39.

Glassner, Barry. 1988. *Bodies.* New York: Putnam.

Green, Lawrence W. 1984. "Health Education Models." Pp. 181–198 in Joseph D. Matarazzo, Sharlene M. Weiss, J. Alan Herd, and Neal E. Miller (eds.), *Behavioral Health: A Handbook of Health Enhancement and Disease Prevention.* New York: Wiley.

Grossman, Michael and Theodore J. Joyce. 1989. "Socioeconomic Status and Health: A

Personal Research Perspective." Pp. 139–162 in John P. Bunker, Deanna S. Gomby, and Barbara H. Kehrer (eds.), *Pathways to Health: The Role of Social Factors.* Menlo Park, Calif.: Henry J. Kaiser Family Foundation.

Guydish, Joseph R., Eve Golden, and Karen Hembry. 1991. "Needle Sharing, Needle Cleaning and Risk Behavior Change Among Injection Drug Users." Pp. 28–42 in James L. Sorensen, Laurie A. Wermuth, David R. Gibson, Kyung-Hee Choi, Joseph R. Guydish, and Stephen L. Batki (eds.), *Preventing AIDS in Drug Users and Their Sexual Partners.* New York: Guilford Press.

Haas, Jennifer S., I. Steven Udvarhelyi, Carl N. Morris, and Arnold M. Epstein. 1993. "The Effect of Providing Health Coverage to Poor Uninsured Pregnant Women in Massachusetts." *Journal of American Medical Association* 269:87–91.

Health Care Financing Review, Office of National Cost Estimates. 1990. "Revisions to National Health Accounts and Methodology." 11(4):42–54.

Hochbaum, Godfrey M. 1958. *Public Participation in Medical Screening Programs: A Sociopsychological Study.* Public Health Service Publication No. 572. Washington, D.C.: USPHS.

Institute of Medicine. 1988a. *The Future of Public Health.* Washington, D.C.: National Academy Press.

———. 1988b. *Prenatal Care: Reaching Mothers, Reaching Infants.* Washington, D.C.: National Academy Press.

Kaplan, George A., Mary N. Haan, S. Leonard Syme, Meredith Minkler, and Marilyn Winkleby. 1987. "Socio-economic Status and Health." Pp 125–129 in Bruce H. Dull and Robert W. Amler (eds.), *Closing the Gap: The Burden of Unnecessary Illness.* New York: Oxford University Press.

Keil, Julian E., Susan E. Sutherland, Rebecca G. Knapp, and Herman A. Tyroler. 1992. "Does Equal Socioeconomic Status in Black and White Men Mean Equal Risk of Mortality?" *American Journal of Public Health* 82:1133–1136.

Kitagawa, Evelyn M. and Philip M. Hauser. 1973. *Differential Mortality in the United States: A Study in Socioeconomic Epidemiology.* Cambridge, Mass.: Harvard University Press.

Klerman, Lorraine V. 1991. *Alive and Well? A Research and Policy Review of Health Programs for Poor Young Children.* New York: National Center for Children in Poverty/Columbia University School of Public Health.

Kronick, Richard. 1991. "Health Insurance, 1979–1989: The Frayed Connection Between Employment and Insurance." *Inquiry* 28:318–332.

Lee, Philip R., Denise Soffel, and Harold S. Luft. 1992. "Costs and Coverage: Pressures Toward Health Care Reform." *Western Journal of Medicine* 157:576–583.

Lefkowitz, D. and A. Monheit. 1991. "Health Insurance, Use of Health Services, and Health Care Expenditures." *National Medical Expenditure Survey Research Findings 12, Agency for Health Care Policy Research.* Pub. No. 92-0017. Rockville, Md.: Public Health Service.

Leichter, Howard M. 1991. *Free to Be Foolish.* Princeton, N.J.: Princeton University Press.

Marmot, M.G., M. Kogevinas, and M.A. Elston. 1987. "Social/Economic Status and Disease." *Annual Review of Public Health* 8:1111–1135.

Mason, James O. 1989. "Improving the Health of Minorities." *Public Health Reports* 104:523–524.

McGinnis, J. Michael. 1990. "Communication for Better Health." *Public Health Reports* 105:217–218.

Mechanic, David. 1989. "Socioeconomic Status and Health: An Examination of Underlying Process." Pp 9–26 in John P. Bunker, Deanna S. Gomby, and Barbara H. Kehrer (eds.), *Pathways to Health: The Role of Social Factors*. Menlo Park, Calif.: Henry J. Kaiser Family Foundation.

National Center for Health Statistics (NCHS). 1991. *Health, United States, 1990*. Hyattsville, Md.: Public Health Service.

———. 1992. *Monthly Vital Statistics Report, Births, Marriages, Divorces, Deaths, 1991*. Vol. 40, no. 120. Hyattsville, Md.: Public Health Service.

Nelson, Melvin D. 1992. "Socioeconomic Status and Childhood Mortality in North Carolina." *American Journal of Public Health* 82:1131–1133.

Novello, Antonia C. 1991. "The Past, Present and Future of Children at Risk." *Journal of Health Care for the Poor and Underserved* 2:1–16.

Pickett, George and William F. Bridgers. 1987. "Prevention, Declining Mortality Rates and the Cost of Medicare." *American Journal of Preventive Medicine* 3:76–80.

Public Health Foundation. 1991a. *Public Health Agencies 1991: An Inventory of Programs and Block Grant Expenditures*. Washington, D.C.: Public Health Foundation.

———. 1991b. *Public Health Chartbook, 1991*. Washington, D.C.: Public Health Foundation.

"Public Health Is in a Bad Way." 1992. *Business Week* (August 17):102–104.

Robertson, Leon S. 1978. "An Instance of Effective Legal Regulation: No Bicyclist Helmet and Daytime Headlamp Laws." *Law Sociology Review* 10:456–477.

———. 1992. *Injury Epidemiology*. New York: Oxford University Press.

Rogers, Everett M. 1983. *Diffusion of Innovations* (3rd ed.). New York: The Free Press.

Rosenbaum, Sara. 1990. "Children and Private Health Insurance." P. 89 in Mark J. Schlesinger and Leon Eisenberg (eds.), *Children in a Changing Health System*. Baltimore: Johns Hopkins University Press.

Rosenblatt, Roger A. (ed.). 1989. "Perinatal Care in Rural America." *Journal of Rural Health* 5:293–297.

Rosenfield, A. and C. Heaton. 1991. *PEW Health Professions Commission Advisory Panel for Public Health*. Philadelphia: PEW Foundation Report.

Rosenstock, Irwin. 1991. "The Past, Present and Future of Health Education." Pp. 39–62 in Karen Glanz, Frances M. Lewis, and Barbara K. Rimer (eds.), *Health Behavior and Health Education*. San Francisco: Jossey-Bass.

Samuelson, Carole. June 9, 1992. Personal Interview.

Schilling, Robert F., Steven P. Schink, Stuart E. Nichols, Luis H. Zayas, Samuel O. Miller, Mario A. Orlandi, and Gilbert J. Botvin. 1989. "Developing Strategies for AIDS Prevention Research with Black and Hispanic Drug Users." *Public Health Reports* 104:2–11.

Sorensen, James L. 1991. "Introduction: The AIDS-Drug Connection." Pp. 3–17 in James L. Sorensen, Laurie A. Wermuth, David R. Gibson, Kyung-Hee Choi, Joseph R. Guydish, and Stephen L. Batki (eds.), *Preventing AIDS in Drug Users and Their Sexual Partners*. New York: Guilford Press.

Starfield, Barbara and Paul Newacheck 1990. "Children's Health Status, Health Risks, and Use of Health Services." Pp. 3–26 in Mark Schlesinger and Leon Eisenberg (eds.), *Children in a Changing Health System*. Baltimore: Johns Hopkins University Press.

Sutherland, John E., Victoria W. Persky, and Jacob A. Brody. 1990. "Proportionate

Mortality Trends: 1950 Through 1960." *Journal of American Medical Association* 264:3178–3184.

Toffler, Alvin. 1990. *Powershift: Knowledge, Wealth and Violence at the Edge of the 21st Century.* New York: Bantam Books.

U.S. Bureau of the Census. 1991. *Statistical Abstract of the United States: 1991.* Washington, D.C.: U.S. Government Printing Office.

———. 1992. *Statistical Abstract of the United States: 1991* (112th ed.). Washington, D.C.: U.S. Government Printing Office.

U.S. Department of Health, Education, and Welfare (USDHEW). Public Health Service. 1979. *Healthy People: The Surgeon General's Report on Health Promotion and Disease Prevention.* Washington, D.C.: U.S. Government Printing Office.

U.S. Department of Health and Human Services. (USDHHS). Public Health Service. 1981. *Health United States.* Washington, D.C.: U.S. Government Printing Office.

———.1990. *Health Status of the Disadvantaged: Chartbook 1990.* Washington, D.C.: U.S. Government Printing Office.

———. 1991a. *Health United States and Prevention Profile.* Washington, D.C.: U.S. Government Printing Office.

———. 1991b. *Healthy People 2000: National Health Promotion and Disease Prevention Objectives.* Washington, D.C.: U.S. Government Printing Office.

U.S. General Accounting Office (GAO). 1991. *AIDS-Prevention Programs: High-Risk Groups Still Hard to Reach.* Report to the Chairman, Subcommittee on Human Resources and Intergovernmental Relations, Committee on Government Operations, House of Representatives. Washington, D.C.: GAO.

U.S. Public Health Service (USPHS). Office of Disease Prevention and Health Promotion. 1992. *A Public Health Service Progress Report on Healthy People 2000: Violent and Abusive Behavior.* Washington, D.C.: USPHS.

———. 1993. *Strategic Plan to Combat HIV and AIDS in the United States.* Washington, D.C.: USPHS.

Wallack, Lawrence W. 1991. "Media Advocacy: Promoting Health Through Mass Communication." Pp. 370–386 in Karen Glanz, Frances M. Lewis, and Barbara K. Rimer (eds.), *Health Behavior and Health Education.* San Francisco: Jossey-Bass.

Watters, J.K., M. Downing, P. Case, J. Lorrick, Y.T. Cheng, and B. Fergusson. 1990. "AIDS Prevention for Intravenous Drug Users in the Community: Street Based Education and Risk Behavior." *American Journal of Community Psychology* 18:587–596.

White, Sara L. and Susan K. Maloney. 1990. "Promoting Healthy Diets and Active Lives to Hard-to-Reach Groups: Market Research Study." *Public Health Reports* 105:224–231.

Wilkinson, Richard G. 1992. "National Mortality Rates: The Impact of Inequality." *American Journal of Public Health* 82:1082–1084.

6

The Cashier Complex and the Changing American Labor Force

TERESA A. SULLIVAN

Most theories of social change are built upon analyses of historical events, with propositions that predict under what conditions the future will be similar to, or be different from, the past. The historical events most often used to formulate theories concerning the labor force have been the Industrial Revolution in Europe and the subsequent industrialization of other continents. In such analysis, social change theory has emphasized the question of how much the countries that recently industrialized will resemble, and how much they will differ from, advanced industrial countries.

A more muted theme concerns the future of the labor force in the United States and in other advanced industrial countries. For example, will the recent widespread adoption of electronic technology eventually have effects that rival the Industrial Revolution (Hodson and Sullivan 1990)? Predictions of future labor force composition are based on analogies from the Industrial Revolution, and they emphasize one of two effects: either social dislocation and the lessening of skill requirements for jobs in the short run or an increase in productivity and development of skilled jobs in the long run. Depending upon which of these two products they emphasize, analysts of social change have presented conflicting outcomes for the future labor force of developed countries.

An optimistic viewpoint, exemplified by writers such as Bell (1973), forecasts the development of an information society in which many more workers are employed in knowledge-based occupations and professions. Under this framework, a better-trained labor force would enjoy more pleasant working conditions, more stimulating work, and higher salaries and benefits. The implication for the United States would be growth in the high-paying service jobs such as professional services, telecommunications, and finance and a resulting increase in productivity.

A more pessimistic conclusion, such as that presented by Braverman (1974), emphasizes how the owners of capital systematically reduce labor costs by de-skilling present employees and recruiting new ones with lower levels of skills and training. This may be seen as a partial consequence of the new technology that brought about the Industrial Revolution and eroded the market position of the craft worker. According to this proposition, contemporary innovations in technology will be deployed to reduce the cost of labor. Rather than leading to service jobs with high levels of skill, this scenario suggests that the new technology will lead to the development of low skilled, low paying jobs in personal or distributive services. This unfolding of events would tend to emphasize short-run dislocations, and it assumes that capitalists today will behave much as did the capitalists of the Industrial Revolution in applying technology.

Which of these two approaches better describes the American situation of the 1980s depends, in part, on whether the short-run or the long-run effect of technology is emphasized. Descriptions of dual or segmented labor markets explicitly recognize that several effects may work in consort, bifurcating the labor force into those whose jobs are improved by technology and those whose jobs require persons of lower skill levels.

Another approach to the issue is to examine the characteristics of newly created jobs. One particular concept, the ''cashier complex''—the tendency for labor force growth to be concentrated in a set of middle-level jobs that share some of the same characteristics as those of cashiers—is employed in this analysis. It is useful in understanding the types of employment that are projected to create the greatest number of new jobs in the American labor force during the 1990s. Patterns of labor demand and labor supply and the deployment of technology result in new jobs that are more available to women and to minorities, but that are generally low-paying and often part-time positions. The cashier complex enhances the understanding of those labor force changes that are influenced by a continuing shift into a service market, substitution of capital for labor, the lessening of skill requirements for workers, and the shifting proportion of demographic groups among entry-level workers.

Cashiers and the Cashier Complex

The principal economic trends that characterized the 1980s labor force did not really end until the 1990s. The business cycle slowed down around the end of the 1980s as a recession began. From the perspective of this recession, one can learn more about what occurred during the preceding decade. As the economy contracted, the number of employed persons declined by 340,000, from about 117.91 million workers to 117.57 million workers.

The data, from the United States Bureau of Labor Statistics (BLS), are shown in Table 6.1. By examining these data, one can determine the demographic

Table 6.1
Economic Changes during the 1992 Recession

Number of employed persons, June 1992   117,574,000

Number of employed persons, 1990   117,914,000

Difference   -340,000 (job loss)

Decomposition of loss by demographic group:

decline in employed teenagers aged 16-19: -1,071,000

decline in employed men aged 20+   -136,000

increase in employed women aged 20+   +867,000

Net job loss   -340,000

Source: Calculated from U.S. Department of Labor statistics (1992a), *Monthly Labor Review* 115,
   no. 9 (September), table 4, 62–63. Monthly data are seasonally adjusted. June was used because
   it was the month of lowest recorded employment during the recession in 1992.

groups that have been most affected by the recession. Employed teenagers ages
16–19 were the hardest hit; their numbers declined by 1,071,000. Employed
men ages 20 and older decreased by 136,000. By contrast, the number of employed women ages 20 and over increased by 867,000 (Goodman, Antczak, and
Freeman 1993).

Other data gathered by the BLS assess the accuracy of occupational forecasts
in the summer of 1992 (Rosenthal 1992). The greatest error in the BLS projections—a 56 percent underprojection—was for cashiers. The actual growth in
the number of cashiers during the decade of the 1980s was 1,040,000. Given
that the average proportion of all cashiers who were female during the 1980s
was about 83 percent, 863,000 new jobs were created for new women cashiers,
almost the same number by which employment for adult women grew. These
figures do not mean that all 863,000 new women employees were hired as
cashiers; rather the data illustrate the continuing changes in labor supply and
demand that affect the labor force. Although there are risks in making generalizations from aggregated data, this statistical coincidence may justify examining the cashier complex. Because such jobs tend to be distinctive in terms of
the demographic composition of their incumbents, their creation also facilitates
the diversified composition of the labor force.

Jobs in the cashier complex tend to employ larger-than-average proportions of women workers and minority workers. This fact implies that the most rapidly growing demographic segments of the labor force, women and minorities, benefit from job growth. But the jobs themselves are not characteristically highly paid, nor are they well-established career positions. Closer examination of the cashier complex jobs provides a better picture of some potential labor market issues in the 1990s. In the remainder of this chapter, the author examines the changes in labor demand that led to the cashier complex, characteristics of the cashier complex jobs, the effect of technology on these jobs, and the demographic implications of such change.

Occupations, Demand, and Supply

Cashier complex jobs are important because they account for a large proportion of new jobs; moreover, they employ large numbers of entry-level workers. The growth of such jobs points to underlying shifts in the economic structure. In general, the number of people employed in a specific occupation represents a balance of labor demand and supply. As this chapter will argue, the characteristics of the cashier complex jobs result from a combination of two situations: high employer demand and high worker supply, or "Type I" jobs. Four combinations of supply and demand can be identified:

• Type I: high demand, high supply
• Type II: high demand, low supply
• Type III: low demand, high supply
• Type IV: low demand, low supply

Figure 6.1 presents this typology in heuristic form.

Occupational Type I is a combination of high demand and high supply, leading to a growth of jobs. By making this type problematic, the author intends to analyze areas of the labor force that will experience growth. Type I positions are characterized as the cashier complex jobs shown in the top panel of Table 6.2. By contrast, much of the recent literature on the sociology of work has focused on other demand-supply combinations represented in Figure 6.1, because they are most likely to lead either to unemployment (e.g., steelworkers) or to occupational change (e.g., bookkeeping machine operators).

Type II jobs result from high demand with low supply, a condition that leads to changes in occupational content or organization. Some occupations shown in the second panel of Table 6.2 (e.g., paralegals and registered nurses) can be considered examples of Type II occupations. Type II occupations increase in number, but the growth is limited by worker supply. One theoretically interesting aspect of the high demand and low supply condition is that it may lead to the substitution of occupational incumbents from adjacent fields, the substitution of technology for labor, or the eventual downgrading of the required skill level.

Figure 6.1
Heuristic Diagram of Occupational Types (examples in parentheses)

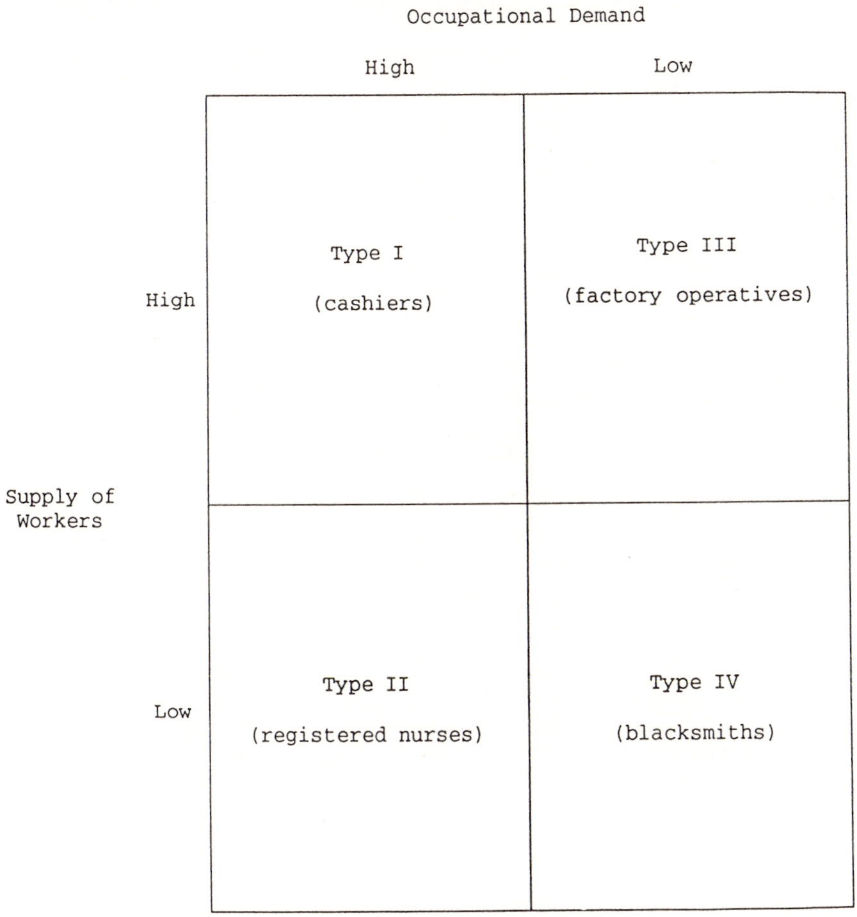

Occupational Demand

	High	Low
High	Type I (cashiers)	Type III (factory operatives)
Supply of Workers		
Low	Type II (registered nurses)	Type IV (blacksmiths)

Source: see text.

For example, in rural areas of the United States, a lack of medical doctors to meet health care needs has led to the substitution of occupational specialists such as osteopaths, nurse practitioners, or pharmacists providing medical advice and primary care. Rural hospitals now use electronic links with metropolitan-area teaching hospitals for diagnostic and laboratory services and for expert advice to compensate for this shortage.

The Type III condition, low demand and high supply, results from market factors of interest to sociologists because of the adverse social effects. This is especially true for occupations in which demand has fallen. Low demand and high supply lead to unemployment or underemployment. Some examples include

Table 6.2

Ten Occupations with the Largest Job Growth and the Ten Fastest-Growing Occupations, 1990–2005 (numbers in thousands)

Largest Job Growth

Occupation	Employment 1990	2005	Numerical Change	Percent Change
Salespersons, retail	3,619	4,506	887	24.5
Registered nurses	1,727	2,494	767	44.4
Cashiers	2,633	3,318	685	26.0
Office clerks	2,737	3,407	670	24.5
Truckdrivers	2,362	2,979	617	26.1
General managers	3,086	3,684	598	19.4
Janitors, cleaners	3,007	3,562	598	19.4
Nursing aides[a]	1,274	1,826	552	43.4
Food counter workers[a]	1,607	2,158	550	34.2
Waiters, waitresses	1,747	2,196	449	25.7

Fastest Job Growth

Occupation	Employment 1990	2005	Numerical Change	Percent Change
Home health aides	287	550	263	91.7
Paralegals	90	167	77	86.2
Systems analyst[a]	463	829	366	78.9
Personal aides	103	183	80	76.7
Physical therapist	88	155	67	76.0
Medical assistants	165	287	122	73.9
Operations research analysts	57	100	42	73.2
Human services workers	145	249	103	71.2
Radiologic technicians[a]	149	252	103	69.5
Medical secretaries	232	390	158	68.3

[a]Includes closely related occupations

Source: Adapted from Silvestri and Lukasiewicz (1991), tables 3 and 4, pp. 81–82.

skilled steelworker and other manufacturing production specialties. Many workers with these occupational skills lost their jobs in the industrial restructuring that followed factory closings in the Midwest. When demand dropped, these workers were often unable to relocate into an industry that could use their skills.

Finally, Type IV jobs, with low demand and low supply, such as blacksmiths, are obsolete occupations resulting from displacement due to rapid technological development. Bookkeeping machine operators, a clerical occupational specialty, have been replaced by other occupational groups who perform the same tasks but with different and more efficient technology. Thus, Type IV occupations are of relatively little numerical import to the labor force.

Recent Job Growth and Occupation

To influence young people's education and training choices, school and other counselors often emphasize the "growth" industries and occupations. Such jobs include computer programmer, radiology technician, and similar service jobs related to the latest technology. A list of such occupations appear in the bottom panel of Table 6.2. Many of these occupations are Type II jobs, where demand currently outstrips supply. Such jobs do indeed appear on the BLS list of the fastest growing occupations, because they have experienced or are projected to record the fastest rate of growth. For those occupations affected by the most recent technology, however, the rate of growth is a percentage that is calculated on a very small base. Thus, the expected 86 percent increase in paralegals is based on a 1990 figure of only 90,000 workers.

Cashiers, retail salespersons, and other occupations in the cashier complex will experience the largest growth in terms of the numbers of new jobs created. In 1990, 23.8 million people held one of the cashier complex jobs, a figure that represents 20.1 percent of the civilian labor force. By the year 2005, the ten occupations listed in the top panel of Table 6.2 are expected to produce 6,373,000 new jobs. The growth in these occupations is estimated to range between 19 and 44 percent. The effect of such growth will be significant because relatively large, growing occupations are involved. In contrast, the fastest growing jobs proportionately are projected to produce only 1,381,000 new jobs between 1990 and 2005.

Type I cashier complex jobs represent a shift of employment into the service sector. Of the top ten occupations, seven are concentrated in the service industries. Two occupations—janitors and cleaners and truck drivers—although found in manufacturing, are most likely to be located in the transportation, business services, and personal services industries. General managers may be employed in any type of industry, but because services are the fastest growing industrial sector, new general managers are most likely to be employed in these. To better understand the composition of the labor force during the 1990s, it is important to give attention to those occupations where growth is rapid only in relation to small base numbers.

Job Characteristics of the Cashier Complex Jobs

The cashier complex jobs have common traits that suggest the roots of job growth in the 1990s. These traits are part-time status, off-shifts of work, job content changes as technology by-products, and generally low levels of pay, benefits, and job security. Most of these occupations require relatively low levels of training and have few barriers to entry, thus establishing many of these positions as potential entry-level jobs.

Such traits are generally characteristic of less desirable jobs within the economy. Cashier complex jobs can be considered ''generic jobs,'' in that they require occupational skills that many different types of employers seek and that many workers possess. High demand is therefore balanced by high supply. However, high demand is not necessarily translated into high salaries or good benefit packages.

Supply is relatively high because most Type I cashier complex occupations require relatively low levels of specific training. Moreover, some individuals displaced from Type III jobs, including craft and skilled manufacturing workers, may find Type I jobs the only ones available to them, thus increasing the supply for the Type I jobs. The relatively large supply of workers, and their dispersion among many employing firms, imply that these occupations are likely to garner only low levels of occupational power (Fraser 1987).

There are two possible exceptions to these generalizations. The more notable exception is registered nurse, an occupation that requires specific training either in a hospital training program or a formal college nursing program and a successful outcome in a licensure examination. Demand for registered nurses remains high, and the employment opportunities include not only hospitals, nursing centers, and physicians' offices, but also workplaces and schools. Indeed, the imbalance of supply and demand may be sufficient to consider nursing a Type II job. Nursing is also one occupation for which employers are most likely to seek the admission of immigrant workers on the grounds of a labor shortage. Immigration also is one way to increase the supply of nurses without necessarily increasing salaries and other working conditions.

The limited supply of trained nurses might lead to more occupational power, given that nursing is a profession with strong occupational organizations. The occupational power of nursing remains less than might be possible, however, partly because of the varied orientations of nurses toward professionalization and the formal representation within collective bargaining agreements. The lack of a single, clear strategy and the diversity of workplaces tends to reduce the occupational power that nurses might otherwise command.

The occupation of truck driver is a second possible exception to the traits of the cashier complex jobs. The demand for truck drivers is strong, but it is diffuse both in terms of the skills demanded and the nature of the employers. As coded in the BLS data, drivers of vehicles from pickup trucks to eighteen-wheelers are included, thereby covering a variety of working conditions. Moreover, truck drivers are employed in a variety of industries as well as large and small firms. A significant portion of this occupational group also consists of entrepreneurs who own their own trucks.

Some truck drivers are required to have specialized skills. Technical schools prepare over-the-road truck drivers, but light trucks can be driven with only a commercial driver's license or, in some cases, with an ordinary driver's license. The Teamster's Union has given occupational power to at least some truckers, but the union's propensity to become a general union and the number of unorganized workplaces have mitigated against stronger occupational power for truck drivers.

Because the cashier complex jobs will account for a larger proportion of the labor force in the future, the working conditions prevalent for these jobs will become more common. In the following discussion, four characteristics of the cashier complex jobs will be discussed: part-time nature, working new shifts, low compensation, and changing job content.

Part-Time Status. In 1992, approximately 18 percent of the labor force worked part-time, including 15 million workers who were voluntarily part-time workers. Another 6.3 million workers were part-time workers for economic reasons. The workers in this latter group have been characterized as underemployed because they desire more work, but full-time work is unavailable or job hours have been cut because of material shortages and a slowdown in work.

The percentage of cashier complex workers who work part-time is much higher. About 40 percent of new department stores' sales jobs are part-time, and one-third of these jobs are seasonal, offering employment for three months or less every year (Hodson and Sullivan 1990). Such seasonal work is usually during the Christmas shopping season, although in some parts of the United States tourist activity may dictate seasonal employment (Hartmann, Kraut, and Tilly 1986). While the average number of weekly hours in the private sector in 1992 was 34.3, within the service sector this average was 32.4 hours, among retail sales workers, the average hours worked weekly were only 28.6 (U.S. Department of Labor 1992a, p. 82).

Analysis of retail trade indicates that many of the new cashier jobs are part-time. An influx of women into the labor force and the relocation of retail outlets away from the central city have encouraged retail outlets to expand the workday to include later hours during the week and to open on Sundays. Many retail malls now require occupant stores to be open the same hours the mall maintains, often twelve hours a day during regular weeks, with extended hours during holiday seasons. Retail merchants have such hours to be competitive, but by law, merchants may not require employees to work the extended hours. Faced with the alternative of paying overtime or hiring additional workers, many merchants have chosen to use part-time shifts of four hours each, while some have developed three shifts of four hours each, with only a manager working full-time. In some cases, managers work overlapping six-hour shifts but still do not work a full forty-hour work week.

In comparison to the 1980s, this development underscores an important trend in the labor market of the 1990s; high demand does not necessarily mean equal demand throughout day and night hours. The same forces that encourage part-time work also encourage more off-shift work (Applebaum 1987).

Off-Shifts of Work. The phrase "normal business hours" conveys the normative expectation that working hours occur during the daylight hours. A global economy, however, must be a twenty-four-hour-a-day economy. Moreover, serving customers involves maintaining store hours when potential customers are not themselves working. Thus, expansion of the normal workday into the evening and night hours is occurring. Among full-time workers, 17.8 percent work other than the day shift, an increase of 2.7 million workers since 1985 (U.S. Department of Labor 1992b). Cashier complex jobs generally show lower proportions on the day shift. Seventy-two percent of truck drivers, 69 percent of janitors and cleaners, 68 percent of retail sales workers, 67.6 percent of cashiers, 64 percent of registered nurses, 63 percent of nurse's aides, and 55 percent of waiters, waitresses, and food counter, fountain, and related employees work other than daytime hours. The most rapidly growing jobs are also scheduled for night, evening, and rotating shifts (U.S. Department of Labor 1992b).

In retail sales, 8.6 percent of the workers work on evening shifts, 2.9 percent are on night shifts, 7.8 percent work rotating shifts, 11.2 percent are on irregular shifts, and 1.3 percent have another arrangement. These patterns are consistent with the nature of the demand for retail sales workers outlined above. Not only are retail sales workers most likely to be part-time, but their shifts are likely to be in the evenings, on weekends, or a combination of shifts throughout the week. Some are "on call" for whenever the boss needs additional help.

Even the 85 percent of the labor force on the day schedule may find their work hours altered by arrangements such as flextime, a different kind of "off-shift" that gives the worker some discretion in scheduling a full work week around a core of basic hours specified by the employer. Flextime is popular with workers who need to accommodate child care needs, those who desire to avoid traffic congestion, or those who have specific hours for leisure. In 1985, 9.1 million workers worked flextime; by 1992, that number had grown to 12.1 million and included 15 percent of the full-time work force. During this period, women made the fastest gains, with 14.5 percent of U.S. women working flex-time hours (U.S. Department of Labor 1992b).

Flextime is usually associated with a full-time job, and it is most prevalent in the federal government, where 27 percent of workers have flextime. But flextime can also affect cashier complex jobs; about one-fifth of sales workers (Type I) have flextime hours. When a large proportion of the full-time labor force has flextime, there are additional demands for services during the early morning and late evening hours.

Low Pay, Benefits, Job Security. In general, high demand is assumed to lead to high wages. But the high demand for Type I cashier complex type jobs is balanced by a high supply of workers. Evidence of this can be found by examining those industries in which cashier complex jobs are currently being created. In 1992, for example, when the general average earnings in the private sector were $10.58 per hour, the earnings in retail trade averaged only $7.10 per hour (U.S. Department of Labor 1992a). Part-time work status also is associated with lower earnings, and employers generally do not provide benefits such as health care, insurance, and paid sick leave to part-time workers.

Technology and Job Content Changes

Cashiers have been affected by the introduction of electronic technology into retail sales. In particular, the "smart" cash registers have enlarged the function of the cashier's job while requiring lower skill levels. A smart cash register linked to bar code scanners automatically reads the price, adjusts the available inventory, and prepares statistical summaries of purchases. The smart cash register may also have electronic links for check and credit card verification, and for connecting to remote supplier or warehouse sites (Sullivan 1990, pp. 20–21).

Use of bar codes means that cashiers are no longer required to know the prices of most items scanned. Scanning also eliminates the need for most keyboarding. Taxes and discounts are calculated and registers are programmed to make changes automatically. Some cashiers have icons rather than numbers on their cash registers, such as in fast-food establishments where representations of pictures of shakes, fries, and burgers are displayed on the cash register. Thus, the cashier only needs to remember the flavor of the shake or soda the customer orders.

Advanced technology frees the cashier to perform other skilled tasks. Not all customers know what they want and, in theory, the cashier should have more time for answering questions, demonstrating merchandise, or assisting customers in other ways. In practice, however, this rarely happens, because the cost of the technology leads to a reduction in staffing. In many retail shops, the cashier is the only employee who is visible, and customers must direct their inquiries to the cashier. Direct service to the customer thus becomes secondary to the efficiency of ringing up sales. Moreover, because the cashier handles money belonging to the establishment, special precautions are often taken to insure its safety. Occasionally this is done by closed-circuit television monitors, but more frequently it is accomplished by rules about when the cashier may leave the cash register unattended. As a consequence, some cashiers are unable to move from their assigned site to assist customers who have questions.

Such arrangements suggest that the skill levels of cashiers have been reduced. Cashiers no longer are required to have good arithmetic abilities, and they may not even need to know how to make change. Discounts and taxes are calculated automatically by the computerized cash register, and the change may even be delivered automatically. Language skills comprehension is reduced by the scanning and icon technologies, and the effective reduction of direct service to the customers further reduces the need for language abilities. Honesty and the ability to distinguish denominations of currency remain characteristics of the job, but future electronic monitoring and new scanning procedures may soon make these characteristics optional or obsolete.

Thus, technology has changed the cashier's job in a number of ways. The cashier task may be more comprehensive because it includes inventory control and credit verification, but the skills required to perform it have been reduced to a minimum. Staffing needs are reduced by the substitution of the smart cash register for clerical personnel, which in turn affects direct service to the customer. As these changes progress, the potential supply of cashiers increases because the job skills are so minimal.

Nevertheless, the cashier complex jobs seem to be affected by technology according to the described pattern: technology is substituted for labor to the maximum extent practicable, and there is an irreducible amount of direct human labor required. Examples of this type include waiters and waitresses and food counter, fountain, and related workers. Prepackaging, microwave ovens, and other machinery used in the restaurant business have effectively reduced the skills required of food preparers (Reiter 1991). One need not qualify as a chef or as a skilled cook to work in a fast-food establishment. The specialization in product, the application of industrial techniques to food production, and product standardization through franchise agreements have removed variation, as well as creativity, from the tasks (Ritzer 1993). However, not even changes in the social organization of restaurants, such as the substitution of table services through the use of buffets, self-service beverages, and salad bars, can completely reduce the need to hand a finished food product to the customer.

Thus, the cashier complex jobs exist in an environment in which technology is replacing workers, nominally enlarging the job of the cashier complex worker, and reducing the skill level required. Although new technology often improves working conditions, the cashier complex jobs have become more isolated and less autonomous. These generic jobs, while open to many workers, pay lower wages and have little occupational power.

The Cashier Complex and Demographic Changes

Cashiers constitute an occupation that has become somewhat less gender segregated. According to the 1990 census, there were 2,641,592 female cashiers and 682,360 male cashiers. Ten years earlier, 1,801,100 female cashiers and 332,100 male cashiers were employed. These figures represent a 47 percent increase among women, and a 105 percent increase among men, respectively. As a result of the increase from 15.5 percent of the labor force to 20.5 percent among men, the proportion of women fell from 84.4 percent to 79.5 percent (U.S. Bureau of the Census 1983; 1993).

The occupation has also become more racially diverse (Sullivan 1989). In 1980, 14.4 percent of the cashiers were non-white, of which 8.4 percent were black women, 1.6 percent were black men, and 3.5 percent were women from other racial categories. Only a fraction of a percent were Asian, Pacific Islander, or American Indian males (U.S. Bureau of the Census 1983). By 1990, 22.7 percent of the cashiers were non-white, including 11.7 percent black women and 2.5 percent black men, while 6.3 percent of the women and 2.2 percent of the men were from other racial categories (U.S. Bureau of the Census 1993). Cashier complex jobs have thus opened up many job opportunities for women and minorities. In the labor force as a whole, 10.1 percent of workers are black and 6.9 percent are Hispanic. The median age for male cashiers is only 22 years and for female cashiers it is 20.1, indicating an occupation that is probably entry-level or part-time (U.S. Bureau of the Census 1993).

According to 1990 census data, the mean earnings for cashiers were $9,355 for men and $6,082 for women. Table 6.3 shows the median income for cashiers,

Table 6.3
Mean Earnings of Part-Time Cashiers, by Sex and Race, 1989 (workers who worked at least 27 weeks and on a part-time schedule of 34 hours per week or less)

Race	Sex		Female/Male Ratio
	Males	Females	
White	$5787	$5673	0.98
Black	$5202	$5192	1.00
Other	$6744	$6389	0.95

Source: U.S. Bureau of the Census (1993). Weighted data for persons with positive earnings only.

by race and sex, who worked at least a half year and part-time in 1989. Although men of every racial group earned slightly more than women of the same group, the ratio between the two is closer to parity than in the labor force as a whole. However, this finding does not hold for cashiers who work at least half of the year and who are full-time. Among these workers, the mean earnings for men are much higher at $18,616 versus $11,975 for women. This ratio, with women earning about 65 percent of what men earn, is closer to the ratio found in the labor force as a whole. The range of mean salaries for men is from $13,870 for other races to $19,956 for whites, and for women the range is from $11,623 for black women to $12,048 for white women.

These data illuminate an important fact about cashier complex jobs. The demographic characteristics of new workers recruited to these occupations closely resemble those of entry-level workers. This finding is not surprising, because the cashier complex consists of many entry-level jobs that require minimal skills. However, to assume that equity in recruiting is equivalent to equity in compensation would be misleading. Instead, the hours of work each week condition not only how much income is received, but also how much parity is found among workers from different demographic groups. There is substantial parity among the part-time workers. Among the full-time workers, however, the familiar pattern emerges of males earning up to one-third more per year, and of whites earning more than workers from other racial groups.

Thus, if the cashier occupation is taken as an indicator for the conditions that characterize a group of jobs, cashier complex jobs are likely to offer parity only at the lowest levels of compensation. As workers gain full-time status, the pattern of inequity in the labor force reasserts itself and is reproduced among the workers in this job. This is an important pattern to understand and to interpret, for what appears to be greater equity in the composition of the occupation disappears under closer analysis.

CONCLUSIONS

Americans have observed the disappearance of high-paying manufacturing jobs during the last decade and a concomitant replacement with low-skill, low-paying jobs. The cashier complex concept is useful to analyze such change in terms of supply and demand conditions of the labor force, the characteristics of labor demand, and the effects of technology in the workplace. Although the cashier complex results in more jobs for women and minority group members, the demographic segments of labor supply are growing, and the relatively low levels of pay suggest that these jobs are at best adequate. Aspirations of the American worker for high-paying, satisfying, and relatively autonomous jobs are not likely to be achieved by the expansion of cashier complex jobs.

In terms of social change in the labor force, the cashier complex offers an admonition against easy generalization. Such jobs can incorporate the new information technology to enlarge the job and to increase productivity within the enterprise. However, the result is that cashier complex jobs simultaneously represent a deskilling of current workers with lower skill levels required of future workers.

REFERENCES

Applebaum, Eileen. 1987. "Restructuring Work: Temporary, Part-Time, and At-Home Employment." Pp. 268–310 in H.I. Hartmann (ed.), *Computer Chips and Paper Clips,* vol. 2. Washington, D.C.: National Academy Press.

Bell, Daniel. 1973. *The Coming of Post-Industrial Society.* New York: Basic Books.

Braverman, Harry. 1974. *Labor and Monopoly Capital.* New York: Monthly Review Press.

Fraser, Bryna. 1987. "New Office and Business Technologies: The Structure of Education and (re) Training Opportunities." Pp. 348–72 in H.I. Hartman (ed.), *Computer Chips and Paper Clips,* vol. 2. Washington, D.C.: National Academy Press.

Goodman, William, Stephen Antczak, and Laura Freeman. 1993. "Women and Jobs in Recession: 1969–92." *Monthly Labor Review* 116 (July):26–35.

Hartmann, Heidi I., Robert Kraut, and Louise Tilly (eds.). 1986. *Computer Chips and Paper Clips,* vol. 1. Washington, D.C.: National Academy Press.

Hodson, Randy and Teresa A. Sullivan. 1990. *The Social Organization of Work.* Belmont, Calif.: Wadsworth.

Reiter, Ester. 1991. *Making Fast Food: From the Frying Pan into the Fryer.* Montreal: McGill-Queen's University Press.

Ritzer, George. 1993. *The McDonaldization of Society.* Newbury Park, Calif.: Pine Forge Press.

Rosenthal, Neal H. 1992. "Occupational Employment." *Monthly Labor Review* 115:32–48.

Silvestri, George and John Lukasiewicz. 1991. "Occupational Employment Projections." *Monthly Labor Review* 114:64–69.

Sullivan, Teresa. 1989. "Women and Minority Workers in the New Economy: Optimistic, Pessimistic, and Mixed Scenarios." *Work and Occupations* 16:393–415.

———. 1990. "The Decline of Occupations." Pp. 13–31 in Maureen T. Hallinan, David M. Klein, and Jennifer Glass (eds.), *Change in Societal Institutions.* New York: Plenum.

U.S. Bureau of the Census. 1983. Public Use Microdata Samples for the 1980 Census. Machine-readable data set.

———. 1993. Public Use Microdata Samples for the 1990 Census. Machine-readable data set.

U.S. Department of Labor. 1992a. "Current Labor Statistics." *Monthly Labor Review* 115:63–113.

———. 1992b. "Workers on Flexible and Shift Schedules." U.S. Department of Labor, Press release 6692-491 (August 14).

7

Urban Redevelopment and the Post-Industrial City: The Persistence of Gentrification in Central Cities, 1980–1990

FRANK HAROLD WILSON

BACKGROUND

Urban redevelopment broadly refers to structural changes and interventions designed to eliminate urban blight, improve the urban environment and its institutions, and upgrade the quality of life for city residents. Publicly initiated and assisted programs to improve cities, such as those focused on revitalizing central business districts, rehabilitating or conserving existing structures, providing for upgraded housing, commercial, industrial, and public buildings, and the clearing of slums, are commonly referred to as "urban renewal" (Abrams 1971, p. 332). Federal urban renewal programs, such as the Housing Acts of 1937, 1949, and 1954, recognized the goals of slum clearance and public housing, urban redevelopment, comprehensive planning, and conservation respectively (Greer 1965). By the late 1960s and 1970s, new urban renewal initiatives led to public recognition of the continuing challenges of traditional federal urban renewal in addressing exacerbating problems, such as employment, housing, and service decline in older cities, and a growing consensus that federally conceived and directed programs had limitations in helping cities in diverse circumstances. Federal institutional interventions, such as the Community Development Block Grant program (CDBG), Urban Development Action Grants (UDAG), and State and Small Cities Community Development Block Grants, recognized, in principle, the competing challenges of reducing governmental taxes, spending, and programs while improving city economies, housing, service delivery systems, and quality of life.

Gentrification is a process of urban redevelopment that occurs when middle-class families move into declining central city neighborhoods, and the housing in these neighborhoods is upgraded through rehabilitation and apartment conversions (Clay 1979; Gale 1984; Smith 1986; Zukin 1987; Wittberg 1992). Sometimes called ''private urban renewal'' (Zeitz 1979) or ''urban revitalization'' to underscore the initiative role of private market forces as distinct from public sector investments, gentrification has important possibilities of increasing homeownership, tax bases, reinvestment, ambience, historic and aesthetic values, and the social class and racial/ethnic diversity of cities. Government leaders, real estate developers, the media, and new homebuyers praise gentrification for renewing the declining neighborhoods and for providing a requisite for economic integration. Yet, while gentrification contributes to these upgrading outcomes of increased middle-class homeownership, taxes, and an improved quality of life (Urban Land Institute 1980; Kasarda 1980; Anderson, Levy, and Reingold 1987), the larger context of economic restructuring and housing change, in which this revitalization occurs, frequently is subject to rising housing costs, tightening of renter markets, speculation, and displacement (Grier and Grier 1980; Le Gates and Hartman 1986; Marcuse 1986; Feagin and Parker 1990). Gentrification is one process of the new urbanization that also coexists with the in-migration of racial minorities, the concentrated ghetto poverty of the underclass, and long-term trends of suburbanization.

The 1980s represent a pivotal period for examining urban redevelopment, in general, and gentrification, specifically. While the literature on urban revitalization suggests that important changes in many older U.S. central cities occurred through central business revitalization and gentrification during the 1960s and 1970s (Lipton 1977; Gale 1984; London, Lee, and Lipton 1986; London 1992), it is not clear how these changes persisted through the 1980s. The economic, urban development, housing, and population changes affecting gentrification remain controversial and subject to different interpretations. This chapter is intended to offer some insights on these issues by evaluating the population and housing changes that occurred in the largest U.S. cities between 1980 and 1990 and by using these sociological facts as a context for examining gentrification. Data from the U.S. Census of Population and Housing will inform this discussion.

The organization of this chapter is threefold: First, changes in the population and housing of U.S. cities experiencing revitalization are documented and described. Second, these population and housing changes are analyzed and evaluated in the context of economic restructuring, regional development, and post-industrial urbanization. Third, the implications of these changes for theory, research, and policy are discussed.

AMERICAN CITIES IN TRANSITION: POPULATION CHANGES, 1980–1990

During the post–World War II years, American cities were characterized by divergent trends. Older central cities located in the Northeast and Midwest, which earlier had concentrations of manufacturing, wholesaling, and retailing functions, lost many of these functions to the suburbs that offered competitive prospects for economic and employment growth. Metropolitan growth, reflected in part by the decentralization of economic activities, new suburban housing construction, and population movements to the suburbs appeared to signal decline and deterioration in central cities. By the 1970s, metropolitan areas of the Southern and Western United States were characterized by rapid gains in industries, services, employment, and population growth. Although these metropolitan areas were also characterized by larger trends of suburbanization of population growth, the central cities in these regions were growing. Through central business district development, the radial expansion of new housing, and annexations, these cities grew dramatically upward and spatially outward.

The primary population redistribution trends characterizing central cities between 1970 and 1980 reflect these post–World War II metropolitan patterns. Central city populations, as a consequence of net-migration losses, remained almost stationary nationally. While population in suburbs increased nearly 16 million—from 83.7 to 99.6 million (19 percent increase)—and population in nonmetropolitan areas increased 7 million—from 47.3 to 54.1 (15 percent increase)—central cities grew only .6 million nationally—from 72.2 to 72.8 million (0.9 percent increase) (U.S. Bureau of the Census 1989). These national trends should not obscure regional and individual variations, however. During the 1970s, metropolitan areas in the Northeast and Midwest experienced central city losses and suburban gains. In declining metropolitan areas of the Northeast and Midwest, small rates of suburbanization and negative migration resulted in these metropolitan areas experiencing population losses. In other older Northeast and Midwest metropolitan areas, the large scale of suburbanization was evident in metropolitan-area population growth. In older metropolitan areas of the South and West, central cities experienced smaller losses because of suburbanization and population increases. In the newer metropolitan areas in the South and West, the scale of central city and suburban population was large and rapid (Frey and Speare 1988, pp. 196–210). These demographic trends can be accounted for by net gains in interregional movement into the South and West and net losses in interregional movement within the Northeast and Midwest. Intermetropolitan movement was from the largest metropolitan areas to other large- and intermediate-size metropolitan areas.

Secondary population trends characterizing central cities are suggestive of the reversal of central city population decline and the potential to be realized through revitalization. Although many of the largest cities were characterized by net losses, central cities experienced absolute and relative increases of in-migrants and absolute decreases of out-migrants during the 1970s. According to Nelson (1988, p. 55) the number of migrants in central cities increased from 6.5 million between 1970 and 1975 to 6.9 million between 1975 and 1980. At the same time, out-migration decreased from 13.6 to 13.2 million. The selectivity of these movements was evident in the largest decreases of out-migration among professionals and whites (Nelson 1988, p. 65). This slowed rate of population loss in central cities was accompanied by a deceleration in the income disparity between central cities and suburbs through the mid-1970s (Gale 1984, p. 48). These stay-in-the-city movements appear largely to be made up of components of intermetropolitan movers who may move directly to the central city from other metropolitan areas and mobile urbanites who change residences within the central city. In Washington, D.C. between 1975 and 1980, approximately 50 percent of all white movers in selected revitalizing community areas were intermetropolitan movers (from outside the MSA) and 30 percent were residentially mobile (Wilson 1992, p. 135).

During the 1980s, national population patterns for central cities indicated a continuation of the larger regional developments, in the growth of Southern and Western Sunbelt areas over slow growing and declining Frostbelt areas of the Northeast and Midwest. In metropolitan areas, suburbs continued to grow more rapidly than central cities. Yet, simultaneously, there was an emergent secondary trend of bicoastal development during the 1980s that transcended the conventional Sunbelt-Frostbelt characterizations (Frey 1990, p. 16). In this development, recent metropolitan population growth increased most rapidly in the Atlantic Coast and Pacific Coast regions, while metropolitan areas in the interior (or Heartland) regions of the Midwest, South, and Rocky Mountains experienced reduced growth. In many large metropolitan areas, central city population loss has slowed, stabilized, or grown. The intersection of each trend is essential to understanding the complexity of central city growth, in general, and gentrification, specifically.

Census figures show that central cities experienced larger population growth during the 1980s than in the 1970s. Nationally, central city populations grew by 5 million people—from 72.8 million in 1980 to 77.8 million in 1990. The magnitude of this decade's growth can be observed by comparing change differentials. Between 1980 and 1990, the rate of change for central cities nationally (6.9 percent) was more than seven times the 1970–1980 rate of 0.9 percent (see Table 7.1). Although these increases can be attributed in part to an increase in the number of MSAs, this growth is representative of the new urbanization.[1] Central cities located in newer metropolitan areas of the South and West experienced population growth, and a number of central cities in the Northeast and Midwest also had population increases. It is noteworthy that despite decade-long central city population increases, central city populations increased less in terms of absolute and relative numbers than did suburban and larger metropolitan areas. While the U.S. population in suburbs grew roughly 16 million (or 15.3 percent) from 1980 to 1990, metropolitan-area population increased more than 20 million (11.7 percent).

By examining the decade differentials between 1970–1980 and 1980–1990, tendencies of stabilization in central city populations can be noted. Table 7.1 shows that during the 1980s, the distributional share of national population in central cities changed less (−0.8) than suburbs and rural nonmetropolitan areas. When the direction of these rates are compared to the 1970 period when central

Table 7.1

U.S. Population for Metropolitan and Nonmetropolitan Areas, 1970–1990

	POPULATION (MILLIONS)			RATE OF CHANGE	
	1970	1980	1990	1970-80	1980-90
Metropolitan Statistical Areas (MSAs)	155.9	172.5	192.7	10.6	11.7
Central Cities	72.2	72.8	77.8	0.9	6.9
Outside Central Cities	83.7	99.6	114.8	19.0	15.3
Nonmetropolitan Areas	47.3	54.1	55.9	15.1	3.3
United States Population	203.4	226.5	248.7	11.4	9.8

PERCENTAGE DISTRIBUTION

				CHANGE IN PERCENT	
	1970	1980	1990	1970-80	1980-90
Metropolitan Statistical Areas (MSAs)	76.6	76.1	77.4	-.5	1.3
Central Cities	35.4	32.1	31.3	-3.3	-.8
Outside Central Cities	41.2	44.0	46.1	+2.8	+2.1
Nonmetropolitan Areas	23.4	23.9	22.6	+.5	-1.3
United States Population	100.0	100.0	100.0		

Sources: U.S. Bureau of the Census (1989), table G; U.S. Bureau of the Census (1992a), Summary Tape File 2C (General Population Characteristics).

city losses occurred (−3.3), no other residential settlement experienced this rate of positive growth.

City population growth occurred more rapidly in the intermediate-sized cities. Consequently, by the end of the decade, the national and regional hierarchies of cities demonstrated a pattern of decentralization consistent with that of the previous decade. In the six cities larger than 1 million population, this growth was only .3 million (1.7 percent) between 1980 and 1990. Because Dallas and San Diego surpassed the 1 million mark during the decade, the adjusted growth for cities of this size shows that a larger increase of 1 million population through 1988 indicate slow growth (.6 million, 5.5 percent), while cities of less than 10,000 population increased at a rate of 2.5 percent (.7 million increase), and in cities of 10 to 25,000, a rate 4.5 percent increase (.9 million). In cities of 100 to 250,000, the population increased 10.8 percent (1.8 million); in cities of 250 to 500,000 the population increased 11.9 percent (1.4 million). The most rapid growth was among cities between 50 and 100,000, with an increased population of 3.6 million residents (20.5 percent increase).[2]

GROWING AND TRANSITIONAL CITIES

Disaggregation of population change for the largest cities allows growth, reversal, and decrease to be described. Table 7.2 illustrates these population changes for the fifty largest U.S. central cities between 1970 and 1990. A comparison of the continuity or discontinuity between the 1970–1980 and 1980–1990 rates indicates that three relatively discernible patterns exist: (1) central cities experiencing a continuity of population growth (growing cities), (2) central cities that experienced increases during the 1980s after decreases during the 1970s (recently growing cities), and (3) central cities that experienced population declines since 1970 (transitional cities).[3] The population changes in these cities result from diverse patterns of net migration that are positive for growing cities, vary between small positive and negative net migration in recently growing cities, and are negative for transitional cities.

Growing cities are almost wholly identified as newer Sunbelt cities located in the South and West. Economically, these cities have national, regional, and subregional diversified service centers, functional nodal centers, government-education centers, industrial-military centers, and a mining industrial center. Characterized by expanding, rapidly growing infrastructures and annexing communities, these cities include San Diego, Los Angeles, Long Beach, San Jose, Honolulu, Phoenix, Tucson, Albuquerque, Houston, Dallas, Austin, San Antonio, El Paso, Oklahoma City, Tulsa, Nashville-Davidson, Miami, Jacksonville, Charlotte, and Columbus. Columbus, Ohio, which has annexed communities, is the lone non-Sunbelt exception to this pattern. The largest population increases occurred in Los Angeles, San Diego, San Jose, Jacksonville, and Austin, but the rates of growth were also rapid in Charlotte, San Diego, Phoenix, and Jacksonville.

After two decades of growth, some of these large population centers slowed in their growth. Houston, for example, grew at a rate of 2.2 percent during the 1980–1990 period after recording a growth rate of 29 percent during the 1970s. Other cities in which dramatic decreases also occurred include Albuquerque, Tulsa, and Honolulu. While revitalization and gentrification occurred in all growing cities, these processes frequently differ from conventional models of neighborhood revitalization and gentrification.

Recently growing cities are largely older cities located in the Northeast, Midwest, and West. The economic structures are comprised exclusively of national, regional, and subregional diversified service centers of corporate activities, government, universities, and high-technology industries: Boston, New York, San Francisco, Oakland, Portland, Seattle, Fort Worth, Omaha, and Indianapolis. The largest absolute increases occurred in New York, Portland, and Fort Worth. Because the infrastructures of these cities are largely built up and annexation is limited, further radial expansion is less than within the growing cities. In older cities such as Boston, New York, and San Francisco, new building construction

Table 7.2
Population Change in 50 Largest U.S. Central Cities, 1970–1990

	Population 1970(1000s)	Population 1980(1000s)	Population 1990(1000s)	%Change 1970-80	%Change 1980-90
New York	7,782	7,071	7,323	-10.4	3.6
Chicago	3,367	3,005	2,787	-10.8	-7.3
Los Angeles	2,816	2,967	3,485	5.5	17.5
Philadelphia	1,949	1,688	1,586	-13.4	-6.0
Houston	1,233	1,595	1,631	29.2	2.2
Detroit	1,511	1,203	1,023	-20.5	-14.9
Dallas	844	904	1,007	7.1	11.4
San Diego	697	876	1,111	25.5	26.8
Phoenix	582	790	983	30.9	24.4
Baltimore	906	787	736	-13.1	6.5
San Antonio	654	785	936	20.1	19.2
Indianapolis	745	701	731	-4.9	4.4
San Francisco	716	679	724	-5.1	6.6
Memphis	624	646	610	3.6	-7.8
Washington, D.C.	757	638	607	-15.7	-4.9
San Jose	446	637	782	38.4	7.1
Milwaukee	717	636	628	-11.3	-0.9
Cleveland	751	574	506	-23.6	-11.8
Columbus, Ohio	546	565	633	4.6	12.0
Boston	641	563	574	-12.2	1.9
New Orleans	593	557	497	-6.1	-10.8
Jacksonville	529	541	673	7.3	24.4
Seattle	531	494	516	-7.0	4.5
Denver	515	491	468	-4.5	-4.9
Nasheville-Davidson	448	456	511	7.0	12.1
St. Louis	622	453	396	-27.2	-12.6
Kansas City, Mo.	507	448	435	-11.7	-2.9
Atlanta	497	425	394	-14.1	-7.3
El Paso	322	425	515	32.0	21.2
Pittsburgh	520	424	370	-18.5	-12.7
Oklahoma City	366	403	445	9.5	11.9
Cincinnati	453	385	364	-15.0	-5.5
Fort Worth	393	385	448	-2.1	16.4
Minneapolis	434	371	368	-14.6	-0.8
Portland, Ore.	383	366	437	-3.6	19.4
Honolulu	325	365	377	12.4	3.3
Long Beach	359	361	429	0.7	18.8
Tulsa	332	361	367	9.3	1.7
Buffalo	463	358	328	-22.7	-8.4
Toledo	384	355	333	-7.4	-6.2
Miami	335	347	358	3.6	3.2
Austin	252	345	465	36.3	34.8
Oakland	362	339	372	-6.2	9.7
Albuquerque	244	332	384	35.7	16.9
Tucson	263	331	405	25.7	22.4
Newark	382	329	275	-13.8	-16.4
Charlotte	241	314	396	30.2	26.1
Omaha	347	312	336	-10.2	7.7
Louisville	361	298	269	-17.5	-9.7
Birmingham	301	284	266	-5.5	-7.7

Sources: U.S. Bureau of the Census (1971), table 22; U.S. Bureau of the Census (1981), table 26; U.S. Bureau of the Census (1991a), table 40.

is constrained in the direction of greater intensification, utilization, and renovation of existing land uses.

On the other hand, these cities contain some of the most advanced cases of administrative centralization and concentration in their central business districts. Central business district revitalization and neighborhood revitalization in these cities exemplify classic instances of urban renewal and the more accentuated and definitive processes of growth and decline that form the bases for conventional conceptualizations of gentrification.

Older, transitional cities are located in the Northeast, Midwest, and South that have economic structures made up of regional, subregional, and specialized function centers. Although many are centers of corporate activities, government, universities, and research, most cities hold old manufacturing centers. For this reason, the discontinuity between central business district revitalization and neighborhood revitalization is generally greater in these centers.

It is important to note that while older transitional cities experienced consecutive decades of population loss, the rate of decrease experienced during the 1980s slowed in sixteen cities (80 percent): Chicago, Detroit, Philadelphia, Baltimore, Washington, D.C., Atlanta, Milwaukee, St. Louis, Kansas City, Minneapolis, Cleveland, Cincinnati, Pittsburgh, Buffalo, Toledo, and Louisville. Some cities, such as Washington, D.C., Atlanta, and Minneapolis, have continuities with respect to central business district revitalization and changes in population and housing characteristics. On the other hand, New Orleans, Denver, Newark, and Birmingham experienced stronger rates of decrease during the 1980s.

In the following sections, the complexity of recent housing and population changes affecting gentrification will be examined through a comparison of central cities characterized by growth, recent growth, and transition.

GENTRIFICATION DURING THE 1980s:
A COMPARATIVE ANALYSIS

Gentrification is expected to be greatest in central cities located in metropolitan areas undergoing economic, housing market, and socio-demographic change. Although some evidence suggests gentrification exists in nearly all of the largest cities, this process appears most salient in national and regional administrative centers experiencing office construction in the central business districts to accommodate a rapidly growing concentration of managerial and professional occupations. These national and regional centers mark the post-industrial transformation to newer economies in which services and government have replaced manufacturing as the cornerstone of the economy. Regional and subregional cities, which are specialized in manufacturing, have been slow to experience the gentrification process (Lipton 1977; Schill and Nathan 1983; Palen and London 1984; Berry 1985; London, Lee, and Lipton 1986; Smith and Williams 1986; Friedenfels 1992).

The dynamics of urban development and redevelopment, as reflected in the housing markets of gentrifying cities, are characterized by complex supply-side changes. Cities with older housing markets have experienced the growth of recent new upper-middle and middle-class home construction, condominium conversions, luxury apartments, and similar revitalization developments. Accompanying these changes is a demand-side trend of the housing market marked by the members of the baby boom generation who are currently seeking housing at affordable prices. Housing in older gentrifying neighborhoods is now viewed as a viable investment.

City and neighborhood gentrifications are similarly characterized by the transformations of their social structure as reflected in the socio-demographic facts. Gentrifying areas are generally made up of incoming upper-middle and middle-income persons working in administrative/managerial and professional occupations (Clay 1979; Gale 1984; Le Gates and Hartman 1986). These persons are primarily white, single persons, co-residential householders, and families without children (Gale 1984; Wilson 1992). Since the incoming populations in gentrifying neighborhoods are made up of smaller middle-class households who replaced working-class households, transition neighborhoods are composed of smaller households with members who consume larger amounts of housing and space. Because the previous residents were lower-middle and working-class persons who more frequently rented, the conversion of these properties to upper-middle class homeownership during gentrification has resulted in the dislocation of the previous residents. Although the revitalization-related rate of displacement among blacks is higher than the average (Clay 1979), most successions in gentrification involve white households replacing whites (Spain, Reid, and Long 1980; Gale 1984).

The census data may validate conceptualizations and hypotheses relating to gentrification through 1990. The units-of-analysis for this comparison are a group of central cities that include Boston, New York City (Manhattan), Newark, Philadelphia, Cincinnati, Indianapolis, Chicago, Minneapolis, Washington, D.C., Charlotte, Atlanta, New Orleans, San Diego, Los Angeles, San Francisco, and Seattle. Although gentrification is sometimes examined as a micro-level phenomenon, the macro-level dynamics of housing and population relevant to gentrification may be explained most directly with reference to models of urbanization. For these reasons, the primary unit-of-analysis in this comparison is central cities that are representative of regions experiencing variable patterns of population change. The structural linkage used to examine these patterns is the changing supply-side of housing on population changes.

Gentrification and Housing Change

Upgrading factors of recent housing construction, gentrification, and clearance of obsolescent and deteriorating units result in city housing markets where homeownership, sale values, and the tax base are increasing. Three-fourths of these cities (n = 12) had homeownership increases, with the largest rate of homeownership increase occurring in New York City (134 percent), Charlotte (36 percent), San Diego (19 percent), and Boston (19 percent). In New York City, most of the increase in homeownership occurred because of a conversion of previous renter-occupied apartments into cooperatives and condominiums. Seattle, San Francisco, Los Angeles, Washington, and Indianapolis had moderate increases in the range of 3 to 9 percent. Slower growth in the number of homeowner units is found in Minneapolis (0.3 percent), Atlanta (0.1 percent), and New Orleans (0.1 percent). However, homeowner housing units actually decreased in Chicago, Philadelphia, and Cincinnati resulting in a loss in homeownership ranging from −0.1 to −2.5. In Newark, homeowner units decreased 10 percent (see Table 7.3).

New housing construction is the primary factor that accounts for additions to the housing supply. In growing centers, housing starts are significant. Los Angeles had 96,590 new unit building permits authorized between 1980 and 1986, representing 8 percent of the 1980 housing stock. The housing built during 1986 was valued at $16.8 billion. In New York City (Manhattan), 31,907 new units were authorized between 1980 and 1986 and, during this same period, Chicago authorized 21,918 new units. In other recently growing older cities, new housing construction accounted for a small but important component of housing upgrading. Between 1980 and 1986, Seattle had 13,254 new units authorized, and 12,917 units were built in New Orleans, 11,574 in Philadelphia, 9,425 in San Francisco, 9,167 in Atlanta, and 8,566 in Boston. In Washington, D.C., a hotbed of gentrification during the 1970s, only 5,861 units were authorized (U.S. Bureau of Census 1991a).

In the older transitional central cities characterized by decreasing housing markets, new housing construction is secondary to demolitions and abandonment. In Cincinnati, housing losses of 2 percent were offset by 2,855 new units; in Newark, housing losses of 16 percent were accompanied by 1,982 new units authorized from 1980 through 1986 (U.S. Bureau of Census 1991a).

Residential properties appreciated most rapidly in Northeastern and Western cities. In New York and Boston, new construction, apartment conversions, and gentrification increased the median value of homeowner properties rapidly upward. In 1980, the median value for homeowner units in Manhattan was $92,400; by 1990, the median value had increased to $487,300, a 427 percent increase. In Boston, the value of homeowner units increased from $36,000 to $161,400, a 348 percent increase. Newark, which in 1980 had a low-to-moderate-income homeowner market, experienced an increase from $31,500 to $110,000 (249 percent increase). In San Francisco and Los Angeles, new construction and revitalization resulted in property value increases at the rates of 188 and 147 percent respectively. San Diego and Seattle were not far behind in the middle-income markets, with property value increases of 112 and 111 percent.

Atlanta and Washington are the strongest cases of rapidly appreciating home-

Table 7.3
Comparisons of Population and Housing Changes in Selected Cities

	Boston	New York	Newark	Philadelphia
1. Population, 1980	562,994	1,428,285	329,248	1,688,210
2. Population, 1990	574,283	1,487,536	275,221	1,585,577
3. % Pop. Change, 1980-90	2.0	4.1	-16.4	-6.0
4. Households, 1980	218,457	704,502	110,912	619,781
5. Households, 1990	228,464	716,422	91,552	603,075
6. % Household Change, 1980-90	4.6	1.7	-17.5	-2.7
7. Families, 1980	116,374	295,143	78,255	412,967
8. Families, 1990	115,927	301,041	62,641	378,045
9. % Families Change, 1980-90	-0.4	1.9	-19.9	-8.5
10. Housing, 1980	241,444	754,796	121,387	685,629
11. Housing, 1990	250,863	785,127	102,473	674,899
12. % Housing Change, 1980-90	3.9	4.0	-15.6	-1.6
13. Owners, 1980	59,504	54,785	23,403	378,097
14. Owners, 1990	70,544	128,037	21,115	373,601
15. % Owners Change, 1980-90	18.6	133.7	-9.8	-1.2
16. Renters, 1980	158,953	649,717	87,509	241,684
17. Renters, 1990	157,920	588,385	70,437	229,474
18. % Renters Change, 1980-90	-0.6	-9.4	-19.4	-5.0
19. Median Value (Owner), 1980	$36,000	$92,400	$31,500	$23,500
20. Median Value (Owner), 1990	$161,400	$487,300	$110,000	$49,400
21. % Value Change, 1980-90	348.3	427.4	249.2	110.2
22. Median Rent, 1980	$189	$239	$178	$168
23. Median Rent, 1990	$546	$478	$385	$358
24. % Rent Change, 1980-90	189.9	100.0	116.3	113.0

	Chicago	Minneapolis	Indianapolis	Cincinnati
1. Population, 1980	3,005,061	370,951	700,807	385,457
2. Population, 1990	2,783,726	368,383	731,327	364,040
3. % Pop. Change, 1980-90	-7.3	-0.8	4.4	-5.6
4. Households, 1980	1,903,407	161,858	260,167	157,677
5. Households, 1990	1,025,174	160,682	291,946	154,342
6. % Household Change, 1980-90	-9.7	-0.7	12.2	-2.1
7. Families, 1980	705,952	82,946	181,012	90,644
8. Families, 1990	631,894	77,671	187,617	82,699
9. % Families Change, 1980-90	-10.5	-6.4	3.6	-8.8
10. Housing, 1980	1,174,703	168,859	283,322	172,659
11. Housing, 1990	1,133,039	172,666	291,946	169,088
12. % Housing Change, 1980-90	-3.5	2.3	3.0	-2.1
13. Owners, 1980	425,865	79,655	153,334	60,673
14. Owners, 1990	425,259	79,845	165,584	59,172
15. % Owners Change, 1980-90	-0.1	0.3	7.9	-2.5
16. Renters, 1980	667,542	82,203	106,833	97,004
17. Renters, 1990	599,915	80,837	126,362	95,170
18. % Renters Change, 1980-90	-10.1	-1.7	18.3	-1.9
19. Median Value (Owner), 1980	$45,800	$52,600	$35,000	$40,800
20. Median Value (Owner), 1990	$78,700	$71,700	$60,800	$61,900
21. % Value Change, 1980-90	71.8	36.3	73.7	51.7
22. Median Rent, 1980	$184	$209	$179	$159
23. Median Rent, 1990	$377	$390	$342	$283
24. % Rent Change, 1980-90	104.9	86.6	91.1	77.9

Table 7.3 (Continued)

	Washington	Charlotte	Atlanta	New Orleans
1. Population, 1980	638,333	314,447	425,478	557,515
2. Population, 1990	606,900	395,934	394,017	496,938
3. % Pop. Change, 1980-90	-4.9	25.9	-7.3	-10.9
4. Households, 1980	253,143	146,967	149,621	206,435
5. Households, 1990	249,634	156,729	155,752	188,235
6. % Household Change, 190-90	-1.4	6.6	4.1	-8.8
7. Families, 1980	133,643	106,510	89,254	132,927
8. Families, 1990	122,087	101,116	86,737	118,026
9. % Families Change, 1980-90	-8.6	-5.1	-2.8	-11.2
10. Housing, 1980	276,984	124,069	178,826	226,452
11. Housing, 1990	278,489	170,430	182,754	225,573
12. % Housing Change, 198 -90	0.5	37.4	2.2	-0.4
13. Owners, 1980	89,846	64,481	67,057	81,970
14. Owners, 1990	97,108	87,411	67,126	82,279
15. % Owners Change, 1980-90	8.1	35.6	0.1	0.1
16. Renters, 1980	163,297	53,336	95,496	124,465
17. Renters, 1990	152,526	71,078	88,626	105,951
18. % Renters Change, 1980-90	-6.6	33.3	-7.2	-14.9
19. Median Value (Owner), 1980	$68,800	$45,800	$33,000	$50,400
20. Median Value (Owner), 1990	$123,900	$81,300	$71,700	$69,600
21. % Value Change, 1980-90	+80.1	+77.5	+115.8	+38.1
22. Median Rent, 1980	$207	$180	$148	$153
23. Median Rent, 1990	$441	$377	$352	$277
24. % Rent Change, 1980-90	+113.0	+109.4	+137.8	+81.0

	Los Angeles	San Francisco	Seattle	San Diego
1. Population, 1980	2,966,850	678,974	493,846	875,538
2. Population, 1990	3,484,793	723,959	516,259	1,110,549
3. % Pop. Change, 1980-90	17.5	6.6	4.5	26.8
4. Households, 1980	1,135,230	298,956	219,469	321,060
5. Households, 1990	1,217,258	305,584	236,702	405,976
6. % Household Change, 1980-90	7.2	2.2	7.8	26.4
7. Families, 1980	693,694	140,490	114,123	201,438
8. Families, 1990	758,974	141,906	112,969	249,498
9. % Families Change, 1980-90	9.4	1.0	-1.0	23.8
10. Housing, 1980	1,189,475	316,608	230,039	341,928
11. Housing, 1990	1,299,813	328,471	249,032	406,096
12. % Housing Change, 1980-90	9.3	3.7	8.3	18.8
13. Owners, 1980	457,375	100,786	111,951	157,595
14. Owners, 1990	479,752	105,497	115,709	196,153
15. % Owners Change, 1980-90	4.9	4.7	3.4	24.5
16. Renters, 1980	677,855	198,170	107,518	163,465
17. Renters, 1990	737,537	200,087	120,993	209,943
18. % Renters Change, 1980-90	8.8	0.9	12.5	28.4
19. Median Value (Owner), 1980	$96,100	$103,900	$65,100	$89,800
20. Median Value (Owner), 1990	$244,500	$298,900	$137,900	$189,400
21. % Value Change, 1980-90	154.4	187.7	111.8	110.9
22. Median Rent, 1980	$229	$266	$232	$249
23. Median Rent, 1990	$544	$613	$425	$560
24. % Rent Change, 1980-90	137.6	130.5	83.2	124.9

Sources: U.S. Bureau of the Census (1992b), Summary Tape File 3A; U.S. Bureau of the Census (1981).

owner markets outside the Northeastern and Western cities. During the 1970s, the appreciation in value of homeowner properties in Washington, D.C. was among the highest in the nation (187 percent). During the 1980s, however, appreciation decreased to 80 percent. Chicago and Indianapolis experienced rates comparable to some Southern cities (72 and 74 percent), whereas Cincinnati, New Orleans, and Minneapolis experienced the smallest decade property value increases (51, 38, and 36 percent respectively).

The renter-occupied markets in ten cities experienced a decrease in available housing units. Although it is difficult to generalize across cities how much of these losses resulted from apartment conversions, as opposed to wastage through abandonments and demolition, the apartment conversion appears to be stronger in gentrifying cities where continuous population growth occurred. In transitional cities, wastage increases in renter markets has been significant. Available renter units decreased in Newark (-19 percent), New Orleans (-15 percent), Chicago (-10 percent), New York (-9 percent), Atlanta (-7 percent), Washington (-7 percent), and Philadelphia (-5 percent) respectively. In Minneapolis and Cincinnati, rental losses were approximately 2 percent and in Boston 0.6 percent. It is instructive to note that these markets experienced only small rent increases. In most cities, the median rent was less than \$400 a month. Boston, with an upturning and tight middle-class renter market, was the lone exception to this pattern. In the growing cities, renter-occupied units have been stable or increasing. Such renter increases are noted for Charlotte (33 percent), San Diego (28 percent), Indianapolis (18 percent), Seattle (13 percent), Los Angeles (9 percent) and, to a lesser extent, San Francisco (1 percent). In West Coast cities, increases occurred for units priced above \$500 a month.

Gentrification and Population Change

A direct relationship exists between the housing changes and changes in population and types of households (see Table 7.3). Central cities characterized by housing growth are also characterized by stable or growing numbers of households. Nine of the growing and recently growing cities fit this pattern: Boston, New York, Charlotte, Atlanta, Indianapolis, San Diego, Los Angeles, San Francisco, and Seattle. Only Washington, D.C. and Minneapolis broke from this transitional cities pattern with stable and growing housing markets and small household rate decreases. Conversely, five central cities characterized by decade-long housing losses experienced population decreases, namely Newark, Philadelphia, Cincinnati, Chicago, and New Orleans. In Cincinnati (-2.1 percent), these decreases are correlated to changes in the housing supply. Although the rate of housing loss was much more rapid in Newark than in other cities, the number of housing losses were greater in Philadelphia and Chicago.

Cities experiencing stable and growing numbers of households usually are characterized by specific socio-demographic features: First, families make up a stable component of the social structure. Where not growing, the decreases in families are small ($-.4$ to -3 percent). Second, single-person households can be noted. Growing and recently growing cities have an increasing number of single, middle-class households. On the other hand, some transitional cities are characterized by a loss of families, households, and single individuals. Families leaving central cities are less frequently replaced by other families, and the attractive conditions for a middle-class singles lifestyle are absent. These include the attractions of various public amenities such as parks, libraries, museums, and universities within safe walking distance and high-grade retail activities and services including restaurants and entertainment.

Gentrification and Social Class Change

Changes in housing and population characteristics are reflected in the data that indicate the administrative and professional classes are succeeding and replacing the blue-collar and service-sector classes.[4] With the exception of three cities, 1990 levels of administrative and professional classes were larger than the U.S. averages (26 percent). The greatest relative concentrations were in New York (Manhattan) (47.6 percent), Washington (39.1 percent), Charlotte (37.8 percent), Seattle (36.3 percent), and San Francisco (34 percent). Rates of growth for the middle classes were strong in Boston, New Orleans, Charlotte, Seattle, and San Diego, which surpassed national rates (38.1 percent). Only Philadelphia, Chicago, and Newark had lower than national distributions and lower rates of increases. These cities continue to have strong industrial and working-class characteristics (see Table 7.4).

Social class transformation can be examined by the extent to which the middle class is replacing blue-collar residents. The effects of deindustrialization, and suburbanization in particular, affected blue-collar workers; 70 percent of cities experienced blue-collar losses. These cities include Boston, New York, Newark, Philadelphia, Washington, Chicago, Minneapolis, Indianapolis, Cincinnati, Atlanta, New Orleans, and Seattle. Large-scale blue-collar losses were not region-specific. Indeed, substantial losses occurred in Northeastern, Midwestern, Southern, and Western cities. The social class transformation can be observed through comparisons of change differentials between the administrative/professional and blue-collar classes. Between 1980 and 1990, the national differential in growth rates between administrative/professionals (38 percent) and blue-collar workers (3 percent) was substantial and significant. More than 80 percent of these cities (n = 13) experienced greater-than-average differentials in the rate and extent to which their middle classes are coming to exceed working classes. Cities such as Los Angeles, San Diego, and Charlotte did experience significantly larger additions of blue-collar workers than the national average. In New York, Washington, San Francisco, and Seattle, the larger size of administrative and professional classes in 1990 contributes to this discrepancy. In New Orleans, Chicago, Cincinnati, and Philadelphia, rapid losses among blue-collar classes and close-to-average rates of administrative- and professional-class growth char-

Table 7.4
Social Class Changes for Selected Central Cities, 1980–1990

	Boston	New York	Newark	Philadelphia	Chicago
Admin./Prof. 1980	66,660	291,118	13,523	126,399	245,887
Admin./Prof. 1990	94,477	366,541	14,922	161,640	302,246
% Change 1980-90	41.7	25.9	10.3	27.8	22.9
% Admin./Prof. 1990	32.1	47.6	14.1	24.8	25.0
Blue Collar 1980	51,103	103,041	48,415	184,920	402,922
Blue Collar 1990	46,259	85,533	38,799	150,944	319,774
% Change 1980-90	-9.4	-16.9	-19.9	-18.3	-20.6
% Blue Collar 1990	16.0	11.1	36.8	23.2	26.5
Service 1980	47,109	93,353	18,402	98,158	177,727
Service 1990	49,953	93,356	18,926	106,201	182,737
% Change 1980-90	6.0	0.0	2.8	8.2	2.8
% Service 1990	17.3	12.1	17.9	16.3	15.1

	Minneapolis	Indianapolis	Cincinnati	Washington	Charlotte
Admin./Prof. 1980	50,074	72,111	38,974	97,151	41,037
Admin./Prof. 1990	61,179	99,615	46,533	118,853	62,264
% Change 1980-90	22.2	38.1	19.4	22.3	51.7
% Admin./Prof. 1990	31.8	27.1	29.2	39.1	37.8
Blue Collar 1980	43,316	92,982	42,532	43,484	42,171
Blue Collar 1990	34,775	86,825	33,279	36,105	47,795
% Change 1980-90	-19.7	-6.6	-21.7	-16.9	13.3
% Blue Collar 1990	18.1	23.6	20.9	11.8	29.0
Service 1980	30,025	44,361	27,724	52,103	18,924
Service 1990	30,142	49,860	26,396	50,518	25,801
% Change 1980-90	.4	12.4	-4.8	-3.0	36.3
% Service 1990	15.7	13.6	16.6	16.6	15.7

	Atlanta	New Orleans	Los Angeles	San Francisco	Seattle	San Diego
Admin./Prof. 1980	42,277	38,974	358,835	98,255	71,789	100,598
Admin./Prof. 1990	50,469	56,908	455,922	133,941	103,056	170,697
% Change 1980-90	19.3	46.0	27.1	36.3	43.5	69.7
% Admin./Prof. 1990	28.8	30.6	27.3	34.7	36.3	32.5
Blue Collar 1980	44,175	57,113	381,626	57,549	56,021	76,914
Blue Collar 1990	36,334	33,858	437,797	59,083	47,121	95,448
% Change 1980-90	-17.7	-40.7	14.7	2.7	-15.9	24.1
% Blue Collar 1990	20.7	18.2	26.2	15.3	16.6	18.1
Service 1980	33,421	39,144	178,223	54,665	33,938	53,508
Service 1990	31,285	35,675	232,629	60,586	36,787	73,035
% Change 1980-90	-6.4	-8.9	30.5	10.8	8.3	36.4
% Service 1990	17.9	19.2	13.9	15.7	12.9	13.9

Sources: U.S. Census of Population (1992b), Summary Tape File 3A; U.S. Census of Population and Housing: Census Tracts, 1980, table P-10.

acterize this transition. In San Francisco, Los Angeles, San Diego, and Charlotte, increases in blue-collar and middle-class growth was dominant.

While service classes are larger than the U.S. average (13.4 percent) in most of these cities, the residential status of service-class households is in transition. Decade-long changes show 13 cities had less than the U.S. rate of increase (21.7) for service workers. Only in Los Angeles, San Diego, and Charlotte did the growing economies result in the addition of service classes in excess of the national average. The largest number of these cities experienced rates of increase that were less than half (10 percent and less) the U.S. rates. Four cities, namely Washington, Atlanta, New Orleans, and Cincinnati, experienced losses in service-class households.

Gentrification and Racial/Ethnic Change

There are at least three models that may explain the status of majority and minority groups in the changing contemporary American city. These models are based on different assumptions of the underlying logic of economic and housing growth, the changing internal spatial structure of the city, and the status of different social class and racial groups. These models are based on different assumptions relating to the historic, regional, and cultural factors of urbanization including growth, gentrification, and transition.

Growth of cities should be favorable to the in-movement and demographic growth of different racial and ethnic groups. This scenario is possible because the economic structures of national, regional, and subregional administrative centers increased in scale and diversified business and employment opportunities. Concomitantly, the growing housing markets are favorable to new construction, upgrading, and the filtering-down of older housing. Gentrification in growing cities may involve new construction of higher priced luxury homes and condominiums or the renovation of previously declining properties to middle-class occupancy. Conversions occur in the homeowner market and less frequently involve renter markets. Although revitalization in growing cities causes displacement of some populations, the possibilities of housing for these groups are accommodated within central cities.

Gentrification suggests that changes in cities should be favorable to the in-movement and growth of selective racial and ethnic groups and the out-movement and population decreases of other racial and ethnic groups. Gentrification occurs because administrative centers have specialized economic structures that favor the growth of upper-middle and middle-income administrative/managerial and professional classes. Because the possibilities of new housing construction in these cities are limited, the dynamics of housing upgrades center on gentrification and apartment conversions. A decline in working-class residences and the dislocation of renters result. Growth is zero-sum, and for this reason segmented housing markets tighten especially for moderate- and low-income renters.

In transitional cities, population changes are indicative of a smaller future city as reflected in population decreases and out-movement across nearly all racial and ethnic groups. While the economies of these national, regional, and subregional centers enhance administrative/managerial and professional occupational growth, they have not necessarily translated into "stay-in-the-city" movements among middle classes. Gentrification is an emergent trend dwarfed by patterns of suburbanization and concentrated poverty. Central business districts in emergent gentrifying cities may experience new construction and revitalization, but the housing markets in such transitional cities are initially characterized more by deterioration, abandonment, and demolitions than new construction and apartment conversions. These cities come closest to the "Islands of Renewal in Seas of Decay," characterized by Berry (1985). According to Berry, what distinguishes the loose housing markets in transitional cities from tighter housing markets in more rapidly gentrifying cities is the absence of significant central business district growth centralizing professional and white-collar jobs (Berry 1985, p. 95).

Structural changes in transitional cities include patterns of racial and ethnic change (see Table 7.5). Among the most rapidly growing cities such as Los Angeles, San Diego, and Charlotte such changes generally involve the growth of majority white and minority black, Hispanic, and Asian-American populations. Between 1980 and 1990, the absolute size and rates of minority populations exceeded whites. In recently growing and transitional cities, where housing upgrading occurs and middle classes increase under zero-sum conditions, these racial changes are most notable. New York's growth in racial and ethnic diversity has continuities with the rapidly growing cities. Population increases among whites, Hispanics, and Asians took place in Washington, D.C., which also recorded a loss in the black population.[5]

Six cities experienced losses of white and black populations accompanied by increases of Hispanic and Asian populations, namely, Chicago, Philadelphia, Atlanta, New Orleans, San Francisco, and Newark. In Northern and Western cities, the in-movement and growth of Hispanic and Asian populations is exceeding that of whites and blacks, while in Southern cities, increases of Hispanic and Asian populations are smaller and more selective. In this cluster of cities, whites constitute a majority only in Philadelphia and San Francisco.

A second cluster of cities, where gentrification has been accompanied by the growth of minority populations and decreases of white populations, is Boston, Cincinnati, Minneapolis, and Seattle. Still, whites continue to represent a majority population ranging from 58 to 78 percent.

THE CHANGING DEMOGRAPHIC AND HOUSING STRUCTURE IN REVITALIZING CENTRAL CITIES, 1980–1990

Changes and differentials in population and housing across regions, metropolitan areas, and central cities are related to the changing social structure of American society. From a macro-sociological perspective, these recent changes are correlated with the restructuring of the American economy and specific economic redevelopment of cities. Both developments hold important implications for macro-economic and housing public policy.

The Restructuring of the American Economy

Since 1970, the U.S. economy has experienced structural changes that have important consequences for regional, metropolitan, and central city growth.

Table 7.5
Racial and Ethnic Populations for Selected Cities, 1980–1990

	Boston	New York	Newark	Philadelphia	Chicago
White Pop. 1980	393,937	841,204	101,417	983,084	1,490,217
White Pop. 1990	360,875	867,227	78,771	848,586	1,263,524
% Change 1980-90	-8.4	3.1	-22.3	-13.7	-15.2
% White 1990	62.8	58.3	28.6	53.5	45.4
Black Pop. 1980	126,229	311,326	191,743	638,878	1,197,001
Black Pop. 1990	146,945	326,967	160,885	631,936	1,087,711
% Change 1980-90	16.4	5.0	-16.1	-1.0	-4.2
% Black 1990	25.6	22.0	58.5	39.9	39.1
Hispanic Pop. 1980	36,068	336,247	61,254	65,570	422,061
Hispanic Pop. 1990	61,955	386,630	71,761	89,193	545,842
% Change Hispanic	71.7	14.9	17.2	36.0	29.3
% Hispanic 1990	10.8	26.0	26.1	5.6	19.6
Asian Pop. 1980	15,150	72,884	2,366	17,764	69,191
Asian Pop. 1990	30,388	110,629	3,281	43,522	104,118
% Change 1980-90	100.6	51.8	38.7	145.0	50.5
% Asian 1990	5.3	7.4	1.2	2.7	3.7

	Minneapolis	Indianapolis	Cincinnati	Washington	Charlotte	Atlanta
White Pop. 1980	323,832	540,294	251,144	171,768	211,980	138,025
White Pop. 1990	288,967	554,423	200,285	179,667	259,760	122,327
% Change 1980-90	-10.8	2.6	-12.3	4.6	22.5	-11.4
% White 1990	78.4	75.8	60.5	29.6	65.6	31.0
Black Pop. 1980	28,433	152,626	130,467	448,906	97,627	282,911
Black Pop. 1990	47,948	165,570	138,132	399,604	125,827	264,262
% Change 1980-90	68.6	8.5	5.9	-11.0	28.9	-6.6
% Black 1990	13.0	22.6	37.9	65.8	31.8	67.1
Hispanic Pop.1980	4,684	6,145	2,988	17,679	3,418	5,842
Hispanic Pop.1990	7,900	7,681	2,386	32,710	5,571	7,525
% Change Hispanic	68.7	24.9	-20.1	85.0	61.4	28.8
% Hispanic 1990	2.1	1.1	.7	5.4	1.4	1.9
Asian Pop. 1980	4,104	3,792	2,216	6,636	2,367	2,000
Asian Pop. 1990	15,723	6,852	4,030	11,214	7,211	3,498
% Change 1980-90	283.1	80.7	81.9	69.0	204.6	74.9
% Asian 1990	3.3	.9	1.1	1.8	1.8	.9

	New Orleans	Los Angeles	San Francisco	Seattle	San Diego
White Pop. 1980	236,967	1,816,683	395,082	392,766	616,796
White Pop. 1990	173,554	1,841,182	387,783	388,858	745,406
% Change 1980-90	-26.8	1.3	-1.8	-1.0	20.8
% White 1990	34.9	52.8	53.6	75.3	67.1
Black Pop. 1980	308,149	505,210	86,414	46,755	77,700
Black Pop. 1990	307,728	487,674	79,039	51,948	104,261
% Change 1980-90	-0.1	-3.5	-8.5	11.1	34.2
% Black 1990	61.9	13.9	10.9	10.1	9.4
Hispanic Pop.1980	19,219	815,989	83,373	12,646	130,610
Hispanic Pop.1990	17,238	1,391,411	100,717	18,349	229,519
% Change Hispanic	-10.3	70.5	20.8	45.1	75.7
% Hispanic 1990	3.5	39.9	13.9	3.6	20.7
Asian Pop. 1980	7,332	196,024	147,426	36,613	57,207
Asian Pop. 1990	9,678	341,807	210,876	60,819	130,945
% Change 1980-90	31.9	74.4	43.0	66.1	128.8
% Asian 1990	1.9	9.8	29.1	11.8	11.8

Sources: U.S. Bureau of the Census (1981, 1992b).

Employment within industries such as steel, tools, automobiles, and clothing experienced significant declines as a consequence of globalization, deindustrialization, automation, devolution, and decentralization. At the same time, new growth areas are integrated around corporate services, government, high-tech manufacturing, and support services activities that involve decision-making and information processing. Such economic growth patterns during the 1970s and 1980s also were accompanied by changes in energy and transportation. A number of cities opened or planned to develop light-rail mass transit systems for commuters and increase air transit for trade.

The role of federal and state governments in economic restructuring through program expenditures and employment opportunities has varied by region and metropolitan area. The growth of cities during the post–World War II period has been altered by a redirection of federal expenditures from industrial centers to capital cities (Caroll and Meyer 1983). Federal defense spending became a central factor in the ascendancy of aerospace-related military-industrial complexes in new growth, especially in the South and West, whereas industrial decline occurred in defense-related manufacturing centers located in the Northeast and Midwest (Hall and Markusen 1992, p. 53). As a result, a larger proportion of federal public works funds were appropriated to the South and West, thereby improving the infrastructures of these states.

Although the primary trend characterizing regional economic restructuring during the post–World War II decades has favored the South and West, there was an emergent secondary trend of bicoastal development occurring during the 1980s. Recent metropolitan growth occurred most rapidly in the Atlantic Coast and Pacific Coast regions, while the interior regions of the Midwest, Rocky Mountains, and South experienced reduced growth. This economic restructuring is underscored by the enhancement of global, national, and regional economies.

During the 1980s, gentrification appears to have been more dynamic in central cities of the Atlantic Coast and Pacific Coast regions. Cities such as Boston, New York, and Washington and newer cities, such as Los Angeles, San Francisco, Seattle, and San Diego, experienced extensive economic revitalization evidenced by the growth of corporate and government managerial/administrative and professional activities, public infrastructural developments, and housing upgrading. Cities such as Chicago, Philadelphia, New Orleans, Minneapolis, Indianapolis, Cincinnati, Charlotte, and Newark are experiencing central business district revitalization and gentrification. Yet neighborhood revitalization lags, because these cities made the transition to a service economy at a later date, are less integrated into national and international economies, and city housing markets are less attractive to middle-class professionals.

URBAN REDEVELOPMENT AND SPATIAL REORGANIZATION OF THE POST-INDUSTRIAL CITY: THE PERSISTENCE OF CENTRALIZATION AMIDST METROPOLITAN DECENTRALIZATION

For most of the post–World War II period, metropolitan-area populations decentralized, moving to the suburbs. These population movements were geographic shifts that created changes in social relations because of the increasing population size, relocation of manufacturing, wholesale, and retail markets from the central city, increased income, and different consumption patterns of a growing middle class. Although restructuring was a primary cause for this urban redevelopment, housing factors also influence this spatial reorganization. Government subsidized, low interest housing programs, such as FHA and VA mortgage loans, channeled the demand for housing away from central city neighborhoods toward newly developed outlying and suburban communities. In growing housing markets, older neighborhood housing filtered down to working-class residents. In the absence of a middle class, the increasing visibility of Euro-American villages, black ghettos, and Hispanic barrios have underscored the problems of concentrated poverty and polarization upon which the imagery of contemporary cities is based.

Urban development factors relevant to the decline of central city populations during these post–World War II years are readily identified: First, the focus of federal urban renewal programs involved the revitalization of central business districts (CBDs) (Greer 1965). Low-grade CBD and central-area residential land uses were cleared and replaced with office, commercial, and luxury apartment buildings (Gans 1966). This revitalization occurred simultaneously with the development of new corporate and government functions. The concentration and centralization of administrative, financial, and legal firms, and the development of the tourist and convention industries, marked an important shift in the central business district from a commercial to administrative center.

Second, urban redevelopment policies since the end of World War II addressed the problems of physical deterioration through slum clearance. However, the demolition of older housing through urban renewal and highway development programs was not accompanied by federal initiatives to construct new housing for those dislocated.

Third, post–World War II federal mortgage programs engaged in appraisal ranking practices such as redlining biases against housing in declining and racially mixed neighborhoods. Investments prominent in newer, growing, racially homogeneous, and white suburban communities were generally unavailable to residents of these older neighborhoods. Redlining, when augmented by private market disinvestment, contributed to the depreciation, deterioration, and abandonment of these neighborhoods (Jackson 1980).

Finally, influenced by the racial segregation in central city housing markets, the succession of increasing segments of neighborhoods from white to black occupancy, and the white flight to suburban housing markets beginning in the 1950s, large sectors of central city housing markets became racial ghettos (National Advisory Commission on Civil Disorders 1968). The concentration of other social problems such as declining employment, unemployment, deteriorating municipal services, and escalating crime would become important reasons for the flight of the middle- and working-class families to the suburbs.

Since the 1970s, macro-economic changes put into motion a countertrend of centralization that has implications for the reorganization of the internal spatial structure of central cities and movements of population. First, central city economies that experienced declining manufacturing and commercial activities have increasingly experienced reinvestment through the development of office, hotel, and residential properties. These investments involve international financing. This international and national competition for central business land has driven the traditional logic of the growing city dramatically.

Second, since the late 1970s, private redevelopment projects in central cities have been augmented by federal subsidies in the form of UDAGs tax abatements, and historic preservation tax credits (Feagin and Parker 1990, pp. 134–137). Although these subsidies are universally targeted and are designed to improve depressed areas, the spatial implementation of the projects has been uneven. Central business districts contiguous to middle-class neighborhood housing have benefited more.

Third, increasing land costs, available financing, changing tax laws, and rising prices provide developers with incentives to construct upper-grade housing in growing central cities. Rapid increases in property values and rent prices reflect this upgrading and the growth of middle-class residents.

Fourth, rising costs of new central city and suburban housing constrain many first-time homebuyers who desire inexpensive housing in older neighborhoods. Although frequently in "transition areas," older housing units are centrally located and within access of central business districts, universities, and cultural activities. Other properties such as factories, warehouses, and schools in transition areas are being renovated into middle-class condominiums and cooperatives.

Fifth, in response to community mobilized housing movements of the 1970s, Congress recognized the viability of Community Development Corporations (CDCs), mandated federal funding for these CDCs through the CDBG program, and enacted the Home Mortgage Disclosure Act (1975) and the Community Reinvestment Act (1977) (Keating, Rasey, and Krumholz 1990, pp. 210–211). These measures required that conventional lending institutions, which during earlier post–World War II years had redlined older neighborhoods, now invest in housing in these same neighborhoods where CDCs formed.

Sixth, rising energy costs for transportation and home heating fuel may be changing the logic of decentralized and suburban living. Although outlying land remains cheaper, the post-industrial city may require less separation of work and home. Norms of accessibility now replace spacious living quarters and excessive consumption as the urban ideal.

Such macro-sociological trends in administrative concentration, reinvestment, gentrification, and apartment conversions represent variable processes that are most dynamic and visible in bicoastal cities, ranking among the leading centers of the changing global and national urban systems. Examples of these primary centers include New York, Boston, Washington, San Francisco, Los Angeles, and Seattle. The recent data suggest, however, that regional and subregional centers also are experiencing these housing and population developments albeit on a smaller scale. Cities such as Chicago, Philadelphia, Atlanta, New Orleans, San Diego, Minneapolis, Indianapolis, Cincinnati, and Charlotte exemplify this persistent gentrification process.

CONCLUSION

The population and housing changes of the 1980s are useful to form the conceptualizations and hypotheses of gentrification. Largest central cities in which gentrification is prominent are largely growing cities located near the Atlantic and Pacific coasts, which house national and regional diversified service centers of corporate activities, government, universities, and new high-technology industries. Each city also has dynamic housing markets that are undergoing upgrading. Regional and subregional centers, which are located primarily in the Heartland, are characterized by stronger traditional manufacturing and population decreases; these centers appear to be experiencing more emergent patterns of gentrification with smaller scale housing market upgrading.

Supply-side upgrading of housing in most large cities results from new construction, gentrification, and apartment conversions. It is significant that these cities had homeownership increases and that in most older coastal cities, property values appreciated rapidly. This appreciation has important implications for city tax bases. Although revitalization resulted in the dislocations of renter units, the net result does not necessarily mean that a tightened renter market exists. In older, metropolitan centers, the rent squeeze disproportionately affects the supply of moderate- and low-income renter housing units. Such supply-side housing changes are consistent with hypotheses of gentrification that assume a zero-sum logic between renter and owner housing growth. In newer metropolitan centers, gentrification occurs within markets that accommodate both renter and homeowner housing growth.

Structural housing changes and social class dynamics are highly correlated, in that young professional people succeed members of the blue-collar and service classes. Thus, a growing concentration of the middle class has led to a decrease in housing for members of the working and service classes. These developments are most advanced in the national and regional diversified service centers. In regional and subregional centers, which are strongly based on manufacturing and contain relatively larger working classes, growth of the middle class has been slower. Racial and ethnic changes are characterized by three distinct patterns: (1) cities in which white and black populations decreased and Hispanic and Asian populations grew, (2) cities where black, Hispanic, and Asian populations increased and the white population decreased, and (3) cities in which white and minority populations grew. It is instructive that in only Washington, D.C. and Los Angeles were 1980–1990 racial population changes characterized by white growth and black decline.

Population changes associated with neighborhood revitalization remain favorable to the growth of single and smaller households than for larger families. In general, single and small households residing in cities of growth are characterized by stable numbers of families. On the other hand, some transitional cities experience a loss of population as well as a loss of households. Both the population and housing changes in these cities are associated with broad, complex macro-economic changes.

Two theoretical models account for the formation and growth of gentrification: (1) urban ecology and (2) new urban sociology. These models differ with respect to assumptions of the underlying logic of urbanization, the causes of gentrification, the salient variables and relationships, and the effects of gentrification.

From the ecological perspective, the salience of changing socio-economic and lifestyle characteristics such as class, earnings, race, age, and type of household, as well as central city revitalization and older neighborhoods, are hypothesized as favorable to gentrification. The in-movement and growth of selective populations into cities, such as white middle-class professional baby boomers, have created a demand for what was previously identified as a declining housing market (Myers 1990). From a macro-level ecological perspective, the growth of new office construction in central business districts, high technology and the service oriented businesses, and the convention-tourism and cultural entertainment industries have affected revitalization (Berry 1985; Kasarda 1988). Displacement is minimized by growing housing markets, a filtering process, and social mobility. Although ecological theorists recognize the possibilities of gentrification, the empirical research influenced by these conceptualizations through the 1980s found only limited evidence for gentrification and displacement (Sumka 1979; Long 1980; Spain 1981; Nelson 1988).

New urban sociology theorists argue that corporate industrial capitalism is responsible for the growth of the international, national, and regional systems of cities and the restructuring of urban space (Zukin 1980; Fainstein et al. 1983; Logan and Molotch 1987; Gottdiener and Feagin 1988). Gentrification is defined as a process of urban transformation characterized by the movement of capital into suburbs and the growth of rent gaps in central cities, deindustrialization and the centralization of administrative, professional, and other white-collar employment, new forms of cultural consumption and human capital, and uneven patterns of investment and disinvestment (Smith and Williams 1986; Zukin 1987; Feagin and Parker 1990). More critical in their perspectives, the new urban theorists view gentrification as a macro-level process of urban redevelopment in which financiers, speculators, developers, and growth machines play a central role. Gentrification across metropolitan areas varies according to the extent which central cities are advanced and dynamic parts of the new international economy and division of labor and city governments create opportunities for reinvestment. Although theorizing based on the new urban sociology has predicted a much greater presence of gentrification and displacement than found in ecological theories (Marcuse 1986; Le Gates and Hartman 1986), the empirical research informing these has usually been based on case studies.

The complexity of gentrification requires an explanation that links different levels of sociological analysis including patterns of individuals and households, neighborhood and community change, and patterns of urban spatial and housing market restructuring. Although both the ecological and new urban sociology perspectives are used independently, neither model offers a sufficient explanation. A more holistic explanation would incorporate both models to explain gentrification. Salient among the questions that have not been sufficiently answered by either model are the identification of changing housing-demography relationships and the variable relationships among supply-side factors and the redistribution of populations by race, class, and lifestyle.

Finally, a number of questions and hypotheses related to demographic and structural change raised in this paper require further research. Among these questions is why does gentrification continue to be more advanced in cities located on the two coasts (the bicoastal hypothesis)? At issue is whether this occurrence is a result of population size, density, and heterogeneity, or whether factors such as city history, politics, economy, and culture influence gentrification. A second issue pertains to changes in urban development and housing and how these can explain the growth of middle classes between 1980 and 1990. Downtown redevelopment, new construction, homeownership, and conversions are relevant processes, but the relationship between these macro-level factors and social class, lifestyle, and racial change is unclear. Third, identification of micro-level demand-side changes in migration and residential movement in cities and gentrifying community areas and the relationship between these shifts and socio-demographic factors such as income, occupation, race, and age remains unclear. Further analysis of in-movement, stability, and displacement will be useful for better understanding the dynamics of how contemporary urban redevelopment differentially affects the social and residential mobility of groups in central cities and vice versa.

NOTES

1. There were 518 central cities within MSAs in 1986, representing an increase of eight cities compared to 1980 (U.S. Bureau of the Census 1989, p. 18).

2. By 1988, intermediate-sized cities (25,000–50,000, 50,000–100,000, and 100,000) made up 39 percent of the U.S. city population in comparison to 29 percent in the large-

sized cities (500,000–1 million and greater than 1 million) and 32 percent in small cities (under 10,000 and 10,000–25,000). In 1970, 34 percent of the population lived in the intermediate-, 32 percent in the large-, and 33 percent in the small-sized cities respectively (U.S. Bureau of the Census 1991, p. 34).

3. The fourth possible pattern of 1970s population growth, followed by 1980s population decline had only one central city—Memphis, Tennessee. Memphis' population patterns lagged but are similar to Southern cities such as Louisville, Birmingham, and New Orleans.

4. The blue-collar class in this comparison consists of precision production, craft, repairs, operators, fabricators, and laborers categories. Service class consists of private household, protective, and other service categories. Technical, sales, and administrative support and farming, forestry, and fishing occupations are excluded from the analysis.

5. Washington, D.C. and Los Angeles are the only two cities in this comparison where white population increases were accompanied by black population decreases. The gentrification-related racial changes in Washington, D.C. during the 1970s are documented in studies by Lee, Spain, and Umberson (1985) and Wilson (1992).

REFERENCES

Abrams, Charles. 1971. *The Language of Cities: A Glossary of Terms.* New York: Viking Press.
Anderson, Kurt, Daniel Levy, and Edwin Reingold. 1987. "Spiffing Up the Urban Heritage." *Time* (November 23):72–83.
Berry, Brian J.L. 1985. "Islands of Renewal in Seas of Decay." Pp. 69–98 in Paul Peterson (ed.), *The New Urban Reality.* Washington, D.C.: Brookings Institute.
Caroll, Glenn and John Meyer. 1983. "Capital Cities in the American Urban System: The Impact of State Expansion." *American Journal of Sociology* 88:565–578.
Clay, Phillip. 1979. *Neighborhood Renewal: Middle Class Resettlement and Incumbent Upgrading in American Neighborhoods.* Lexington, Mass.: Lexington Books.
Fainstein, Norman, Susan Fainstein, Richard Child Hill, and Peter M. Smith (eds.). 1983. *Restructuring the City: The Political Economy of Urban Redevelopment.* New York: Longman.
Feagin, Joe and Robert Parker. 1990. *Building American Cities: The Urban Real Estate Game.* Englewood Cliffs, N.J.: Prentice-Hall.
Frey, William H. 1990. "Metropolitan America: Beyond the Transition." *Population Bulletin* 45:1–42.
Frey, William H. and Alden Speare. 1988. *Regional and Metropolitan Growth and Decline in the United States.* New York: Russell Sage Foundation.
Friedenfels, Roxanne. 1992. "Gentrification in Large American Cities from 1970 to 1980." Pp. 63–94 in R. Hutchinson (ed.), *Research in Urban Sociology,* vol. 2. Greenwich, Conn.: JAI Press.
Gale, Dennis. 1984. *Neighborhood Revitalization and the Postindustrial City.* Lexington, Mass.: Lexington Books.
Gans, Herbert. 1966. "The Failure of Urban Renewal." Pp. 537–557 in James Q. Wilson (ed.), *Urban Renewal: The Record and the Controversy.* Cambridge, Mass.: MIT Press.
Gottdiener, Mark and Joe Feagin. 1988. "The Paradigm Shift in Urban Sociology." *Urban Affairs Quarterly* 24:163–187.

Greer, Scott. 1965. *Urban Renewal and American Cities.* Indianapolis: Bobbs-Merrill.

Grier, George and Eunice Grier. 1980. "Urban Displacement: A Reconnaissance." Pp. 252–269 in Shirley Laska and Daphne Spain (eds.), *Back to the City.* New York: Pergamon.

Hall, Peter and Ann R. Markusen. 1992. "The Pentagon and the Gunbelt." Pp. 53–76 in A. Kirby (ed.), *Urban Affairs Annual Reviews,* vol. 40. Newbury Park, Calif.: Russell Sage Foundation.

Jackson, Kenneth T. 1980. "Race, Ethnicity, and Real Estate Appraisal." *Journal of Urban History* 6:419–452.

Kasarda, John. 1980. "The Implications of Contemporary Redistribution Trends for National Urban Policy." *Social Science Quarterly* 61 (December):373–400.

———. 1988. "Economic Restructuring and America's Urban Dilemma." Pp. 56–84 in Mattei Dogan and John D. Kasarda (eds.), *A World of Giant Cities.* Beverly Hills, Calif.: Russell Sage Foundation.

Keating, W. Dennis, Keith P. Rasey, and Norman Krumholz. 1990. "Community Development Corporations in the United States: Their Role in Housing and Urban Redevelopment." Pp. 206–218 in W. van Vliet and J. Weesep (eds.), *Urban Affairs Annual Reviews,* vol. 36. Newbury Park, Calif.: Russell Sage Foundation.

Le Gates, Richard and Chester Hartman. 1986. "The Anatomy of Displacement in the United States." Pp. 178–203 in N. Smith and P. Williams (eds.), *Gentrification of the City.* Boston: Allen and Unwin.

Lee, Barrett, Daphne Spain, and Debra J. Umberson. 1985. "Neighborhood Revitalization and Racial Change: The Case of Washington, D.C." *Demography* 22:581–591.

Lipton, S. Gregory. 1977. "Evidence of Central City Revival." *Journal of the American Institute of Planners* 43:136–147.

Logan, John R. and Harvey L. Molotch. 1987. *Urban Fortunes: The Political Economy of Place.* Berkeley: University of California Press.

London, Bruce. 1992. "Land-based Interest Groups and Gentrification: Corporate Capital, Competitive Capital, and Urban Neighborhood Change." *Research in Urban Sociology* 2:47–62.

London, Bruce, Barett Lee, and S. Gregory Lipton. 1986. "The Determinants of Gentrification in the United States: A City-level Analysis." *Urban Affairs Quarterly* 21:369–387.

Long, Larry. 1980. "Back to the Countryside and Back to the City in the Same Decade." Pp. 61–76 in S.B. Laska and D. Spain (eds.), *Back to the City: Issues in Neighborhood Revitalization.* New York: Pergamon Press.

Marcuse, Peter. 1986. "Abandonment, Gentrification, and Displacement: The Linkages in New York City." Pp. 153–177 in N. Smith and P. Williams (eds.), *Gentrification of the City.* Boston: Allen and Unwin.

Myers, Dowell. 1990. "The Emerging Concept of Housing Demography." Pp. 3–34 in Dowell Myers (ed.), *Housing Demography.* Madison: University of Wisconsin Press.

National Advisory Commission on Civil Disorders. 1968. *Report of the 1968 National Advisory Commission on Civil Disorders.* New York: Bantam Books.

Nelson, Kathryn. 1988. *Gentrification and Distressed Cities: An Assessment of Trends in Intrametropolitan Migration.* Madison: University of Wisconsin Press.

Palen, John and Bruce London (eds.). 1984. *Gentrification, Displacement, and Neighborhood Revitalization.* Albany: State University of New York Press.

Schill, Michael and Richard Nathan. 1983. *Revitalizing America's Cities: Neighborhood Reinvestment and Displacement.* Albany: State University of New York Press.

Smith, Neil. 1986. "Gentrification, the Frontier, and the Restructuring of Urban Space." Pp. 15–34 in N. Smith and P. Williams (eds.), *Gentrification of the City,* Boston: Allen and Unwin.

Smith, Neil and Peter Williams (eds.). 1986. *Gentrification of the City.* Boston: Allen and Unwin.

Spain, Daphne. 1981. "A Gentrification Scorecard." *American Demographics* 3:14–19.

Spain, Daphne, John Reid, and Larry Long. 1980. "Housing Successions Among Blacks and Whites in Cities and Suburbs." *Current Population Reports.* Series P-23, No. 101. Washington, D.C.: U.S. Government Printing Office.

Sumka, Howard. 1979. "Neighborhood Revitalization and Displacement: A Review of the Evidence." *Journal of the American Planning Association* 45:480–487.

Urban Land Institute. 1980. *Downtown Development Handbook.* Washington, D.C.: Urban Land Institute.

U.S. Bureau of the Census. 1971. *Statistical Abstract of the United States: 1971.* Washington, D.C.: U.S. Government Printing Office.

———. 1981. *Statistical Abstract of the United States: 1981.* Washington, D.C.: U.S. Government Printing Office.

———. 1989. "Patterns of Metropolitan Area and County Population Growth: 1980 to 1987." *Current Population Reports.* Series P-25, No. 1039. Washington, D.C.: U.S. Government Printing Office.

———. 1991a. *City and County Data Book, 1989.* Washington, D.C.: U.S. Government Printing Office.

———. 1991b. *Statistical Abstract of the United States: 1991.* Washington, D.C.: U.S. Government Printing Office.

———. 1992a. *U.S. Census of Population, 1990.* Summary Tape File 2C (General Population Characteristics). Washington, D.C.: U.S. Government Printing Office.

———. 1992b. *U.S. Census of Population, 1990.* Summary Tape File 3A (Detailed Population Characteristics). Washington, D.C.: U.S. Government Printing Office.

Wilson, Frank Harold. 1992. "Gentrification and Neighborhood Dislocation in Washington, D.C.: The Case of Black Residents in Central Area Neighborhoods." Pp. 113–144 in R. Hutchinson (ed.), *Research in Urban Sociology,* vol. 2. Greenwich, Conn.: JAI Press.

Wittberg, Patricia. 1992. "Perspectives on Gentrification: A Comparative Review of the Literature." Pp. 63–94 in R. Hutchinson (ed.), *Research in Urban Sociology,* vol. 2. Greenwich, Conn.: JAI Press.

Zeitz, Eileen. 1979. *Private Urban Renewal: A Different Residential Trend.* Lexington, Mass.: Lexington Books.

Zukin, Sharon. 1980. "A Decade of the New Urban Sociology." *Theory and Society* 9: 575–601.

———. 1987. "Gentrification: Culture and Capital in the Urban Core." *Annual Review of Sociology* 13:129–147.

8

Poverty in the Midst of Plenty

KIRSTEN K. WEST

INTRODUCTION

The 1980s started out in a recession, followed by a period of economic expansion. For seven consecutive years, from 1983 to 1990, real per-capita income increased. The decade was one that brought more people into the top distribution of income. Yet, it was also a decade where the proportion of children living in poverty rose in thirty-three states. It was a decade that saw reductions in public assistance programs and growth in the percentage of full-time workers who earned less than the officially defined threshold level for poverty.

In this chapter, the size and characteristics of the population in poverty in the 1980s is examined. Whatever position one may take to explain poverty, it is essential to understand the size and characteristics of the poor population. Only then can one begin to grasp the complexity of the problems and appreciate why disparate views on poverty have emerged. To understand the trends, an assessment of the income distribution is offered. Similarly, the size and characteristics of the population that is working, yet not earning sufficient wages to be above the official poverty threshold, is examined. Finally, to put the findings in perspective, the concept of relative income is introduced.

THE SIZE OF THE POPULATION IN POVERTY

The national poverty rate showed a slight decrease in the 1980s. In 1980, the rate was 13 percent. By 1989, the rate had decreased to 12.8 percent. However, in absolute numbers, there were more people in poverty in 1989 than in 1980.

During that time period, the number of poor in the United States rose by 2.3 million, or 7.7 percent, from 29.3 to 31.5 million.[1]

Compared with the earlier decade, a 7.7 percent increase is high. Between 1970 and 1979, the number of people in poverty rose by only .6 million, or 2.5 percent. Similarly, the 1980s saw fluctuations in the poverty rate that were more dramatic than those observed in the 1970s. The rate increased steadily until 1983, where it peaked at 15.2 percent before starting a gradual decline. The curve for 1970 to 1979 was much more stable.

The number of persons in poverty is not on a declining course. On the contrary, it continues to rise. According to the figures released for 1990, the number of poor people rose by 2.1 million in 1990. The poverty rate was 13.5 percent in 1990 and 14.2 percent in 1991, when another 2.1 million was added to the population in poverty. As of September 1992, 35.7 million people in America were living below the official poverty line.

The distribution of poverty is not the same for subgroups in the population. Thus, only when this distribution is examined does one get a comprehensive picture of the size of the population in poverty. The persons below the official poverty line represent diverse groups in the population. Place of residence, race and ethnic background, age, and family status are useful demographic groupings when trying to capture this diversity. The groupings show that poverty touches every demographic group in the United States, but some groups are touched more heavily than others.

Historically, the Northeast has had the lowest poverty rate and the South the highest rate. This pattern persisted in the 1980s. In 1980, the poverty rate in the South was 16.5 compared to an average rate of 11.3 for the other three regions. By 1980, the rate for the South was 15.4; the West showed 12.5 percent, the Midwest had a rate of 11.9 percent, and the Northeast was at 10 percent. The same pattern emerged in 1990.

The farm population had a 17.5 percent poverty rate in 1980, compared to 12.7 percent for the nonfarm population. In 1989, and again in 1990, there was not much difference between the two groupings. The 1989 percentages were 12.9 for farm and 11.1 for nonfarm populations.

Metropolitan areas had a lower rate than nonmetropolitan areas in both 1980 and 1989. In 1980, the percentages were 12 and 15.7 respectively. In 1989, the figures were 11.9 for metropolitan areas compared with 15.4 for nonmetropolitan areas. In 1990, the poverty rate was 12 in metropolitan areas and 15.7 in nonmetropolitan areas.

Central cities had higher poverty rates than suburban areas. The rate in central cities was 17.2 in 1980, 18.1 in 1989, and 19 in 1990. The suburban rate remained around 8 percent for the three time periods considered.

Poverty estimates computed at the state level should not be used to rank the states, because the poverty measure does not adjust for local differences in the cost of living. Also, observed differences may be due to sampling variability. However, the rates are useful for observing patterns at the state level.

Table 8.1
Ten States with High Poverty Rates, 1980, 1989, and 1990

1980 State	Rate	1989 State	Rate	1990 State	Rate
Miss.	24.3	Louisi.	23.3	Miss.	25.7
Arkansas	21.5	Miss.	22.0	Louisi	23.6
Alabama	21.2	New Mex.	19.5	D.C.	21.1
D.C.	20.9	Alabama	18.9	New Mex.	20.9
New Mex.	20.6	Tennes.	18.4	Arkansas	19.6
Louisiana	20.3	Arkansas	18.3	Alabama	19.2
Tennessee	19.6	D.C.	18.0	West Va.	18.1
Kentucky	19.3	Texas	17.1	Kentucky	17.3
So. Dako	18.8	S.Car.	17.0	Tenn.	16.3
So.Car.	16.8	Kentucky	16.1	S.Car.	16.2

Source: U.S. Bureau of the Census (1991c).

The pattern in Table 8.1 is observed among the ten states with the highest rates.

In 1980, with exception of South Dakota (Midwest) and New Mexico (West), the states with the highest poverty rates were in the group of states representing the South. In 1989, New Mexico was the only non-Southern state in the high poverty rate group. This was the situation in 1990 as well. It is clear that there are poverty pockets throughout the nation. Large parts of the South still suffer high rates. Inner cities have more poor people than other urban areas, and non-metropolitan areas have higher rates than metropolitan areas.

The differences among race and ethnic groups are more striking than the differences among the states for any one race. While about one in ten among the white population falls in this category, almost one in three among blacks and one in four among Hispanics fall below the poverty level. (It should be noted that persons of Hispanic origin may be of any race). This pattern persisted throughout the decade.

In 1980, 10.2 percent of the white population fell below the poverty line. By 1989, the percentage was 10. The same figures for the black population show a slight improvement over the decade, from 32.5 percent in 1979 to 30.7 percent in 1989. Among the population of Hispanic background, the percentage was 25.7 in 1980 and 26.2 in 1989.

Even though there are disproportionately more poor among the black and the Hispanic population, most poor people are white. In 1989, there were 20.8 million whites below the poverty level, compared with 9.3 million blacks, and 5.4 million Hispanics. In 1990, there were 22.3 million whites, 9.8 million blacks, and 6 million Hispanics below the poverty level.

The young and the adults of working age experienced sharp increases in the poverty rate until 1983. In 1980, more than 18.3 percent of children under the age of 18 lived below the poverty line. By 1983, the percentage had climbed to 22.3, and by 1989, the rate decreased to 19.6 percent. That figure implies that in 1989 12.6 million of the nation's children lived in poverty.

The poverty status among the adult population of working age increased from 10.1 percent in 1980 to 10.2 percent in 1989, with a peak of 12.4 percent in 1983. Only the elderly experienced a decline; in 1980, the rate was 15.7 and by 1989, this rate had declined to 11.4 percent, or 3.4 million elderly. The elderly population did not participate in the high rates experienced in 1983 by other population subgroups. Their poverty rate for 1983 was 13.8 percent.

Thus, in the 1980s, poverty rates were particularly high for the very young, somewhat lower for the elderly, and lowest for the 25–64-year-olds. In 1989, about one in five children and one in nine elderly lived in poverty, compared with one in ten among the adults of working age. By 1990, the rate for children remained the highest of the three age groups. Children under the age of 18 constituted 40 percent of the poor population.

A complex relationship exists between poverty levels and the presence or absence of children under 18. Poverty rates vary not only according to the number of children in the family but also by their ages. In general, the more children in the family and the younger the children, the greater the likelihood that they will be in families without adequate income to place above the poverty threshold. In particular, single parenthood and the presence of children under the age of 6 raise the likelihood of being in poverty.

Throughout the decade, families with a female householder and no husband present remained at much greater risk of falling below the poverty line than families with married-couple individuals. In 1989, some 32.2 percent of all poor people lived in families headed by a woman, down slightly from 32.7 percent in 1980. In comparison, though there are fewer families of this type, the percent below poverty with a male householder and no wife present was 11 in 1980 and 12.1 in 1989.

If presence of children under 18 in the household is considered, single-parent families (female householder) had a poverty rate of 42.9 percent in 1980 and 42.8 percent in 1989. For single fathers with children under 18, the rate was 18 in 1980 and 18.1 in 1989.

The feminization of poverty is not new to this decade. Data from the University of Michigan Panel Study of Income Dynamics show that in the 1970s the persistently poor were heavily concentrated in the female-headed households (Duncan et al. 1984). Persistently poor was defined as being in poverty for eight

Table 8.2
Poverty Rates by Educational Attainment, 1980 and 1989

Education	1980	Poverty Rate 1989
Householder who had not completed eighth grade	24.9	25.5
Householder who completed eighth grade	13.1	15.9
Householder who had 1-3 years of high school	16.2	19.2
Householder who had graduated from high school	8.0	8.9
Householder who had completed one or more years of college	3.7	3.6

Source: U.S. Bureau of the Census (1991a), table 752.

or more years during the time period 1969–1978. The gender difference has been attributed to the higher average incomes of males (Zopf 1989).

With 6.2 percent below poverty levels in 1980 and 5.6 percent in 1989, married-couple families fared better throughout the decade than families with a single head of household, primarily because both spouses worked for wages. The poverty rate for the married-couple families with children under 18 was 7.7 and 7.3 percent respectively.

Though most married-couple families have been much better off financially than their unmarried counterparts, a rate of 7.3 percent implies that there were more than 1.8 million families with children under 18 in this situation in 1989. As observed by Ellwood (1988), this means that half the poor children in America are living in two-parent homes, and that most of the children now in poverty started out life in two-parent households.

It is the expectation that poverty rates should be related to the level of educational attainment and that an increase in the number of years of school completed would result in lower poverty rates for an individual. This pattern prevailed in the 1980s. However, as shown in Table 8.2, though the level of poverty decreases as the level of educational attainment increases, poverty is found among all educational groups.

In 1990, it was again the finding that the more education, the lower the percentage in poverty. For persons who did not complete high school, the percentage was 21.8; high school graduates had a 9.3 percent poverty rate, and persons with a college degree were at 3.8 percent.

In sum, the demographics of the poor population in 1980 and 1989 examined in this section show that poverty characteristics remained largely unchanged from the beginning to the end of the decade. Poverty is found within all sub-populations throughout the nation. However, the likelihood of being poor is greater for a black young unmarried female without a high school diploma who lives in the South with one or more children under the age of 6 than for any other subpopulation. Also, only the elderly seemed to have experienced a decline in poverty in the 1980s.

THE DEFINITION OF POVERTY

The poverty rate referenced in this section has been defined as the proportion of the total population below official poverty thresholds. The definition has several restrictions: First of all, it consists of a set of money-income thresholds that vary by family size and composition. Developed by the Social Security Administration in the early 1960s, the measure was based on the U.S. Department of Agriculture's economy plan meant to reflect different consumption requirements. The consumption requirements were based on family size and composition, the age of the householder, as well as the location of the family's residence—farm or nonfarm.

The poverty measure was revised in 1969 to base annual adjustments in the threshold levels on changes in the Consumer Price Index (CPI) rather than on changes in the cost of food. A further revision was implemented in 1980, when the distinction between a farm and nonfarm household was eliminated. In addition, the poverty matrix was extended to families with nine and more members. A detailed description of the poverty index is provided in Orshansky (1965a, 1965b).

As a reference point, the average threshold for a family of four persons was $8,414 in 1980. In 1989, the level was $12,674. In 1990, the average poverty threshold was $13,359 for a family of four; the threshold for a person living alone was $6,652. For nine and more members, it was $26,848.

The official poverty definition has several limitations. It is based only on reported pretax cash income, excluding capital gains. As such it is subject to underreporting and may not correctly reflect the resources available to a family.

The measure does not count in-kind benefits such as food stamps, housing subsidies, medical care assistance, and aid for education. Starting in the 1980s, research has been conducted at the U.S. Bureau of the Census to measure the effect of including the value of noncash benefits and taxes on income in the poverty measure. Though the number of poor may be overstated depending on the way in which noncash assistance is valued, the experimental calculations show that if all noncash benefits were counted and capital gains and taxes were then deducted, the poverty rate would still have been rising over the past decade (U.S. Bureau of the Census 1986).

The measure does not adjust for local differences in the cost of living, and it does not include the total U.S. population. It excludes inmates of institutions, armed forces members in barracks, and unrelated individuals under 15 years of age. Furthermore, the measure is based on a single year. It has been noted that a single year may not be a reasonable period of time over which to measure resources and needs. The measure compares annual family income with annual needs, not long-term needs.

When reviewing the characteristics of the poor, it should also be kept in mind that the data are gathered from a cross section of the population and that the same people are not necessarily poor from one year to the next. There is movement in and out of poverty.

The University of Michigan's Panel Study of Income Dynamics (PSID), which followed 5,000 people across the nation in an annual interview, documents these observations. The longitudinal study began in 1968, and its findings underscore the importance of distinguishing between those who are in poverty for a relatively short time period compared to those who are permanently poor.

According to one study based on the PSID, between 1969 and 1978, at least one-quarter of the U.S. population experienced poverty of short-term duration. They lived in poverty in at least one out of the ten years studied (1969 to 1978). About 5.4 percent were poor for a duration of at least five years, and .7 percent were poor all ten years. The respondents moved in and out of poverty as they changed jobs and as their family situations changed. Poverty need not be a permanent condition (Duncan et al. 1984).

CAUSES OF POVERTY

There are many different views on what causes poverty. These views range from liberal to strictly conservative. Liberals tend to argue that poverty is brought about by lack of job opportunities. The more conservative view perceives poverty as resulting from failure to stay in school or marriage. The debate among scholars is equally diverse (Duncan et al. 1984; O'Hare 1985). In simplistic terms, some hold that poverty can be attributed to characteristics of individuals including their values and attitudes, while others hold that the causes of poverty are to be found within the social structure, not within the individual.

In the first view, some adhere to the school of thought expressed in the "culture of poverty" literature, where certain attitudes and values are seen as keeping families poor. Poverty is passed on from one generation to the next (Lewis 1971), and poverty assistance further undermines the work ethic and people's desire to work (Murray 1984). Others contend that inadequate job skills, or lack of human capital, are at the root of the problem (Becker 1981). Some proponents of this view focus on the productivity of the individual and see poverty as a function of low individual productivity.

In the second view, it is the social structure and, in particular, the economic structure that creates poverty (Harrington 1962, 1984). The labor market restricts the opportunities of the low wage earner. It is lack of job opportunities and low wages that cause poverty (Schiller 1984). In the following sections, the empirical foundations of these views are examined. First, the relationship between work status and public assistance is presented.

WORK STATUS AND FINANCIAL ASSISTANCE

Though poverty rates increased over the decade, public aid payments did not. In 1980, 6.5 percent of the population received public assistance in the form of Federal Supplemental Security Income (SSI) and Aid to Families with Dependent Children (AFDC). In 1989, the percentage was 6.1 (U.S. Bureau of the Census 1991a, p. 372).

In general, there are three types of programs to help equalize incomes: (1) social insurance, (2) means tested income transfer, and (3) targeted education and training. The first type includes Social Security, Medicare, and unemployment insurance. Poor people draw primarily from the second group, which includes AFDC and SSI. The third type includes programs such as Head Start and the Job Corps, which were cut severely in the 1980s.

The principal cash assistance program for the aged and disabled poor is SSI. However, benefits received from this program equal only about 75 percent of the poverty line for a person living alone and only 89 percent for an elderly couple. The financial picture is only slightly better for those elderly people who also receive Social Security payments. Often, even the combined benefits from Social Security payments and SSI are not enough to reach the poverty line. In 1987, combined Social Security and SSI benefits were sufficient to place an individual above the poverty line in only four states; for couples, the combined benefits were enough to lift them out of poverty in only eleven states (U.S. Congress 1989).

In the previous section, it was noted that the elderly of retirement age, 65 and over, saw a decline in poverty. This decline has been attributed to indexing Social Security retirement payments to rise with inflation. However, the adjustment is not enough to alleviate poverty. Elderly people are generally poor, because the benefits they receive are too low to lift them out of poverty.

Similarly, the increase in poverty rates among the nonelderly, particularly children, has been associated with the failure of AFDC payments to keep up with inflation. AFDC is the principal program to assist poor, single-parent families. Until 1990, states had the option to deny AFDC benefits to poor families with children in which both parents were present. Benefit levels for AFDC are not indexed for inflation, and the values of the benefits declined from 1980 to 1990. It is estimated that the median decline in real AFDC benefits for a family of three was 37 percent between 1970 and 1989 (U.S. Congress 1989).

Overall, in the public assistance debate, it is often overlooked that public

Table 8.3
Sources of Reported Income of Poor Families, 1980

Type of Income Number	Number of Poor Families with This Type of Income (1,000s)	% of Total of Families
Total	6,217	10.3
Earnings	3,762	7.2
Other	4,985	9.5
Social Security	1,320	9.5
Public Assistance*	2,269	63.6
Suppl. Security Income*	589	35.7
Other Transfer Programs*	770	7.4
Dividends and Interest	1,457	3.5
Other*	861	6.1
No income	131	100.0

*Public assistance consists of Aid to Families with Dependent Children and general assistance. Supplemental Security Income is for the needy, blind, and disabled. Other transfer programs refer to unemployment insurance, workman compensation, and veterans' payments. Finally, the category "other" includes pensions, alimony, child support, and annuities.
Source: U.S. Bureau of the Census (1982), table 35.

assistance does not go to only poor people and that many poor people receive no or only limited financial assistance. As seen in Table 8.3, in 1980, more than 60 percent of families in poverty reported income from earnings, and only 63 percent of public assistance went to poor families. This pattern prevailed over the decade. At no time was the share of the reported income derived from public assistance more than a quarter. Furthermore, what is particularly noteworthy, many poor people received no public assistance. In 1989, more than 25 percent of the population below the poverty level did not receive cash public assistance. In reality, throughout the decade, most of the population in poverty continued to live in families where a householder worked. In both 1980 and 1989, close to 50 percent of family householders below the poverty level worked, and nearly half of these workers reported working full time (50 to 52 weeks).

LOW INCOME

As indicated previously, many poor people are in families where the householders work full time year-round. Yet, the wages they earn are not sufficient to provide for themselves or their families at an adequate *standard of living*.

Using data from the 1985 CPS to study the causes of poverty, Ellwood (1988) confirmed this observation. Three categories of persons in poverty were examined: persons with low wages, unemployed persons, and disabled persons. The category "low wage earners" was found to have the largest percent distribution of poor families. Looking at two-parent poor families, the family type who should be least likely to fall below the poverty threshold, Ellwood found that 21 percent fell in the category "disabled"—with no one working. About 35 percent did not work full time. However, 44 percent of the poor families had at least one person working full time year-round. These families earned wages that were too low to place them above the officially defined poverty threshold.

To understand more fully the prevalence of poverty in the midst of plenty, the following section examines the size and distribution of the population with low income who are in poverty.

The Census Bureau defines low earnings as wages below the official government poverty level for a family of four, regardless of whether there are four members in the wage earner's family. By definition, the age group examined here is the population of working age (i.e., the ages 16 to 64). The definition excludes people who are unable to participate in the labor force. Furthermore, a worker with low earnings will not be in poverty if the worker's total family income exceeds the appropriate poverty level. Finally, an individual can earn low wages but be above the specified poverty threshold level.

The data presented in this section are provided by the 1980 and the 1990 March supplements to the *Current Population Survey,* as reported in *Current Population Reports,* Series P-60, No. 178. The focus is on able-bodied workers attached to the labor market full time.

In 1979, about 11.4 percent of the white population had low earnings, compared to 18.5 percent among blacks and 19.5 percent among Hispanics. For white male workers, the percentage was 7.2 compared with 19.8 for females. For black male workers, the percentage was 14 compared with 24.3 among females. Finally, for Hispanics, the percentages with low earnings were 13.4 for males and 32.2 for females.

In 1989, the percentages with low wages were 15.7 for whites, 21.2 for blacks, and 27.6 for Hispanics. The gender differences observed at the beginning of the decade persisted at the end of the decade. Regardless of race or ethnic origin, males constituted a lower percentage in the low wage earner category than females.

In 1990, white male workers with full-time year-round employment had the lowest percent with low earnings, namely 13 percent. The same rate for their female counterparts was 23.6 percent. Black males in this category had a rate of 28.2 percent, compared with 28.5 percent for black females. Finally, 23.6 percent of Hispanic males with full-time year-round employment fell in the low wage category, compared with 37 percent for females workers of Hispanic origin.

The 1980s saw a rise in the level of educational attainment in the population among workers with low wages. In 1979, 32.4 percent of full-time, year-round workers with low annual wages had less than twelve years of school completed.

In 1989, this percentage was 23.2. More than 46 percent of the low wage earners had completed high school in 1979. This percentage increased to 48.8 by 1989. Finally, the percentage of full-time, year-round workers with low annual earnings who had thirteen or more years of school completed was 21.4 percent in 1979 but 28.0 percent in 1989.

Overall, the higher the level of education, the less likelihood of falling in the low wage earner category. However, more education does not mean escape from low wages. Since 1979, the likelihood of a full-time worker having low annual income has increased sharply within each educational category. In the less than twelve years of education category, the percentage of low wage earners was 21.3 percent in 1979 and 32.1 in 1989. Among high school graduates, 13 percent fell in the low wage earner category in 1979, compared to 19.5 percent in 1989. Finally, in the category with thirteen or more years of education, 6.1 percent in 1979 and 8.9 percent in 1989 had low wages.

In 1990, the poverty rate among low income full-time, year-round workers was as follows: 36.1 percent in the category with less than twelve years of schooling, 21.6 percent among high school graduates, and 10.5 percent in the category with thirteen or more years of education. However, earning a low wage does not necessarily place one below the poverty threshold level. Most workers with low earnings were not in poverty during the time period examined. Over the decade, the absolute number of low income workers in poverty increased, but the likelihood of being in poverty actually decreased. It is possible that households sent additional earners into the labor force to offset the low earnings capacity, thus bringing the combined household earnings above the poverty threshold.

In 1979, there were 63.5 million full-time, year-round workers. About 7.5 million of these workers had low annual earnings, and 15.8 percent of these workers were in poverty. In comparison, in 1989, there were 78.7 million workers and 9.9 million with low annual earnings. The percent of full-time, year-round workers with low wages in poverty was 12.7. The 1990 figures show 78.6 million full-time, year-round workers, 14.4 million with low annual earnings and 12.9 percent of the low wage earners in poverty.

As stated, the likelihood of a worker with low earnings being in poverty will depend on a number of factors including his or her family situation. In 1979, the poverty rate was 35.7 percent among husbands in married-couple families working full-time, year-round making low annual earnings. In 1989, the percentage had declined to 22.3. The poverty rate among wives with low earnings was 4.3 percent in 1979, 5.5 percent in 1989. Among female family householders, the percent with low wages in poverty increased between 1979 and 1989 from 26.7 percent to 28.5 percent.

The 1990 figures show the poverty rate to be 21.4 percent for a husband in a married-couple family, 5.5 percent for a wife in a married-couple family, and 27.8 percent for a female family householder, no spouse present. All categories refer to full-time, year-round workers with low annual earnings.

Table 8.4
Unemployment Rates by Industry, 1980 and 1989

Industry*	1980	1989
All Unemployed*	7.1	5.3
Agriculture	11.0	9.6
Mining	6.4	7.9
Construction	14.1	10.0
Manufacturing	8.5	5.1
Transportation and Public Utilities	4.9	3.9
Wholesale and Retail	7.4	6.0
Finance, Insurance and Real Estate	3.4	3.1
Services	5.9	4.8
Government	4.1	2.7

*The label "industry" covers unemployed wage and salary workers. "All unemployed" includes the self-employed, unpaid family workers, and persons with no previous work experience.
Source: U.S. Bureau of the Census (1991a), table 655.

In conclusion, when examining the size and distribution of the population that works full-time, year-round yet still finds itself with earnings that are insufficient to place above the officially established poverty thresholds, one gets a sense of poverty in the midst of plenty. Earned income is a vehicle for staying out of poverty, but in the 1980s that was not always sufficient. The figures reveal that the incidence of poverty did not improve in this decade for workers with low wages.

UNEMPLOYMENT IN THE 1980s

The section on low income workers indicated that many workers are in poverty because they are unable to earn a wage above the poverty threshold level. To this dimension can be added the prospect of being unable to keep such a job for long.

Looking at unemployment rates by industry, the data show that over the decade, the pattern of unemployment remained the highest for construction workers and the lowest for government employees (Table 8.4).

Though unemployment has remained high throughout the decade, unemployment insurance coverage has dropped. In 1988, only 31.5 percent of the unemployed workers nationwide received unemployment insurance benefits in an average month. Furthermore, in 1988, only one state, Alaska, provided extended benefits. The extended benefit program is designed to provide an additional thirteen weeks of aid to jobless workers who live in high unemployment areas, have been out of work for at least six months, and are actively looking for work.

It can further be observed that increases in the number of workers in low paying jobs did not contribute to the prevalence of poverty. Using CPS data for March 1977 and March 1984, Williams (1991) examined the relationship between poverty and the employment structure. It was the finding that during this time period, poverty increased primarily from a decline in employment rates and from increases in poverty within all industries. The growth of service sector employment did not contribute to the increase in poverty.

RELATIVE INCOME

In the previous sections, poverty has been defined in absolute terms. The measures presented rest on some notion of the acceptable shape of the income distribution. Poverty is of course a relative term (U.S. Department of Health, Education and Welfare 1976a, 1976b). For example, by the standards of many developing countries, the poor in the United States might be well off. However, measured by the standard of living enjoyed by most citizens in this country, they are not well-off. Thus, to evaluate the level of poverty, it is of value to study a measure of income inequality such as the concept of relative income, rather than the size of poverty and its distribution in the population.

Relative income is a well-suited measure for studying inequality over time and for comparing population subgroups. The inequality measure that is reported in this section is based on the proportion of the population with either high or low relative incomes. Low relative income is defined as less than one-half of the median income, and high relative income is defined as at least twice that of median income. The median relative income is equal to 1.0. To measure inequality, the proportion with low and high relative wages is compared with the proportion in the "middle" of the distribution.

The inequality measure is based on a monetary definition of income. Thus, it is subject to the same limitations as the poverty rate. Furthermore, changes in aggregate economic activity may affect the distribution of income.

The data for evaluating inequality are from the 1980 and the 1990 March supplements to the *Current Population Survey* as published in the *Current Population Report,* Series, P-60, No. 177. This means that the years 1979 and 1989 can be examined. Relative income has been calculated by the U.S. Census Bureau (1991b) for a twenty-five-year time span at five-year intervals, starting with 1964 and ending with 1989.

The 1989 income distribution showed more inequality than the 1979 distribution. The percent of the population with either high or low income values increased from 31.9 percent to 36.8 percent. Looking at only the percent with low income, it is found that there was an increase from 20 to 22.1 percent.

The distribution of relative income depends on the characteristics of the population. Examining inequality by race and ethic background, it is the finding that the percent of the population with either low or high relative income values increased over the ten-year period for all three population subgroups. In 1989, whites had 18.8 percent of its population in the relative low income category compared to 16.7 percent in 1979. Among blacks, the percentage was 44.1 in 1979 and 43.9 in 1989. Finally, for persons of Hispanic origin, 34.2 percent were in the relative low income category in 1979. By 1989, the percentage was 40.1.

The black and the Hispanic origin population fared worse than the white population throughout the decade. In both population groups, more than 70 percent of the population had below median relative income, compared to about 46 percent for the white population.

The same pattern emerges when low and high relative incomes are examined by age. The distribution became more unequal for the age groups under age 64 but less unequal for the older ages. In 1979, 24.5 percent of the population under 18, 15.1 percent of persons 18 to 64 years, and 36.2 percent of persons 65 years and over had low relative incomes. By 1989, the percentages for the same population age groups were 29.1, 17.3, and 31.5. Thus, the percentage decreased for persons in the oldest age group.

However, when focusing on the relative median income, it is the finding that the population age 64 and over was more likely to have relative incomes below the median level than any other age group in both 1979 and 1989, even though improvements were seen in 1989. In 1979, 72.9 percent have relative incomes below the median level. In 1989, the percentage was 65.7.

During the period 1979 to 1989, the percent with either high or low income increased for all educational groups, showing more inequality in the income distribution. Four groups were compared to reflect educational attainment: (1) those not finishing high school, (2) those completing high school, (3) those completing one to three years of college, and (4) those completing college. In 1979, relative low income figures for the four groups were 29, 11, 8.6, and 5.1 percent. The equivalent percentages for 1989 were 38.4, 15.7, 10.2, and 4.6. Clearly, the persons with low education were worse off than the persons with higher educational attainment in both years, but the range in percentages was larger in 1989 than in 1979.

When the proportion with incomes that are either high or low is examined by family relationship, it is the finding that inequality increased for all categories considered between 1979 and 1989. The poverty rate for children in single head of household families was higher than for children who were living in a married-couple arrangement. The same pattern emerges from the relative income data. For children in married-couple families, the 1979 percentage in the low relative income group was 14.9. In 1989, the percentage was 17.6. This compares to 60.3 percent (1979) and 63 percent (1989) for children who are not in married-couple arrangements. If age of child is taken into consideration, it is the finding that younger children (under 6 years old) who do not live in married-couple families comprise about 71 percent of the relative low income group in both 1979 and 1989.

In this section, the relative income distribution of the population was examined for the years 1979 and 1989. Relative income, a measure of the income inequality in the population, became more unequal over the decade. The increase came about because the percentage with both high and low relative income values increased. One population subgroup, the elderly, appeared to have made some gains over the decade. However, the 1989 low relative income rate for this group was still well above the other age groups. Whites continued to do better than blacks and Hispanics. It was as advantageous in 1989 as it was in 1979 to have some college background and, in particular, to have completed a college education. Children, especially young children, experienced inequality over the decade regardless of their living arrangements.

CONCLUSION

The 1980s started out with a recession and the poverty rates increased, peaking in 1983. With the economic recovery in 1984, the poverty rates started declining again, but the poor population was left permanently behind. By the end of the decade, the number of poor and the poverty rates were lower than the number and rates reached in 1983, yet, the level remained above the rates experienced during the years of economic expansion in the late 1970s.

Is the population better off financially at the end of the decade than it was at the beginning of the decade? The answer is no, if median earnings is used as an indicator. According to the U.S. Bureau of the Census, a civilian male employed full time year-round had a median income of $29,558 in 1980, but this figure decreased to $27,866 in 1990 (1990 CPI-U-XI dollars).

Those who stand 0–25 percent above the poverty line are the near poor. This group, although not poor officially will convert to poor with a relative minor change in income. The size of this group has increased over the decade. Similarly, the gap between the poverty threshold and the average income of poor families has widened. The depth of poverty is deeper.

No matter what income inequality indicator is used to study poverty, the gap between the rich and the poor widened (Ryscave and Henly 1990). Relatively speaking, the poor were worse off at the end of the decade than they were at various times in the past. The income deficit, the difference between total income of families and unrelated individuals below the poverty level and their respective poverty threshold, increased. In the 1980s, the poor got poorer (The League of Women Voters 1988).

Public policies to alleviate poverty did not materialize in the 1980s. Strides were made to raise the minimum wage, but it would take substantial increases to keep a family with a full-time minimum wage worker above the poverty line (Ellwood 1988). Other tax reforms took place, such as the federal Earned Income Tax Credit (EITC) program, but implementation has many limitations.

The EITC program is designed to offset the high burden posed by regressive payroll taxes. It is a refundable tax credit for low income working families with at least one child living at home. Because it assists low income working families, and because other benefits such as AFDC and SSI are not reduced, it is viewed by some as a promising tool for making a dent in poverty (Greenstein and Shapiro 1992). It is, however, a drawback that a federal tax return and a separate schedule have to be filed in order to qualify for the refund from the Internal Revenue Services. Furthermore, the refund is not received throughout the year, but is a lump sum payment after the year is over. Recently, adjustments have been made to take into account family size, but these adjustments do not appear to be adequate to help families with more than two children.

Thus, in the 1980s, there was little evidence to support the notion that public assistance contributes to the incidence of poverty. The prevailing economic structure was not conducive to improving the incidence of poverty in the population. The working age population was faced with lack of job opportunities, low wages, and unemployment. Education no longer served as a safeguard against poverty.

There are many causes and many sources of structural change reflected in the incidence of poverty. These factors are complex and interrelated. The definitions employed in this chapter to describe poverty have been economic in nature and limited to one specific attribute of economic status, that of income. As such, no claim is made that all the aspects of what constitutes being poor in the midst of plenty have been captured. To do so requires a much broader definition of income, one that includes social preferences and psychological conditions. Only then can one begin to evaluate the many views on the causes of poverty.

NOTE

1. Unless referenced otherwise, the data used in this section were obtained from the March supplements to the 1981 and the 1990 *Current Population Survey* (CPS), the two reference points for the year 1980 and 1989. Where appropriate, reference will also be made to 1990 data. The data were published in the U.S. Bureau of the Census, *Current Population Reports,* Consumer Income, Series P-60, No. 133 (1982), No. 171 (1991d), No. 175 (1991c), and No. 178 (1992).

REFERENCES

Becker, Gary. 1981. *A Treatise on the Family.* Cambridge, Mass.: Harvard University Press.

Duncan, Greg J., Richard D. Coe, Mary E. Cochran, Martha S. Hill, Saul D. Hoffman, and James N. Morgan. 1984. *Years of Poverty, Years of Plenty.* Ann Arbor: Institute for Social Research, University of Michigan.

Ellwood, David T. 1988. *Poor Support: Poverty in the American Family.* New York: Basic Books.

Greenstein, Robert and Isaac Shapiro. 1992. ''Policies to Alleviate Rural Poverty.'' Pp. 249–263 in Cynthia M. Duncan (ed.), *Rural Poverty in America.* New York: Auburn House.

Harrington, Michael. 1962. *The Other America: Poverty in the United States*. New York: Penguin Books.

———. 1984. *The New American Poverty*. New York: Holt, Rinehart and Winston.

League of Women Voters Education Fund. 1988. *Unmet Needs: The Growing Crises in America*. Washington, D.C.: The League.

Lewis, Oscar. 1971. "The Culture of Poverty." Pp. 187–220 in Daniel Patrick Moynihan (ed.), *On Understanding Poverty*. New York: Basic Books.

Murray, Charles. 1984. *Losing Ground: American Social Policy 1950–80*. New York: Basic Books.

O'Hare, William P. 1985. "Poverty in America: Trends and New Patterns." *Population Bulletin* 40, no. 3:1–44. Washington, D.C.: Population Reference Bureau.

Orshansky, Mollie. 1965a. "Counting the Poor: Another Look at the Poverty Profile." *Social Security Bulletin* 28 (January):3–29.

———. 1965b. "Who's Who Among the Poor: A Demographic View of Poverty." *Social Security Bulletin* 28 (July):3–32.

Ryscave, Paul and Peter Henly. 1990. "Earning Inequality in the 1980s." *Social Security Bulletin* 53 (December):3–16.

Schiller, Bradley, R. 1984. *The Economics of Poverty and Discrimination*. Englewood Cliffs, N.J.: Prentice-Hall.

U.S. Bureau of the Census. 1982. "Characteristics of the Population Below the Poverty Level: 1980." *Current Population Reports*. Series P-60, No. 133. Washington, D.C.: U.S. Government Printing Office.

———. 1986. "Measuring the Effect of Benefits and Taxes on Income and Poverty." *Current Population Survey,* Consumer Income. Series P-60, No. 164-RD-1. Washington, D.C.: U.S. Government Printing Office.

———. 1991a. *Statistical Abstracts of the United States: 1991*. Washington, D.C.: U.S. Government Printing Office.

———. 1991b. "Trends in Relative Income: 1964 to 1989." *Current Population Reports,* Consumer Income. Series P-60, No. 177. Washington, D.C.: U.S. Government Printing Office.

———. 1991c. "Poverty in the United States: 1990." *Current Population Reports,* Consumer Income. Series P-60, No. 175. Washington, D.C.: U.S. Government Printing Office.

———. 1991d. "Poverty in the United States: 1988 and 1989." *Current Population Reports,* Consumer Income. Series P-60, No. 171. Washington, D.C.: U.S. Government Printing Office.

———. 1992. "Workers with Low Earnings: 1964–1990." *Current Population Reports,* Consumer Income. Series P-60, No. 178. Washington, D.C.: U.S. Government Printing Office.

U.S. Congress. House. 1989. "Background Material and Data on Programs within the Jurisdiction of the Committee on Ways and Means." WMCP 101-4. Prepared for the Committee on Ways and Means by its staff. The 101st Congress, 1st session. Washington, D.C.: U.S. Government Printing Office.

U.S. Department of Health, Education and Welfare. 1976a. *The Measure of Poverty*. Technical Paper II. Washington, D.C.: Office of the Assistant Secretary for Planning and Evaluation.

———. 1976b. *The Measure of Poverty*. Technical Paper III. Washington, D.C.: Office of the Assistant Secretary for Planning and Evaluation.

Williams, Donald R. 1991. ''Structural Change and the Aggregate Poverty Rate.'' *Demography* 28:323–332.

Zopf, Paul E., Jr. 1989. *American Women in Poverty*. Westport, Conn.: Greenwood Press.

9

Cross-Racial Births in the United States, 1968–1988

LOUIE ALBERT WOOLBRIGHT AND
J. SELWYN HOLLINGSWORTH

Increasing numbers of people in the United States confront a dilemma when requested to complete official applications and questionnaires. In the space where individuals are asked to identify their race, these categories typically consist of a single racial or ethnic group. For children of mixed-racial unions, this presents a problem. If one selects a single category, they are in effect denying their true racial heritage. In other words, self-identity is denied. This identity problem is but one of many problems that affect the children of cross-racial unions.

The focal concern of this chapter is to document and analyze the rapid increase in cross-racial births in the United States. This growth reflects, in part, social change in race relations, especially since the 1960s, which has brought about changes in the ways in which people define themselves. This change, as a major basis for self-identification, points to a declining significance regarding the racial category with which people identify.

This problem is not unique to the United States. Amerasian children in Vietnam, for example, have similar identity problems. Of mixed parentage, Amerasians are socially shunned, and they confront discrimination in schools, jobs, and dating (''The Dust of Life'' 1991, p. 56). Amerasians are not accepted as real Vietnamese, but neither are they truly American. The resulting absence of a social identity is problematic in several ways, including one's sense of self-identity and belonging.

This is not the case worldwide. In Latin America, for example, the majority of early settlers were Spanish and Portuguese males. Because of the unsettled and uncertain nature of life in the New World, there was a lack of white females.

Thus, these settlers formed unions and had children with women of indigenous groups. Early on, there was strong discrimination against such *mestizo* (racially mixed) offspring. Gradually, however, this situation abated, so that mestizos now represent the majority, rather than the exception, of most Latin American populations (Morner 1967). Brazil is an example of a country where Negro slaves and their descendants were incorporated into a great melting pot of that society (Smith 1963).

In the United States, many biracial children were conceived as slave owners had their way with slave women. Some of these children eventually were legitimized by their white fathers, but this was not a common occurrence. In fact, until 1870, slaves were counted officially as only three-fifths of a person for purposes of allocating each state's representation in the national legislature (Shryock, Siegel and Associates 1973, p. 253).

Interracial parentage thus has a long history in the United States. Among the first explorers and settlers in what is now the present-day United States, males predominated. As a result, European men cohabited with native American Indian women, thereby producing mixed European and American Indian children. Racial mixing among blacks and whites also appears to have been fairly common. In fact, six U.S. censuses collected information on "mulattoes," or persons of mixed white and black ancestry (U.S. Bureau of the Census 1979).

Nevertheless, mixing of the races was considered to be morally wrong, causing many states to enact laws prohibiting miscegenation, or the mixing of the races. These laws were especially common in the South, where marriages between whites and blacks were forbidden, and on the West Coast, where marriages between Orientals and whites were banned (Ringer and Lawless 1989). Indeed, miscegenation was illegal in forty states (Weinberger 1966; Vander Zanden 1966), and these laws remained in effect until ruled as unconstitutional by the Supreme Court in 1967.

However, even before 1967, racial attitudes were changing in many parts of the country. Events related to World War II led to a rethinking of race relations in our nation. The racial policies of the German Nazis led scholars and policy-makers to question the caste-like racial barriers in the United States. Moreover, the Chinese were our allies during World War II, causing Chinese stereotypes in the United States to change.

Progress in race relations was made first in the military and then in society as a whole. Such progress accelerated during the 1960s, as the Civil Rights movement led to the passage of new laws regulating the interactions between the members of different racial groups. These changes are also reflected in interethnic and interracial marriage and parentage. Alba and Golden (1986) and Lieberson and Waters (1988) note a significant rise in intermarriage between European ethnic groups after World War II. These analysts found that intermarriage was much more common among European groups than it was between white and non-European groups. Also noted was a high rate of intermarriage between American Indians and whites.

One model used to explain the interrelationships between racial and ethnic groups is referred to as the assimilation, or melting pot, model. According to this model, ethnic group members shed their distinctive behaviors and customs and assimilate into the dominant American culture. Lieberson and Waters (1988, p. 162) note that intermarriage is one indicator of the degree of assimilation that occurs. These analysts also note that assimilation is a stimulus for both inter-racial couples and their children. This may occur in a series of steps, as suggested by Gordon (1964), with the final stage being the intermixing of gene pools. In a more general way, interracial marriage and parentage test the boundaries between groups, thereby serving as a measure of both social distance and assimilation.

PROBLEMS EXPERIENCED BY PERSONS OF MIXED RACIAL PARENTAGE

Being of cross-racial heritage presents difficulties for the individuals involved. Perhaps the greatest problem created by biracial births is that of individual self-definition. According to Lieberson and Waters (1988, pp. 162–163), "For the children of intermarriage, the determination of ethnic identity becomes a question and a decision that does not exist for the children of an ethnically homogeneous marriage." Persons of mixed-racial ancestry are, according to the literature, treated as half-breeds, psychologically unstable, social misfits, physically mutated, intellectually inadequate, mongrels, genetic abominations, and degenerates (Motoyoshi 1990).

Stonequist (1937) referred to the racially mixed as marginal people. In a study of half-white, half-black children in London, Wilson (1987) found identity conflict in the children, which she attributed to a lack of acceptance by both families and the general society. Christine Hall (1980) and George Kich (1982) reported that many cross-racial people experience identity confusion because they know they do not belong to a specific racial category. Some individuals experience low self-esteem and frustration. Motoyoshi (1990, p. 85) states that ethnicity determines one's membership in a specific group, and failure to share completely in a group's heritage begs the question of one's membership.

Problems encountered by persons of mixed racial heritage are revealed in the following case studies. The first is that of Minerbrook (1990, p. 44), who reports his pain of having a divided family:

Because my father is black and my mother is white, to my mother's half of the family, I do not exist . . . If you are born to a family like mine, you learn race matters very early. You learn that your life will be valued and governed by rules fundamentally different from those that shape the lives of your white relatives, because your skin is darker, your lips fuller, your hair a different texture. To me, race corrupts the meaning of the word family. And if my white relatives have killed me off in their hearts, I have tried to kill them off no less in mine. . . . In some ways, I believe I have felt the injustice of race hate more keenly than my black friends, because for them, racism didn't reside inside the family.

One Stanford University student, who is Korean and black, reported, "When I got to Stanford, I didn't think of myself as black or Korean or white. I thought of myself as Carl Hicks. But everyone kept labeling me" (Atkins 1992, p 1).

A similar view was expressed by a white/black/American Indian female, who was a Harvard University student: "I hate it when I have to check a box" (Atkins 1992, p. 1).

Another case is that of a second-generation person of mixed descent, who was only one-quarter black. He experienced discrimination from white family members, which strongly affected his self-identity. He appeared to be white, had been reared as a white, and lived in a white suburb in Washington, D.C. When his parents divorced, he was 10 years of age. Because of financial constraints, he and his brother moved with their father to Muncie, Indiana. On the trip, the father revealed that he was not Italian or Greek, as most people thought, but that he was "colored," the son of a black maid and her white boss. The children were told that they, too, were "colored."

The family was taken in by black relatives in Muncie but was totally shunned by the mother's white relatives. When Gregory registered in public school, he was reclassified as "Negro" on the school records. His official transcript contained a statement advising teachers that although Gregory looked white, they should not be fooled by his appearance. Teachers generally considered him to be of no consequence and discouraged him from attempting to excel (Whitaker 1992).

Others attempt to force a racially mixed individual into one racial group: a group in which he/she is not fully accepted. However, individuals who make such a choice are denied the remaining portion of their heritage. Being forced into such categories denies these persons an appropriate view of self. In the United States, until the 1960s, a person with only a minute portion of black blood was considered black. Instructions given to interviewers involved in the 1960 census directed them to "classify as Negro any descendant of a black man, or of a black man and any other race" (Steinfeld 1970, p. 229).

Mahin Root is yet another example of the attempt to force a biracial person to identify as a member of only one race. Having a white father and a black mother, Mahin left unanswered the question of her race when she registered at a North Carolina high school. School officials asked her to make a choice, in part because the Civil Rights Division of the U.S. Department of Education required school systems to report racial data for all students. She declined the request. The family, members of the Bahai faith, explained, "Our family believes very strongly in the oneness of mankind. There is but one race—the human race" ("No Place for Mankind" 1989, p. 17). Although the student was allowed to register, Department of Education officials insisted that her racial classification be reported, using a "rule of reason" or an "eyeball" test.

In the remainder of this chapter, our intent is to focus on mixed-race births and the extent to which such births occur. According to Atkins (1991), 2 percent of all U.S. marriages are interracial, and the number of mixed-race births increased by more than 400 percent between 1968 and 1988. Mixed-race children now account for 3.2 percent of all births in the nation, compared to 0.7 percent in 1968 (Usdansky and Edmonds 1992). The implications of this change also are addressed.

THE PATTERN OF MIXED-RACE BIRTHS IN THE UNITED STATES

The data reported in this chapter are from the National Center for Health Statistics (NCHS). The race of mother and father has been cross-classified to provide some indication of mixed-race children in the United States. Race, based on these NCHS statistics, does not refer to pure racial groups, but to categories best identified as a mixture of racial and ethnic groups.

From 1968 to 1988, NCHS changed some of the reported race categories. For example, births to Filipinos have been coded separately only since 1969. The Other Asian and Pacific Islander category was first used in 1978; before then, Asian and Pacific Islander births were included in the Other Races category. Other Races is a residual category for persons who do not fit any of the other racial classifications used by the NCHS.

In Table 9.1, the percentages of births where the race of father was unknown are reported according to race of mother for 1968 to 1988. Missing data for fathers is attributed to laws that prohibit some states from reporting data for fathers where the birth is to an unmarried woman, unless an affidavit of parentage is filed.

Among every racial group, the percentage of births with the father's race unknown increased over the period 1968–1988, increasing for whites from 3.8 percent in 1968 to 8.7 percent in 1988. The most dramatic increase occurred among blacks and American Indians; almost 40 percent of births to black mothers have no father's race reported, and for almost 30 percent of births to American Indian women in 1988, the race of father is unreported. For the Asian and Pacific Islander groups (except for Hawaiians), the percentage of birth certificates with unknown race of father is low. Thus, missing data for father's race is a recording problem mainly for births to black, American Indian, and Hawaiian mothers.

Table 9.2 shows births by race of mother and father.[1] When the race of the father was unknown, his race was allocated to one of the racial categories, based on the proportional racial distribution of records where the race of father *was* known.

Table 9.1

Percent of Birth Certificates with Race of Father Unknown by Race of Mother: United States, 1968–1988

Year of birth	White	Black	Race of mother American Indian	Chinese	Japanese	Hawaiian	Filipino	Other Asian
1988	8.66	39.32	29.11	1.17	2.77	17.64	3.29	6.69
1987	8.26	37.87	29.15	1.23	2.30	17.44	3.25	5.97
1986	7.86	36.93	28.15	0.96	2.85	18.03	3.22	5.49
1985	7.31	36.61	26.94	0.88	3.26	18.10	3.20	4.75
1984	6.87	36.27	26.77	0.94	2.56	21.21	3.53	4.37
1983	6.57	35.46	25.23	0.98	2.90	21.12	3.68	3.72
1982	6.25	34.92	24.87	0.71	3.06	20.22	3.72	2.95
1981	6.08	34.58	25.99	0.66	2.48	20.53	3.58	2.34
1980	5.98	34.90	27.10	0.79	2.58	20.75	3.42	2.13
1979	5.71	35.20	25.37	0.76	2.52	19.76	3.07	2.23
1978	5.57	35.05	24.69	0.67	2.47	20.21	3.05	2.12
1977	5.32	33.68	24.73	0.76	2.32	19.62	2.81	---
1976	5.07	33.22	23.80	0.53	1.89	17.55	2.94	---
1975	4.85	32.32	23.88	0.63	2.40	17.74	3.62	---
1974	4.39	31.50	22.67	0.71	1.85	15.40	3.03	---
1973	4.37	31.07	19.50	0.86	1.81	15.88	3.02	---
1972	4.18	30.38	17.87	0.70	1.81	15.88	3.02	---
1971	3.89	27.71	18.88	0.67	1.58	13.24	2.72	---
1970	4.06	26.32	18.49	1.25	2.72	13.35	3.72	---
1969	3.85	25.04	17.99	0.93	2.02	13.68	3.14	---
1968	3.75	24.79	15.77	0.63	2.00	13.17	---	---

Source: Unpublished worktables from the National Center for Health Statistics.

White Mothers

Although the percentage of births conceived of non-white fathers is small, the proportion increased from .5 percent in 1968 to 1.97 percent in 1988. In 1968, there were 14,658 fathers of babies born to white women, almost one-half of this total were black fathers (n = 7,244). There were 3,086 births involving American Indian fathers and white mothers.

Among racially mixed children born to white mothers, 49.4 percent had black fathers in 1968, compared to 55.6 percent in 1988. By 1988, births involving fathers in each non-white racial category increased when compared to 1968. The Other Races category declined, perhaps because of a change in NCHS reporting procedure that now delineates Filipino and Other Asian and Pacific Islander fathers separately. Interracial births involving black fathers increased 470 per-

Table 9.2
Births and Percent Distribution by Race of Mother and Father: United States, Selected Years 1968–1988

Race of mother and Year of birth	Number of births	Total births	White	Black	American Indian	Chinese	Japanese	Hawaiian	Filipino	Other Asian	Other races
White											
1988	3094411	100.00	98.03	1.09	0.33	0.05	0.08	0.04	0.11	0.24	0.02
1985	3028337	100.00	98.35	0.86	0.32	0.05	0.08	0.04	0.10	0.18	0.02
1980	2923915	100.00	98.64	0.72	0.28	0.04	0.06	0.04	0.07	0.13	0.02
1975	2572970	100.00	98.99	0.55	0.21	0.03	0.04	0.03	0.06	---	0.08
1970	3105088	100.00	99.37	0.32	0.13	0.03	0.03	0.03	0.04	---	0.05
1968	2922668	100.00	99.50	0.25	0.11	0.02	0.03	0.03	---	---	0.08
Black											
1988	637142	100.00	2.68	97.03	0.08	0.01	0.01	0.01	0.03	0.12	0.03
1985	580306	100.00	2.19	97.57	0.06	0.01	0.01	0.01	0.03	0.08	0.04
1980	566149	100.00	1.50	98.31	0.05	0.01	0.01	0.00	0.02	0.06	0.04
1975	495844	100.00	0.88	99.02	0.03	0.01	0.00	0.01	0.01	---	0.04
1970	560674	100.00	0.71	99.19	0.04	0.01	0.01	0.01	0.02	---	0.03
1968	522804	100.00	0.45	99.49	0.02	0.01	0.00	0.00	---	---	0.02
American Indian											
1988	37004	100.00	37.52	3.19	57.89	0.07	0.16	0.30	0.32	0.53	0.02
1985	33909	100.00	37.39	2.76	58.55	0.10	0.15	0.29	0.32	0.39	0.05
1980	29187	100.00	33.60	2.39	62.99	0.05	0.10	0.31	0.24	0.32	0.00
1975	22664	100.00	26.38	2.07	70.71	0.03	0.07	0.24	0.24	---	0.27
1970	22214	100.00	21.71	1.81	75.82	0.07	0.04	0.15	0.19	---	0.21
1968	21476	100.00	21.48	1.63	76.51	0.01	0.07	0.08	---	---	0.23
Chinese											
1988	21199	100.00	10.59	0.44	0.04	83.92	1.66	0.33	0.48	2.48	0.05
1985	16304	100.00	11.32	0.74	0.14	82.72	1.66	0.51	0.62	2.23	0.07
1980	11558	100.00	12.63	0.78	0.11	80.15	2.59	0.62	0.72	2.28	0.12
1975	7746	100.00	12.65	0.94	0.10	79.46	2.07	1.03	0.83	---	2.92
1970	7028	100.00	11.44	0.89	0.20	80.03	3.03	1.15	0.92	---	2.33
1968	5706	100.00	8.99	0.63	0.07	82.15	2.65	1.31	---	---	4.20

Table 9.2 (Continued)

Source: Unpublished worktables from the National Center for Health Statistics.

Race of mother and Year of birth	Number of births	Total births	White	Black	American Indian	Chinese	Japanese	Hawaiian	Filipino	Other Asian	Other races
Japanese											
1988	8617	100.00	35.88	2.33	0.61	4.23	47.59	4.56	2.88	1.87	0.06
1985	8009	100.00	35.31	2.48	0.50	3.70	49.37	4.58	2.52	1.50	0.04
1980	7438	100.00	31.20	1.85	0.48	3.28	54.24	4.47	2.51	1.93	0.03
1975	6719	100.00	32.33	1.86	0.26	3.19	54.82	3.37	1.74	---	2.44
1970	7732	100.00	27.36	1.97	0.24	2.77	60.62	3.08	1.89	---	2.07
1968	8002	100.00	30.40	1.99	0.10	2.63	58.02	2.93	---	---	3.93
Hawaiian											
1988	5237	100.00	24.16	3.32	1.60	1.95	7.33	45.47	10.36	5.75	0.07
1985	4935	100.00	24.96	3.64	1.98	1.73	7.30	43.54	11.01	5.84	0.00
1980	4651	100.00	23.03	2.98	1.30	2.22	7.79	48.43	10.04	4.21	0.00
1975	3709	100.00	24.02	1.97	2.20	1.87	6.82	47.26	12.09	---	3.77
1970	4286	100.00	25.90	1.88	0.86	2.80	6.89	47.71	10.77	---	3.18
1968	3554	100.00	26.44	1.75	0.52	2.72	5.51	49.58	---	---	13.48
Filipino											
1988	23115	100.00	29.38	4.27	0.38	0.95	1.25	2.07	59.79	1.82	0.09
1985	19951	100.00	27.96	3.85	0.48	0.88	1.12	2.06	61.91	1.63	0.12
1980	13817	100.00	26.89	3.69	0.37	1.15	1.15	2.8	62.38	1.46	0.10
1975	10344	100.00	26.09	3.06	0.28	0.90	1.04	3.04	64.16	---	1.42
1970	8056	100.00	21.58	3.69	0.46	0.77	1.44	3.66	66.94	---	1.44
1969	7396	100.00	22.28	3.15	0.45	0.84	0.98	3.41	66.30	---	2.60
Other Asian and Pacific Islanders											
1988	70326	100.00	14.39	1.77	0.13	0.91	0.33	0.21	0.32	81.58	0.06
1985	54849	100.00	15.53	1.95	0.15	0.96	0.38	0.25	0.32	80.42	0.05
1980	36285	100.00	19.92	2.70	0.16	1.10	0.56	0.28	0.32	74.94	0.03
1978	22594	100.00	27.46	3.23	0.27	1.36	0.67	0.31	0.44	66.24	0.02

cent between 1968 and 1988, albeit the proportion of births involving white mothers increased by less than 6 percent. The number of American Indian, Chinese, Japanese, and Filipino fathers tripled over this same period (310 percent), while the number of Hawaiian fathers almost doubled (102 percent). In addition, Other Asian and Pacific Islander fathers increased by more than 100 percent between 1979 and 1988.

Black Mothers

Lieberson and Waters (1988) note that blacks have the largest rate of inmarriage (99 percent). However, as with babies born to white mothers, the percentage of interracial births involving non-black fathers increased dramatically from .51 percent to 2.97. The number of white fathers increased from 2,400 in 1968 to more than 17,000 in 1988, a change of more than 600 percent.

The proportion of black mothers and interracial fathers is small, but for each individual racial category an increase is observable over time. Babies born to black mothers with Other Asian and Pacific Islander fathers increased markedly between 1978 and 1988, ranking third after both white fathers and black fathers.

Among mixed black-white births, the black father-white mother combination accounted for three-quarters of these births during 1968. By 1988, this proportion had declined to approximately 66 percent. Births to white fathers and black mothers are increasing more rapidly than those to black fathers and white mothers, a finding supported by Tucker and Mitchell-Kernan (1990), who found that men tend to marry those of other racial categories in greater proportions than is the case among women.

American Indian Mothers

More than three-quarters of births to American Indian mothers in 1968 had American Indian fathers. By 1988, this proportion decreased to less than 60 percent, with one-third of the fathers being white. When mixed-race births involve American Indians and whites, white fathers are more common. Black fathers are twice as likely to be involved with American Indian mothers as is the case with black mothers and American Indian fathers.

Births among American Indian mothers has increased considerably, recording 21,000 in 1968 and increasing to 37,000 in 1988. Undoubtedly, this increase can be attributed to the tendency for women to identify themselves as American Indian or as women of mixed blood, when previously they reported themselves as being members of another race.[2]

Chinese Mothers

The U.S. Chinese population increased primarily because of immigration. This increase is reflected in a 272 percent increase in the births recorded to

Chinese mothers during the 1968–1988 period. However, the racial mix of fathers of babies born to Chinese mothers changed little over this same period. In 1968, slightly more than 82 percent of the babies had Chinese fathers, while in 1988, 84 percent were so reported.

Births involving white fathers and Chinese mothers increased from 9 percent in 1968 to 13.8 percent in 1976, but then declined to 10.6 percent in 1988. However, in absolute numbers, such births more than quadrupled during this same period. Mixed white-Chinese children were more likely to have a Chinese mother and a white father in 1988, as opposed to the past, when white mothers and Chinese fathers was a more common occurrence. Among the other groups, Chinese mother-Other Asian or Pacific Islander father is the most prevalent. Chinese mothers have relatively few babies with either black or American Indian fathers.

Japanese Mothers

U.S. Japanese mothers were more likely to have babies with a non-Japanese father in 1988 (52 percent of all births) than they were to have babies with Japanese fathers. By comparison, in 1968, almost 60 percent of the births to Japanese mothers were with Japanese fathers. White fathers accounted for 30 percent of the births to Japanese mothers in 1968, a proportion that increased to almost 36 percent in 1988. The percent of black fathers and Japanese mothers has remained steady, accounting for approximately 2 percent of births. Japanese women are not very likely to bear babies of a father from the Other Races group. In 1988, about 13.5 percent of biracial babies of Japanese mothers had a non-Japanese Asian father.

Hawaiian Mothers

The term Hawaiian refers more to a geographic origin than it does to a distinct racial category. Among Hawaiians, there is a history of a high rate of intermarriage involving different racial and ethnic groups, and this fact has created a mixture of racial origins. In fact, Vander Zanden (1966, p. 326) refers to Hawaii as a "polyracial paradise."

Because Hawaiians consist of a mixture of racial categories, Hawaiian mothers are more likely to have babies with fathers of a different racial category. This fact is reflected in the data between 1968 and 1988, when over 50 percent of the babies born to Hawaiian mothers had non-Hawaiian fathers, except for one year. The lone exception was 1973, when the proportion of Hawaiian fathers (50.9 percent) exceeded that of non-Hawaiian fathers. Throughout this twenty-one-year period, white fathers composed about one-fourth of the total number. Also, the percentage of black, American Indian, Japanese, and Other Asian or Pacific Islander fathers has risen since 1968, while the percentage of Chinese and Filipino fathers has fluctuated up and down during this same period.

Filipino Mothers

The number of Filipinos residing in the United States has risen dramatically since the late 1960s, as has their number of births. As a result, births to Filipino mothers more than tripled between 1969 and 1988. The percentage of births involving both Filipino parents decreased from the 66.3 percent recorded in 1969 to 59.8 percent in 1988. By 1988, almost 30 percent of all children born to Filipino women had white fathers, compared with only 22 percent in 1969. Filipino women have a higher percentage of births with black fathers than with any of the other non-black groups. One reason for this could be that black military personnel stationed at U.S. military bases in the Philippines often marry Filipino women. For children with one Filipino and one black parent in 1988, 987 had black fathers, while 178 had Filipino fathers.

Other Asian and Pacific Islanders

The category of Other Asian and Pacific Islanders includes a diverse and rapidly growing population. This category, which has grown rapidly during the past decade, includes persons from the Asian and Pacific region such as Vietnamese, Cambodians, Laotians, Thais, Koreans, and Asian Indians. Consequently, the number of births to Other Asian and Pacific Islander mothers was over three times as great in 1988 as in 1978. Most Asian and Other Pacific Islander mothers giving birth in 1988 conceived their children with members of their own group. In 1988, only Chinese mothers were as likely to bear children with males who were from the same ethnic group. More than 27 percent of the fathers of babies born to mothers of this group in 1978 were white, compared to 14 percent in 1988. Nevertheless, the number of white fathers in absolute terms increased steadily from 6,204 in 1978 to 10,119 in 1988. Among all other racial categories, the number of other fathers increased while the percent of births with fathers from that group declined. In sum, the number of mixed babies is increasing, but the percentage of mixed babies born to Other Asian and Pacific Islander women is decreasing.

NATIVITY OF MOTHER

The likelihood of interracial marriage and parenthood is lower among women who were not born in the United States (Hwang 1990). Although single men generally experience the highest rates of international migration, many immigrants had already married in their place of origin and the family moved to the United States as a unit. Thus, immigrant mothers are more likely to have mates of the same ethnic/racial group.

The assimilation model predicts that immigrants become assimilated over time and that future generations are more likely to intermarry and become interracial or interethnic parents than are the members of the immigrant generation. As a result, births were tabulated for 1978 and 1988 by nativity of the mother as well as by the race of the mother and father (see Table 9.3).

Among the Asian groups, there is a marked difference in the probability of children being born of interracial parentage, depending on whether the mother was born in the United States or is foreign-born. Less than 50 percent of U.S.-born Chinese (44.3 percent), Japanese (41.0 percent), Other Asian and Pacific Islander (40.3 percent), and Filipino (27.3 percent) mothers reported fathers of the same ethnicity. For births to foreign-born mothers, on the other hand, more than 50 percent of the fathers in all four Asian groups were of the same Asian origin (Chinese—88.5 percent, Japanese—54.9 percent, Filipino—64.9 percent, and Other Asian and Pacific Islanders—84.5 percent). This finding strongly supports the assimilation model.

Much of the interracial parentage involves American-born Asians and whites. For Other Asian and Pacific Islander mothers born in the United States, 46 percent had babies whose fathers were white, while only 40 percent had Other Asian and Pacific Islander fathers. This is much higher than among foreign-born Other Asian and Pacific Islander mothers, where 85 percent of the fathers were of the same group. Among U.S.-born Chinese women, 36 percent conceived babies with white fathers, compared with only 7.7 percent for foreign-born Chinese mothers. Similarly, 44.2 percent of U.S.-born Filipino mothers in 1988 had babies with white fathers, while 27 percent of foreign-born Filipino mothers had babies with white fathers in the same year. However, foreign-born black women are almost twice as likely to bear children with white fathers as are U.S.-born black women. Based on this measure, then, foreign-born blacks appear to be more assimilated than are U.S.-born blacks. Even Asian-born women are more likely to have children with white fathers than with black males.

Except for Filipinos, the percentage of Asian women born in the United States whose children had white fathers increased among all groups between 1968 and 1988, leading to a corresponding decline in the percent of births occurring among parents of the same racial group. Among all Asian groups, for foreign-born mothers, a majority of the babies' fathers were from the same group. The percent with same-group parents for births to foreign-born women remained relatively constant between 1978 and 1988, except for Other Asian and Pacific Islander mothers, where the increase from 1978 to 1988 was 17 percent (68 and 85 percent, respectively).

Since 1978, then, the statistics indicate a rise in interracial parentage among babies of Asian mothers who were born in the United States. By this measure, assimilation of American-born Asian mothers has increased since 1978. Since these groups have a very low level of out-of-wedlock childbearing, this finding also indicates a high rate of intermarriage among American-born women who were having babies between 1968 and 1988.

Table 9.3
Births and Percent Distribution by Race of Mother and Father and Nativity of Mother: United States, 1978 and 1988

Race of mother and nativity	Number of births	Total births	Race of father White	Black	American Indian	Chinese	Japanese	Hawaiian	Filipino	Other Asian and Pacific Islander	Other Races
1978											
U. S. born											
White	2724795	100.0	98.78	0.64	0.28	0.03	0.06	0.04	0.07	0.09	0.02
Black	587197	100.0	1.05	98.83	0.04	0.00	0.00	0.01	0.01	0.03	0.02
American Indian	36038	100.0	30.61	2.00	66.49	0.02	0.14	0.19	0.23	0.26	0.06
Chinese	2199	100.0	28.79	2.77	0.42	46.02	11.42	4.84	3.67	2.01	0.07
Japanese	4536	100.0	25.65	1.10	0.96	5.16	54.93	6.71	4.06	1.35	0.08
Hawaiian	5158	100.0	22.88	2.84	1.23	2.04	6.76	49.10	11.54	3.62	0.00
Filipino	3279	100.0	35.04	4.12	0.88	1.59	5.71	19.11	31.08	2.25	0.22
Other Asian and Pacific Islander	4250	100.0	43.38	5.15	1.08	6.08	2.15	1.69	1.62	33.59	0.15
Other races	294	100.0	36.42	16.29	0.64	0.96	0.96	0.64	0.00	0.32	43.77
Foreign born											
White	365062	100.0	98.54	0.91	0.10	0.06	0.05	0.02	0.09	0.17	0.06
Black	47023	100.0	5.32	94.39	0.03	0.04	0.02	0.00	0.05	0.10	0.04
American Indian	899	100.0	27.07	5.63	63.69	0.00	0.00	0.00	0.47	3.13	0.00
Chinese	18986	100.0	10.66	0.70	0.01	85.02	0.66	0.17	0.47	2.14	0.17
Japanese	4070	100.0	39.17	2.90	0.21	1.36	52.10	0.82	0.94	2.45	0.06
Hawaiian	78	100.0	33.72	2.30	1.15	2.68	0.77	51.72	3.07	4.21	0.38
Filipino	19821	100.0	23.73	3.55	0.28	0.39	0.55	0.39	59.77	1.32	0.02
Other Asian and Pacific Islander	65962	100.0	26.17	3.59	0.22	1.07	0.58	0.23	0.37	68.26	0.01
Other races	2429	100.0	37.11	4.45	0.13	0.64	0.2	0.1	0.1	0.23	57.14

Table 9.3 (Continued)

1988

Race of mother and nativity	Number of births Total births	Race of father White	Black	American Indian	Chinese	Japanese	Hawaiian	Filipino	Other Asian and Pacific Islander	Other Races
U.S. born										
White	100.0	98.02	1.08	0.37	0.05	0.08	0.05	0.11	0.23	0.01
Black	100.0	2.46	97.28	0.08	0.01	0.01	0.01	0.03	0.10	0.03
American Indian	100.0	37.65	3.14	57.85	0.07	0.15	0.30	0.32	0.50	0.02
Chinese	100.0	36.25	1.86	0.28	44.33	10.87	2.70	2.23	1.49	0.00
Japanese	100.0	35.99	1.55	0.78	6.15	40.97	8.14	4.66	1.69	0.07
Hawaiian	100.0	24.14	3.28	1.58	1.93	7.38	45.50	10.42	5.70	0.07
Filipino	100.0	44.20	5.50	1.30	1.17	5.50	12.62	27.28	2.37	0.07
Other Asian and Pacific Islander	100.0	46.17	5.83	0.90	1.37	1.68	1.57	2.01	40.29	0.18
Other races	100.0	32.63	22.46	1.69	0.42	0.00	0.42	0.00	0.85	41.53
Foreign born										
White	100.0	98.12	1.17	0.10	0.06	0.06	0.02	0.12	0.29	0.05
Black	100.0	4.75	94.72	0.04	0.07	0.02	0.00	0.01	0.32	0.06
American Indian	100.0	33.63	4.84	58.98	0.25	0.25	0.25	0.13	1.53	0.13
Chinese	100.0	7.65	0.28	0.02	88.45	0.60	0.06	0.28	2.60	0.06
Japanese	100.0	35.74	3.18	0.43	2.08	54.88	0.65	0.93	2.08	0.05
Hawaiian	100.0	25.71	4.29	2.86	2.86	4.29	44.29	7.14	8.57	0.00
Filipino	100.0	27.07	4.08	0.24	0.92	0.59	0.43	64.85	1.73	0.09
Other Asian and Pacific Islander	100.0	12.39	1.51	0.08	0.88	0.24	0.13	0.21	84.49	0.06
Other races	100.0	17.08	3.32	0.05	0.63	0.16	0.16	0.16	2.32	76.12

Source: Unpublished worktables from the National Center for Health Statistics.

SUMMARY AND CONCLUSIONS

Increased tolerance toward people of other races has resulted in many changes, including an increase in racial intermarriage in the United States. The increase in intermarriage, and subsequently, of interracial people, are suggestive of an interesting demographic shift. In 1968, 0.8 percent of all births in the U.S. involved interracial parents; by 1988, this proportion had almost quadrupled, accounting for 3.1 percent of all interracial births. During this same period, the proportion of biracial births increased for most racial categories of mothers. The exceptions to this trend are found among children born of Chinese and Other Asian and Pacific Islander mothers.

Gordon (1964) suggests that when marital assimilation takes place, the minority group loses its identity in the host society and identifiable assimilation results. Eventually, racial and ethnic group members become absorbed into the dominant society, and distinct racial and ethnic groups disappear. In sum, intermarriage is the *sine qua non* of assimilation.

The U.S. Bureau of the Census currently is predicting growth in the birth rates of minority groups during the next half century. Although no provision is made in the estimates for interracial classifications, perhaps this is a result of a current failure to include multiracial categories in the survey questionnaires. The Bureau predicts that the non-Hispanic white majority, which currently represents 76 percent of the population, will decline to 52 percent by the year 2050. The following predictions posed by Bovee (1993) highlight the projected growth of minority groups by the year 2050:

• Hispanics will increase in size from 9 to 23 percent of the total population;

• Blacks will increase in size from 12 to 16 percent of the total population;

• Asian Americans will increase from 3 to 10 percent of the total population; and

• American Indians will increase from less than 1 percent to more than 1 percent of the total population.

Interracial unions undoubtedly will increase. For the census of 1990, 9.8 million people checked the ''other'' box for race, a 45 percent increase from 1980. For this reason, the census bureau should consider the addition of a multiracial category.

The data presented in this chapter suggest that the population of the United States is becoming more interracial in composition. By extension, these data also suggest that the assimilation of specific racial and ethnic groups into the dominant culture is underway.

With regard to specific racial categories, the data for Asians appear to fit the assimilation model well. Native-born Asians, especially, show a high degree of assimilation. Based on the proportion of children born of interracial parentage involving Asian mothers, over half had children involved whose fathers were not Asian. Even among foreign-born Asians, an increasing rate of interracial parentage has occurred. One reason for the increasing interracial parentage among Asians is that many Asians reside either in Hawaii or in the Western region of the United States, where Asians have relatively high socio-economic status and low levels of residential segregation (Woolbright and Hartmann, 1987). Hawaiians and American Indians also have a high rate of interracial parentage, though both groups are socially disadvantaged.

Unlike other groups, however, blacks do not fit the assimilation model well. A low percentage of children have only one black parent compared with the other non-white groups. One plausible reason for this finding is that blacks generally have low levels of socio-economic status, are residentially segregated, and are more socially segregated than are Asian groups (Woolbright and Hartmann, 1987).

The two racial groups most likely to have same-race births are whites and blacks. Among the Asian groups, the Chinese and Other Asian and Pacific Islanders tend to have the highest proportions of same-race parentage, while more than half of the births to Japanese and Hawaiian mothers were multiracial.

Cross-racial births are more likely to involve white fathers. According to Heer (1980, p. 514), a major determinant of intermarriage is the availability of partners and the relative socio-economic levels of different racial categories. Social distance between white fathers and non-white mothers appears to be decreasing, and, in the case of cross-racial births involving white fathers, such births accounted for 90.3 percent of all multiracial births to black mothers. For other racial categories involving white fathers, the proportion of births were: American Indians, 89.1; Chinese, 65.9; Japanese, 68.5; and Other Asian and Pacific Islanders, 79.4 percent.

As the case studies reported earlier suggest, racial designation is becoming increasingly problematic for a growing number of persons born of mixed-race unions. This fact suggests that a reshaping of current racial categories is required, since an increasing number of Americans belong to more than one racial group. The procedure for such change exists in that the census data indicate that many whites now report themselves to be of American ancestry, rather than as of European ancestry. Given the high levels of social status for Asians and their current rate of interracial births, it is probable that in the future these groups may become assimilated and considered more as ethnic rather than racial groups. The low rate of interracial parentage of blacks, on the other hand, suggests that assimilation will take longer to occur.

NOTES

1. The small number of births where the race of the mother is unknown are excluded from the analysis. In addition, births to mothers of the residual Other Races category are not reported in the tables.

2. The 1990 census reports a large increase among the American Indian population.

However, the increments reported were so large that fertility rates would have had to be extremely high for these increases to occur. A more logical explanation is that more American Indians are declaring themselves as such on census questionnaires.

REFERENCES

Alba, Richard and Reid Golden. 1986. "Patterns of Ethnic Marriage in the United States." *Social Forces* 65:202–223.

Atkins, Elizabeth. 1991. "When Life Isn't Simply Black or White." *New York Times* (June 5):C1, C7.

———. 1992. "Students of Mixed Race Form Bond." *St. Louis Post-Dispatch* (June 25):1, 3.

Bovee, Tim. 1993. "Census Sees Radical Shifts in U.S. Racial, Ethnic Mix." *The Birmingham News* (September 29):5D.

"The Dust of Life (Amerasian Children from Vietnam Coming to the U.S." 1991. *Rolling Stone* (November 14):56.

Gordon, M. 1964. *Assimilation in American Life: The Role of Race, Religion and National Origins.* New York: Oxford University Press.

Hall, Christine C. 1980. "The Ethnic Identity of Racially Mixed People: A Study of Black-Japanese." Doctoral dissertation, University of California at Los Angeles.

Heer, David. 1980. "Intermarriage." Pp. 513–521 in Stephan Thernstrom (ed.), *Harvard Encyclopedia of American Ethnic Groups.* Cambridge, Mass.: Belknap Press.

Hwang, Sean-Hsong. 1990. "The Problem Posed by Immigrants Married Abroad on Intermarriage Research: The Case of Asian-Americans." *International Migration Review* 24:563–576.

Kich, George. 1982. *Eurasians: Ethnic/Racial Identity of Biracial Japanese/White Adults.* Doctoral Dissertation. Berkeley, Calif.: Wright Institute.

Lieberson, Stanley and Mary Waters. 1988. *From Many Strands: Ethnic and Racial Groups in Contemporary America.* New York: Russell Sage Foundation.

Minerbrook, Scott. 1990. "The Pain of a Divided Family." *U.S. News and World Report* (December 24):44.

Morner, Magnus. 1967. *Race Mixture in the History of Latin America.* Boston: Little, Brown.

Motoyoshi, Michelle M. 1990. "The Experience of Mixed-Race People." *The Journal of Ethnic Studies* 18:77–94.

"No Place for Mankind." 1989. *Time* 134 (September 4):17.

Ringer, Benjamin and Elinor Lawless. 1989. *Race-Ethnicity and Society.* New York: Routledge.

Shyrock, Henry S., Jacob S. Siegel, and Associates. 1973. *The Methods and Materials of Demography.* Washington, D.C.: U.S. Government Printing Office.

Smith, T. Lynn. 1963. *Brazil: Its People and Institutions* (3rd ed.). Baton Rouge: Louisiana State University Press.

Steinfeld, Melvin. 1970. *Cracks in the Melting Pot: Racism and Discrimination in American History.* Beverly Hills, Calif.: Glencoe Press.

Stonequist, Everett. 1937. *The Marginal Man: A Study in Personality and Culture Conflict.* New York: Charles Scribner's Sons.

Tucker, Belinda and Claudia Mitchell-Kernan. 1990. "New Trends in Black American

Interracial Marriage: The Social Structural Context.'' *Journal of Marriage and the Family* 52:209–218.

U.S. Bureau of the Census. 1979. *Twenty Censuses: Population and Housing Questions, 1790–1980.* Washington, D.C.: U.S. Government Printing Office.

Usdansky, Margaret and Patricia Edmonds. 1992. ''For Interracial Kids, Growth Spurt.'' *USA Today* (December 11):7A.

Vander Zanden, James. 1966. *American Minority Relations.* New York: Ronald Press.

Weinberger, Andrew D. 1966. ''Interracial Marriage: Its Statutory Prohibition, Genetic Import, and Incidence.'' *Journal of Sex Research* 2:157–168.

Whitaker, Charles. 1992. ''The True Story of an Indiana 'White' Boy Who Discovered That He Was Black.'' *Ebony* 47 (October):88–94.

Wilson, Anne. 1987. *Mixed Racial Children: A Study of Identity.* New York: Allen and Unwin.

Woolbright, Louie and David Hartmann. 1987. ''The New Segregation: Asians and Hispanics.'' Pp. 138–157 in Gary Tobin (ed.), *Divided Neighborhoods: Changing Patterns of Racial Segregation.* Newbury Park, Calif.: Russell Sage Publications.

Concluding Comments

This volume began by stating that three questions serve as a unifying theme for the book's task: (1) What are the major social changes that occurred during the 1980s? (2) What changes in structure created these social changes? (3) What changes result from these changes? Each of these questions is intended to focus attention on issues relating to the interaction between structure and environment, as well as to reflect on the consequences of social change for the present condition.

Calhoun's (1991, pp. 1808–1809) assessment of the sociological approach to the study of social change includes three, though perhaps not entirely separate, approaches: (1) sociologists attempt to establish generalizable patterns in the process of change, (2) sociologists offer explanations of the patterns of cumulative change, and (3) some sociologists argue that no single explanation of social change is powerful enough to account for each and every significant transition in the evolutionary process of change. The contents of this volume appear to lend some support to the contention that each of these approaches is useful to understanding cumulative social change.

These nine chapters have brought together a compendium of knowledge useful for instruction and debate. The policy concerns of the 1990s are highly correlated with the economic, social, and demographic changes experienced during the 1980s. As several of the contributors have shown, demographic change in the United States cannot be understood without some understanding of the effects shaped by changes in the global economy. Structural changes are equally important, especially as these relate to globalization and the influences of technology.

The authors' intent has been to focus on the changing characteristics of the U.S. population and some of the resultant changes in structure. Only a limited number of these important events and processes can be covered in a single volume, but the collective chapters point to the magnitude of this development, progress, process, and function during the 1980s. The implications for the experiences of the 1990s and beyond, as shown by the contributors, are noteworthy. New technologies, supported globalization, race relations, social movements, detection of new diseases, and shifting national politics and economies all have been instrumental in the process of demographic and structural change.

The relationships between technology, economics, political ideology, and changing social attitudes and values clearly affect this process. However, the effects of the dynamic forces on the U.S. society do not exist in a vacuum. The dynamics of demographic and social change are so irrevocably intertwined in the society's fabric that concomitant changes in other sectors will irretrievably result in ripple-like effects. This pervasive change can therefore be observed in all aspects of the American experience, be that at the local, regional, and/or national levels.

REFERENCE

Calhoun, Craig. 1991. "Social Change." Pp. 1807–1812 in Edgar F. Borgatta (ed.), *Encyclopedia of Sociology,* vol. 4. New York: Macmillan.

Author Index

Subject Index

Demographic transition theory, 5, 6–7,
   10
Deskilling of job requirements, 136–138
Division of labor, 3, 10

Economic restructuring, in gentrification,
   158–160
Educational attainment: fertility differentials, 97–98; and low wage earners,
   178–179; and the poverty rate, 173–
   174; and relative income levels,
   182
Elderly population: growth of, 66–69; by
   metropolitan-nonmetropolitan residence, 67; population projections of,
   68; by race, 67; by rural-urban residence, 67
Employment data, 128–130; job growth
   and occupation, 132–133

Fecundity, defined, 86
Fertility: defined, 86; trends, 90–94, 85–
   99
Fertility, differentials, 94–98; by educa-
   tional attainment, 97–98; by income,
   98; by racial differences, 97; by re-
   gional differences, 96–97; by religious
   group differences, 97; by rural-urban
   residence, 94–95, 97
Fertility, measurements of, 86–90; Age-
   Specific Fertility Rate, 89; Crude Birth
   Rate, 87; General Fertility Rate, 87–89;
   Total Fertility Rate, 89–90
Fitness trend, 118

General Fertility Rate, 87–89
Gentrification, 43, 142–166; defined, 164;
   during the 1980s, 149–158; and housing change, 150–154; and population
   change, 154–155; and racial/ethnic
   change, 157–158; and social class
   change, 155–157
Growing cities, 146; recently growing cities, 147–148; transitional cities, 147–
   148

Health: by educational levels, 116; by social class, 116

Health care access, 116–117; decreasing,
   122
Health policy, 120–121
Homeownership, 150–151
Human ecological approach, 7–13
Human ecological paradigm, 8–9
Hutterites, 86

Immigration, 21–22, 23–26; and poverty,
   50; regional differences, 76; as a
   source of population growth, 59
Income: by age, 182; differential fertility
   by, 98; by educational attainment, 182;
   by family relationship, 182–183; low,
   177–180; by race, 182; relative levels
   of, 181–183
Incomes of cashier jobs, 138–139
Infant mortality, 111–113
Infectious diseases, resurgence of,
   121
Internal migration, in the United States,
   11–13, 23–26
Interracial marriages, 188

Labor force, changes in, 121–141
Local health agencies, 104–105
Low wage earners, 178–180; by educational attainment, 178–179; by family
   relationship, 179–180; by race, 178; by
   sex, 178

Metropolitan economic polarization, 52–
   54
Metropolitan-nonmetropolitan residence:
   by age, 67; by race, 76; growth in,
   144–145; poverty levels in, 170
Migration, dynamics of, 23–26
Minority groups. See Race

Neo-Malthusianism, 4, 5–6

Occupation and job growth, 132–133
Occupational typology, 130–132
Occupations, demand and supply, 130–
   132

About the Contributors

LAKSHMI K. BHARADWAJ is Associate Professor of Sociology at the University of Wisconsin at Milwaukee, where he teaches courses on sociological theory, social change, and environmental sociology. Until recently, he served as an Advisory Editor for *Sociological Inquiry*. His most recent publication is an exclusive entry on "Human Ecology and the Environment" in the four-volume *Encyclopedia of Sociology*, edited by Edgar and Marie Borgatta (1992).

DONALD W. BOGIE is Professor of Sociology and Director of the Center for Demographic and Cultural Research at Auburn University at Montgomery, Alabama. He is the author of several Alabama population reports.

STUART A. CAPPER is Associate Professor of Public Health at The University of Alabama at Birmingham, where he also serves as Chair of the Department of Health Care Organization and Policy. His scholarly interests are public health policy and strategic planning, areas in which he has conducted several funded research projects and published research articles, book chapters, and monographs.

DAVID W. COOMBS is Associate Professor in the School of Public Health at The University of Alabama at Birmingham. Dr. Coombs's active research and publication agendas focus on psychosocial factors related to health and illness, alcohol and drug abuse, suicide prevention, and health and disease in low-income populations. In addition to these health interests, he has taught courses, conducted research, and published on change, modernization, and development in Latin America and rural American communities.

HONG DAN is a Ph.D. candidate in the Department of Sociology at Texas A&M University. She holds a master's degree in Sociology from the University of Wyoming. One of her areas of concentration is demography, and she is presently studying the effects of minority status on fertility differences in China.

ELAINE L. FIELDING is Assistant Research Scientist at the Population Studies Center, University of Michigan, and Data Coordinator for the Multi-City Study of Urban Inequality. She recently served as a consultant to the U.S. Department of Housing and Urban Development for the President's National Urban Policy Report. Her main research areas are population distribution, race and ethnicity, housing and residential mobility, and she has addressed such issues as residential segregation by race and class, racial differentials in residential mobility, demographic change in U.S. metropolitan areas, and minority suburbanization patterns.

WILLIAM H. FREY is Research Scientist and Associate Director for Training of the Population Studies Center, University of Michigan. He is also Adjunct Professor of Sociology and a faculty affiliate of the Program in Urban, Technological and Environmental Planning. He was also a Visiting Research Scholar at the International Institute for Applied Systems Analysis (Austria) and the Andrew W. Mellon Research Scholar at the Population Reference Bureau. Dr. Frey has written widely on issues relating to migration, population redistribution, and the demography of metropolitan areas. He is author (with Alden Speare, Jr.) of the 1980 census monograph *Regional and Metropolitan Growth and Decline in the United States* (1988) and the Population Reference Bureau Bulletin, "Metropolitan America: Beyond the Transition" (1990).

J. SELWYN HOLLINGSWORTH is Associate Professor of Sociology at the University of Alabama, where he teaches courses on demographics, modernization in developing nations, and urban sociology. In addition to his Latin American research and teaching activities, he has published in the areas of mental retardation, population change, and modernization, and is currently President of the Alabama-Mississippi Sociological Association.

DENNIS L. PECK is Professor of Sociology at the University of Alabama, where he teaches courses in the areas of deviant behavior, theory, and social problems. Dr. Peck's activities include research and the publication of articles on suicide, accidents, and evaluation research. He served as Editor of *Sociological Inquiry* and as book review editor of *Deviant Behavior*. Recent edited books include *Psychosocial Effects of Hazardous Toxic Waste on Communities* and *Open Institutions: The Hope for Democracy* (with John W. Murphy).

DUDLEY L. POSTON, JR. is Head of the Department of Sociology and the Samuel Rhea Gammon Professor of Liberal Arts at Texas A&M University. He is a demographer and studies demographic issues in China. His most recent book is an edited volume (with David Yaukey) entitled *The Population of Modern China* (1992).

TERESA A. SULLIVAN is Professor of Sociology and Law at The University of Texas at Austin, where she is also Associate Dean of Graduate Studies. A demographer with labor force interests, she is coauthor with Randy Hodson of a textbook on the sociology of work. The author of *Marginal Workers, Marginal Jobs: The Underutilization of American Workers,* she is now investigating "middle-tier" jobs and their impact on the labor force.

KIRSTEN K. WEST is a mathematical statistician at the U.S. Bureau of the Census, where she does research related to the quality of census data and coverage error in the decennial census. Recent publications include *Status Enhancement and Fertility* (with John D. Kasarda and John O. G. Billy), *A Demographic Evaluation of the 1988 Dress Rehearsal Post-Enumeration Survey Results,* and articles in *Survey Methodology Journal* and *Sociological Inquiry.* She received her Ph.D. in Sociology from the University of North Carolina at Chapel Hill.

FRANK HAROLD WILSON is an Assistant Professor in the Department of Sociology and the Urban Studies Program at the University of Wisconsin at Milwaukee. Dr. Wilson's general research interests are in the areas of urban sociology, population, and race and ethnic relations. In addition to gentrification, his research is specifically focused on questions of contemporary black urbanization. He is currently studying the urban redevelopment and housing factors explaining the changing status of concentrated poverty in American central cities between 1980 and 1990. His research has been published in *Research in Urban Sociology, The Urban League Review,* and other journals.

LOUIE ALBERT WOOLBRIGHT is a Senior Analyst with the State of Alabama Center for Health Statistics. Throughout his government career, Woolbright has also been active in scholarly endeavors, publishing articles, chapters, and monographs pertaining to demographic issues such as infant mortality, international comparisons of the health of the elderly, census tract change in racial and ethnic composition, and SMA population projections.

ISBN 0-313-28744-9

EAN

HARDCOVER BAR CODE